WORKBOOK FOR

Greg Haydel
362-2736

THE
NUMBERS
GAME

131 at 1:00 + 2:00

So, since this is a statistics class, grades will be assigned by an unbiased technique—using a random number table.

WORKBOOK FOR
THE
NUMBERS
GAME

Gail Ellen Levy and
Joan Gay Snodgrass
New York University

New York

OXFORD UNIVERSITY PRESS

**To my parents:
for their constant love and support
GEL**

Library of Congress Cataloging in Publication Data

Snodgrass, Joan Gay.
   The numbers game.

   Original ed. published by Williams and Wilkins,
Baltimore.
   Includes index.
   1. Psychometrics.   I. Title.
BF39.S58 1977b   150′.1′82   78-14963
ISBN 0-19-502301-3
ISBN 0-19-502300-5 workbook (by Gail Ellen
   Levy & Joan Gay Snodgrass)

Printed in the United States of America

Preface

This workbook is specifically designed as a companion for the textbook *The Numbers Game: Statistics for Psychology.* When used together these books form a comprehensive vehicle for teaching and learning elementary psychological statistics. This workbook reinforces the concepts and computational procedures presented in the textbook. Further, the exercises in the workbook are crucial to effective learning and understanding of this material.

The first chapter provides self-tests of the mathematical skills necessary for statistical computations. We have often found that students entering elementary statistics courses have convinced themselves that they cannot learn statistics because they have little or no ability in mathematics. This chapter clearly shows the students exactly where their weaknesses and strengths are. For most students it will provide reassurance that statistics does not require advanced mathematical skills. For the students who have some difficulty with these self-tests there are specific rules pertaining to the needed skills. In addition these students will now have specific knowledge as to which of their skills need remediation prior to learning statistics. We hope they will be able to acquire these skills and then proceed with the task at hand.

With the exception of the first chapter, each workbook chapter corresponds to a textbook chapter, thus providing a thorough examination of the student's comprehension. Every chapter is divided into three sections: conceptual questions, problems, and formulas. Conceptual questions test the understanding of statistical principles using a short answer format. Problems present specific experiments and hypothetical though psychologically realistic data which require the utilization of computational procedures to answer questions about these data. For quick reference, formulas are listed in the third section of each chapter except Chapter 7. Because this workbook is a learning tool for the student, the answers to all questions are included at the end of the book.

There are many people I would like to thank for their encouragement and help throughout the writing of this book. In order not to forget anyone, I have included in the examples presented in this book the names of family, friends, and colleagues who have helped me. I am indebted to Susan Barbarisi, whose efficient, tireless typing is largely responsible for the completion of this book. Above all I must give special thanks to my mentor, Gay Snodgrass, for without her invaluable guidance and understanding I would not and could not have written this book.

Gail Ellen Levy

Glossary

Learning statistics is very much like learning a foreign language—it requires the translation of both English and Greek letter symbols into understandable concepts. This glossary presents translations of symbols as they are used in this book. However, students should be aware that statistical notation is not completely standardized and varies somewhat from textbook to textbook. We have attempted here to select the most common usage or the least confusing.

The general rule is to use Greek letters for population parameters and English letters for sample statistics. There are exceptions, however: p is a population parameter, and both η^2 and ϕ are sample correlation coefficients.

ENGLISH LETTER SYMBOLS

a A constant; also, the intercept constant in a linear equation

a_x Intercept constant in a regression equation predicting X from Y

a_y Intercept constant in a regression equation predicting Y from X

b A constant; also, the slope constant in a linear equation

b_x Slope constant in a regression equation predicting X from Y

b_y Slope constant in a regression equation predicting Y from X

C Contingency coefficient

cf Cumulative frequency

$c\%$ Cumulative percentage

cf_{ll} Cumulative frequency up to the lower real limit of a class interval

D Difference between two paired scores or two paired ranks

$\bar{D}$ Mean of the difference scores

df   Degrees of freedom

f Frequency

f_i Frequency in the ith class interval

f_e Expected frequency

f_o Observed frequency

F Test statistic used in the F test and in the analysis of variance

H Test statistic used in the Kruskal-Wallis test

H_0 Null hypothesis

H_1 Alternative hypothesis

i Class interval width

IQR Interquartile range

k A constant

MS   Mean square in the analysis of variance

N Number of subjects or observations in a sample

p Population proportion

p_e Expected proportion

p_o Observed proportion

P Sample proportion

$P(A)$ Probability of event A

$P(A/B)$ Probability of event A conditional on the occurrence of B

PR Percentile rank

q_r Studentized range statistic

Q_1 25th percentile

Q_2 50th percentile

Q_3 75th percentile

r Sample Pearson correlation coefficient

r_{rho} Sample Spearman rank-order correlation coefficient

r_{bis} Biserial correlation coefficient

$r_{pt\ bis}$ Point biserial correlation coefficient

r_{tet} Tetrachoric correlation coefficient

s Sample standard deviation (N formula)

$\hat{s}$ Estimated population standard deviation ($N-1$ formula)

s^2 Sample variance (N formula)

$\hat{s}^2$ Estimated population variance ($N-1$ formula)

$s_{\bar{x}}$ Standard error of a sample mean when σ is estimated

$s_{\bar{x}_1 - \bar{x}_2}$ Standard error of the difference between two sample means when σ is estimated

SE Standard error of a sampling distribution

SS Sum of squares in the analysis of variance

t Test statistic used in the t test and following the distribution of t

T Test statistic used in the Wilcoxon signed ranks test

U Test statistic used in the Mann-Whitney U test

x Deviation score, $X - \bar{X}$

X Any score

$\bar{X}$ Sample mean

X_m Midpoint of a class interval in a grouped frequency distribution

X_{ll} Lower real limit of the class interval containing a score of interest

$\hat{X}$ Raw score on X predicted from Y

Y A score paired with X

$\hat{Y}$ Raw score on Y predicted from X

z Deviation score divided by its standard deviation; also, a test statistic having a normal distribution

$\hat{z}_x$ z score on X predicted from Y

$\hat{z}_y$ z score on Y predicted from X

Z Fisher's Z transform of r

GREEK LETTER SYMBOLS

α (Small alpha) level of significance; probability of a Type I error

β (Small beta) probability of a Type II error

$1 - \beta$ Power

χ^2 (Small chi, squared) test statistic used in the chi-square test and following a chi-square distribution

χ_r^2 Test statistic used in the Friedman test

η^2 (Small eta, squared) correlation ratio

μ (Small mu) population mean

μ_0 Value of the population mean specified by H_0

μ_1 Value of the population mean when H_1 is true

σ (Small sigma) population standard deviation

$\sigma_{\bar{X}}$ Standard error of a sample mean when σ is known

$\sigma_{\bar{X}_1 - \bar{X}_2}$ Standard error of the difference between two sample means when σ is known

σ_P Standard error of a sample proportion

Σ (Capital sigma) summation sign; ΣX is an instruction to add up all the X's in a sample

ρ (Small rho) population Pearson correlation coefficient

ρ_{rho} Population Spearman correlation coefficient

ϕ (Small phi) phi coefficient; also, $\phi(P)$ is the arc sine transform of a sample proportion

Contents

WORKBOOK FOR
THE
NUMBERS
GAME

CHAPTER 1

Statistical Tools

Mathematical concepts are essential to the field of statistics. Without these basic tools statistical concepts would be entirely useless. Fortunately for those who shudder at the thought of manipulating numbers, introductory statistics does *not* require a very sophisticated knowledge of mathematics. Most of you will probably be quite surprised and relieved to find that you already have most of the skills you need. This chapter is designed to help you ascertain which concepts you need to review.

This chapter is divided into five conceptual units. Each unit begins with a short test of some aspect of mathematics which is used in statistical computations. After completing the test in each unit, compare your answers to those at the end of the book. If you have no trouble with these problems, skip ahead to the next unit. If, however, you find that you are not confident of the material covered, review the rules at the end of the unit and try the test again. Use outside sources if you need a more detailed review of these topics.

I. Order of Operations

A. Self-test

1. Supply the parentheses needed to make each equation true.

(a) $12 \div 2 \times 6 - 3 = 18$
(b) $12 \div 2 \times 6 - 3 = -2$
(c) $12 \div 2 \times 6 - 3 = 2$
(d) $12 \div 2 \times 6 - 3 = 33$

2. Indicate whether each of the following equations is true or false.

(a) _____ $(2/3)^2 \cdot 4/9 = (4/9)^2$

(b) _____ $\sqrt{4^2 + 3^2} = \sqrt{7^2}$

(c) _____ $\sqrt{8^2 + 8^2} = \sqrt{16^2}$

(d) _____ $a + b = b + a$

(e) _____ $abc = acb$

(f) _____ $a(b + c) = ab \times ac$

B. Rules for Ordering Operations

1. In addition and multiplication the order of terms is irrelevant. Examples:

(a) $a + b = b + a$
$2 + 3 = 3 + 2$
$5 = 5$

(b) $a \times b = b \times a$
$2 \times 3 = 3 \times 2$
$6 = 6$

2. Operations within parentheses are performed first. Examples:

(a) $(a + b) \times c$
$(4 + 2) \times 5 = 6 \times 5 = 30$

First add $a + b$, and then multiply the result by c.

(b) $a + (b \times c)$
$4 + (2 \times 5) = 4 + 10 = 14$

First multiply $b \times c$, and then add the result to a.

3. An expression under a radical sign is treated as though it were a single number. Execute the operations indicated within the radical sign before calculating the square root. Examples:

(a) $\sqrt{2^2 + 4^2} \neq \sqrt{2^2} + \sqrt{4^2}$
$\sqrt{2^2 + 4^2} = \sqrt{4 + 16}$
$= \sqrt{20}$
$= 2\sqrt{5}$

(b) $\sqrt{2^2} + \sqrt{4^2} = \sqrt{4} + \sqrt{16}$
$= 2 + 4$
$= 6$

4. In a fraction both the numerator and the denominator are treated separately, as though each were encased in parentheses. Example:

$$\frac{a + b}{c \times d} = (a + b) \div (c \times d)$$

5. Raising a fraction to a power is equivalent to raising both the numerator and the denominator to that power. Example:

$$\left(\frac{a}{b}\right)^2 = \frac{a^2}{b^2}$$

II. Inequalities

A. Self-test

1. Indicate whether each of the following statements is true or false.

(a) _____ $3 \times 2 < 3 + 2$

(b) _____ $612 > 599$

(c) _____ $72^2 \leq 72^2$

(d) _____ $61^4 \geq 59^2$

(e) _____ $30^2 \leq 60$

(f) _____ $300/100 > 3000/2000$

(g) _____ $42.9 < 429$

(h) _____ $\sqrt{25} = 5$

B. Definition of Signs

1. $a = b$ means a has the same numerical value as b. Example:

$$2 + 2 = 3 + 1$$
$$4 = 4$$

2. $a < b$ means a is less than b. Example:

$$2 + 2 < 2 + 3$$
$$4 < 5$$

3. $a \leq b$ means a is either less than b or equal to the value of b. Examples:

(a) $2 + 2 \leq 2 + 3$
     $4 \leq 5$
(b) $2 + 2 \leq 3 + 1$
     $4 \leq 4$

4. $a > b$ means a is greater than b. Example:

$$2 + 3 > 2 + 2$$
$$5 > 4$$

5. $a \geq b$ means a is either greater than b or equal to the value of b. Examples:

(a) $2 + 3 \geq 2 + 2$
     $5 \geq 4$
(b) $2 + 2 \geq 3 + 1$
     $4 \geq 4$

III. Addition, Multiplication, and Division of Fractions

A. Self-test

1. Choose whether the expression in column A is equal to the expression in column B or the expression in column C. Indicate your answer by putting a "B" or "C" in the space to the left of the item in column A.

	A	B	C
(a)___	$\dfrac{M}{P} + G =$	$\dfrac{M + GP}{P}$	$\dfrac{M + G}{P}$
(b)___	$G/P + M/L =$	$\dfrac{GL + MP}{PL}$	$G + M/P + L$
(c)___	$\dfrac{M}{P} \times G =$	$\dfrac{M \times G}{P \times G}$	$\dfrac{MG}{P}$
(d)___	$\dfrac{M}{P} \times \dfrac{P}{G} =$	$\dfrac{M}{G}$	$\dfrac{MP}{G}$
(e)___	$\dfrac{G}{P} \div \dfrac{G}{M} =$	$\dfrac{G^2}{PM}$	$\dfrac{M}{P}$
(f)___	$G\left(\dfrac{L}{M}\right) =$	$\dfrac{GL}{GM}$	$\dfrac{GL}{M}$
(g)___	$\dfrac{GL}{MP} \Big/ \dfrac{G}{MP} =$	$\dfrac{G^2L}{MP}$	L
(h)___	$\dfrac{MG}{1} =$	MG	1
(i)___	$\dfrac{G}{L} + 1 =$	$\dfrac{G + 1}{L}$	$\dfrac{G + L}{L}$
(j)___	$PM/(P/M) =$	M^2	$\dfrac{M}{P}$

B. Rules for Addition, Multiplication, and Division of Fractions

1. Two or more fractions can be added together only if they have the same denominator. Example:

$$1/5 + 2/5 = 3/5$$

If two or more fractions must be added together and each has a different denominator, then a *common denominator* must be found. Thus, when adding together 1/5 and 1/6, 30 could be used as the common denominator. In this case $1/5 + 1/6$ would be changed to $6/30 + 5/30$, and the resulting answer would be $11/30$.

2. When multiplying two or more fractions the result is a fraction whose numerator is the product of the numerators and denominator is the product of the denominators. Examples:

(a) $\dfrac{a}{b} \times \dfrac{c}{d} = \dfrac{ac}{bd}$

(b) $a\left(\dfrac{1}{b}\right) = \dfrac{a}{b}$

3. Any number divided by 1 or multiplied by 1 retains its original value. Examples:

(a) $\dfrac{a}{1} = a$

(b) $a \times 1 = a$

4. Any number, other than 0, divided by itself is equal to 1. Examples:

(a) $\dfrac{a}{a} = \dfrac{b}{b} = 1$

(b) $\dfrac{ab}{ac} = 1 \times \dfrac{b}{c} = \dfrac{b}{c}$

5. A fraction indicates division. The fraction a/b means $a \div b$. Dividing one fraction by another can be done by inverting the second number (divisor) and multiplying it by the first (dividend). Examples:

(a) $\dfrac{a}{b} \div \dfrac{c}{d} = \dfrac{a}{b} \times \dfrac{d}{c} = \dfrac{ad}{bc}$

(b) $\dfrac{a}{b} \div \dfrac{a}{b} = \dfrac{a}{b} \times \dfrac{b}{a} = \dfrac{ab}{ba} = 1$

IV. Decimals, Percentages and Scientific Notation

A. Self-test

1. Convert each of the following divisions into decimal form.

(a) $4/5 = $ _.08_

(b) $14/4 = $ _3.2_

(c) $4(3/8) = $ _1.5_

(d) $9 \div 12 = $ _.75_

(e) $5000/8 = $ _625_

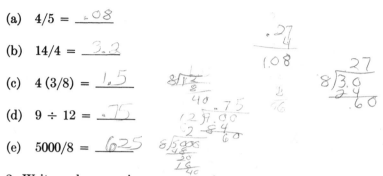

2. Write each expression as a percentage.

(a) $0.032 = $ _3_ %

(b) $(0.2)^2 = $ _40_ %

(c) $(0.1)^3 = $ _10_ %

(d) $0.0046 = $ _1_ %

(e) $11.0/50 = $ _22_ %

(f) $0.006/0.02 = $ _30_ %

3. Use scientific notation to express the following.

(a) $0.00023 = $ 2.3×10^4

(b) $44/2 = $ 1.1×10

(c) $(0.01)(0.2)/0.1 = $ 2×10^2

(d) $(0.6)(0.2)(0.1) = $

(e) $(0.4)^2 = $ .16 16×10^2

(f) $(0.01)^2 = $

B. Rules for Decimals, Percentages, and Scientific Notation

1. Every decimal fraction has a whole number as its numerator and a power of ten as its denominator. Examples:
   (a) $0.1 = 1/10$
   (b) $0.013 = 13/1000$
   (c) $7.2 = 72/10$
   (d) $0.44 = 44/100$

2. To convert a common fraction to a decimal fraction, simply divide the numerator by the denominator. Examples:
   (a) To convert $1/10$ to a decimal fraction perform the division $1 \div 10$. Therefore, $1/10 = 1 \div 10 = 0.1$.
   (b) To convert $4/5$ to a decimal fraction perform the division $4 \div 5$. Therefore, $4/5 = 4 \div 5 = 0.8$.

3. When multiplying two or more decimal fractions, first multiply as you would with whole numbers. Then locate the decimal point in the answer by summing the total number of decimal places in all the factors and counting off from the right. Example:

Suppose you wanted to perform the following calculation: 1.1×0.01. The whole number product is 11×1 or 11. Since there is 1 decimal place in the first factor and 2 in the second, the product has a total of 3 decimal places. We then count 3 places from the right and our answer is 0.011. Alternatively we might have calculated this problem in the following way:

$$1.1 \times 0.01 = 11/10 \times 1/100 = 11/1000 = 0.011$$

4. The percent ($\%$) sign indicates division by 100. To convert a decimal fraction to a percentage, simply move the decimal point two places to the right (i.e. multiply by 100) and then add the percent sign (i.e. divide by 100). Examples:
   (a) $0.0123 = 1.23\%$
   (b) $6.21 = 621\%$

5. Scientific notation refers to the practice of writing a real number as a number between 1 and 10, multiplied by a power of 10. Some of the powers of ten and their equivalent values are
   $10^0 = 1$
   $10^1 = 10$
   $10^2 = 100$
   $10^3 = 1000$
   $10^{-1} = 1/10 = 0.1$
   $10^{-2} = 1/100 = 0.01$
   $10^{-3} = 1/1000 = 0.001$

The power of ten can be found by counting the number of places the decimal point must be moved; movement to the left yields positive powers while movement to the right yields negative powers. Examples:

(a) $11.1 = 1.11 \times 10^1$

(b) $0.00111 = 1.11 \times 10^{-3}$

(c) $1110.00 = 1.11 \times 10^3$

V. Summation

Successful completion of the following exercises requires a knowledge of summation notation and rules. Complete the problems and then check your answers with the key at the end of the book. If you do poorly or if you are unsure why you got the correct answers, refer to Appendix A at the end of the workbook.

A. Self-test

1. Find the expression in column B which is equivalent to each expression in column A.

	A		B
(a) ___	$\displaystyle\sum_{i=1}^{3} \frac{X_i^2}{N}$	(1)	$\dfrac{X_1 + X_2 + X_3}{N}$
(b) ___	$\displaystyle\sum_{i=1}^{3} \frac{(2X_i - X_i)}{N}$	(2)	$\left(\dfrac{X_1}{N}\right)^2 + \left(\dfrac{X_2}{N}\right)^2 + \left(\dfrac{X_3}{N}\right)^2$
(c) ___	$\dfrac{\left(\sum_{i=1}^{3} X_i\right)^2}{N}$	(3)	$\displaystyle\sum_{i=1}^{3} \left(\dfrac{X_i}{N}\right) + \sum_{i=1}^{3} \left(\dfrac{X_i^2}{N}\right)$
(d) ___	$\left(\dfrac{\sum_{i=1}^{3} X_i}{N}\right)^2$	(4)	$\dfrac{1}{N}\left(X_1^2 + X_2^2 + X_3^2\right)$
(e) ___	$\displaystyle\sum_{i=1}^{3} \left(\dfrac{X_i}{N}\right)^2$	(5)	$\dfrac{(X_1 + X_2 + X_3)^2}{N}$
(f) ___	$\displaystyle\sum_{i=1}^{3} \left(\dfrac{X_i}{N} + \dfrac{X_i^2}{N}\right)$	(6)	$\left(\dfrac{X_1 + X_2 + X_3}{N}\right)^2$

2. This is a table of scores for five subjects under four conditions of an experiment. Compute the row sums, the column sums, and the total sum, and record the in them spaces provided.

Subject (i)	Condition (j)				Row Sums
	1	2	3	4	
1	14	8	37	2	$\sum_{j=1}^{4} X_{1j} = 61$
2	17	12	24	7	$\sum_{j=1}^{4} X_{2j} = 40$
3	20	19	15	29	$\sum_{j=1}^{4} X_{3j} = 83$
4	21	26	19	6	$\sum_{j=1}^{4} X_{4j} = 72$
5	28	31	26	12	$\sum_{j=1}^{4} X_{5j} = 77$
Column sums	$\sum_{i=1}^{5} X_{i1} = \underline{}$	$\sum_{i=1}^{5} X_{i2} = \underline{}$	$\sum_{i=1}^{5} X_{i3} = \underline{}$	$\sum_{i=1}^{5} X_{i4} = \underline{}$	$\sum_{i=1}^{5}\sum_{j=1}^{4} X_{ij} = \underline{}$

3. Evaluate the following expressions using the data from the previous exercise.

(a) $\sum_{j=1}^{4} X_{4j} = \underline{}$ (f) $\sum_{j=1}^{2} X_{1j} = \underline{}$

(b) $\sum_{j=1}^{2} X_{3j} = \underline{}$ (g) $\sum_{j=1}^{1} X_{5j} = \underline{}$

(c) $\sum_{j=1}^{3} X_{2j} = \underline{}$ (h) $\sum_{i=1}^{3} X_{i2} = \underline{}$

(d) $\sum_{i=1}^{4} X_{i2} = \underline{}$ (i) $\sum_{i=1}^{4} X_{i4} = \underline{}$

(e) $\sum_{i=1}^{2} X_{i4} = \underline{}$ (j) $\sum_{j=1}^{3} X_{4j} = \underline{}$

B. Rules for Summation

These will be found in Appendix A of this workbook.

CHAPTER 2

Frequency Distributions and Percentile Ranks

A. Conceptual Questions

1. Determine whether the statements below refer to independent, dependent, discrete, or continuous variables and fill in each blank with the appropriate word.

(a) Usually we use statistical tests to analyze ___dependant___ variables.

(b) The number of students in a particular school is an example of a(n) ___discrete___ variable because it can take on only a fixed number of values.

(c) A(n) ___independent___ variable is manipulated by the investigator.

(d) A(n) ___dependent___ variable is the response measured by the experimenter.

(e) A physical measure such as length is an example of a(n) ___continuous___ variable because it can take on any of an infinite number of values.

2. To which measurement scale—nominal, ordinal, interval, or ratio—do the following belong?

14

(a) Numbers indicating win, place, and show in a horse race.
ordinal

(b) The number assigned to each player on a basketball team.
nominal

(c) The number indicating the year (e.g. 1984 B.C.). _interval_

(d) Scores on a multiple choice test. _ratio_

(e) Age measured in years. _ratio_

(f) Temperature measured in degrees Fahrenheit. _interval_

3. In each example below identify the independent and dependent variables. Indicate the appropriate measurement scale—nominal, ordinal, interval, or ratio—for each dependent variable.

(a) A medical researcher, Dr. Barbarisi, investigated the effect of a new drug on reducing high temperatures in patients with pneumonia. She took two groups of rats with pneumonia, measured each rat's temperature, and administered the drug to one (experimental) group and nothing to the other (control) group. Temperatures were taken again 4 hours after the drug was injected. She found that all of the experimental animals now had normal temperatures while all of the control animals still suffered from elevated temperatures.

_____

_____

(b) A leading milk company sponsored a research project on the effect of a child consuming large amounts of milk each day at age 2 on his or her subsequent height and weight. Questionnaires were sent to 500 parents asking how much milk had been drunk by their children at the age of 2, the height and weight of the child at age 10, as well as some demographic information about the family. Based on these replies, 50 children who at the age of 2 drank at least 6 glasses of milk a day were matched (on family socioeconomic status, parents' educational level, etc.) to a group of 50 children who had drunk no more than 1 glass of milk a day during their second year. The height and weight at age 10 of these two groups of children were then compared.

_____

_____

(c) Ms. Chop, an investigator, studied the effect of practice on Graduate
Record Examination scores. She randomly chose 100 college graduates who had taken the exam three times and compared the scores
each student received after taking the first, second, and third tests.

_____

_____

(d) An investigator, Dr. McClure, hypothesized that hunger would increase the likelihood of interpreting ambiguous stimuli as food items.
She presented 50 subjects with a series of ambiguous pictures and
recorded the number of food-related responses made by each subject.
Following this each subject was interviewed and asked how many
hours had passed since he or she had last eaten. Based on this information the subjects were divided into three groups: hungry (had
not eaten for more than 7 hours), moderately hungry (had not eaten
for 2 1/2–6 1/2 hours), or not hungry (had eaten within the previous
2 hours).

_____

_____

(e) Mr. Grupsmith, a gambler, has two systems for winning at the race
track. Unfortunately, each system predicts different winners for most
races. Not knowing which system to adopt, he tries the following
"experiment." For two nights he bets using the first system and on
two other nights (with the same track conditions) he bets using the
second system. (He always bets $10 on every race.) At the end of these
four nights he compares his winnings with the first system to his
winnings with the second system.

_____

_____

B. Problems

Interested in implementing an intensive reading program for his third grade class, Mr. Ohman collected information on the age, IQ, reading level, and reading preference of his 25 students. The data he collected are presented in Table 2.1. Use this information to solve the following problems.

1. Indicate the appropriate scale of measurement for each of the following variables:

(a) Student number _____

(b) Age _____

(c) IQ _____

(d) Reading level _____

(e) Reading preference _____

TABLE 2.1

Age, IQ, Reading Level, and Reading Preference of 25 Third Graders

Subject Number	Age (Months)	IQ	Reading Level[a]	Reading Preference[b]	Subject Number	Age (Months)	IQ	Reading Level[a]	Reading Preference[b]
1	90	104	2	2	14	97	112	2	3
2	96	111	2	1	15	94	145	1	4
3	92	98	3	3	16	87	136	2	2
4	87	132	1	1	17	99	124	1	4
5	84	128	2	1	18	102	130	2	1
6	88	106	3	3	19	103	129	1	3
7	93	126	1	3	20	98	114	2	1
8	99	99	3	2	21	95	103	3	3
9	103	111	2	1	22	89	121	1	5
10	105	120	2	1	23	104	109	2	2
11	108	125	1	2	24	101	101	2	4
12	101	106	1	1	25	96	117	1	5
13	96	99	3	5					

[a] 1 is the highest group and 3 is the lowest.
[b] 1 = Biography, 2 = Novels, 3 = History, 4 = Science, 5 = Science Fiction.

2. Make a table for the frequency distribution of reading preference for the 25 students (using the space provided in Table 2.2). Plot this information as a bar graph (using the graph paper at the end of the chapter).

3. What percentage of the students are in each of the three reading level groups?

(a) Group 1 __36__ %

(b) Group 2 __44__ %

(c) Group 3 __20__ %

$$89.5 + \frac{3\left(\frac{25 \times 25}{1.00} - 5\right)}{2}$$

4. Make a table of the grouped frequency distribution of IQ's based on an interval width, i, of 5. (Use the space provided in Table 2.3.) Plot a histogram of these grouped frequencies using the graph paper at the end of the chapter.*

5. Make a table of the grouped and cumulative frequency distributions of age based on an interval width, i, of 3 months. (Use the space provided in Table 2.4.) For these data plot both the frequency polygon and the cumulative frequency distribution (using the graph paper at the end of the chapter). (Remember to plot cumulative frequencies along the left ordinate and cumulative percentage along the right ordinate.)

* (Note: In this and subsequent examples, the highest interval is always given.)

TABLE 2.2
Frequency Distribution of Reading Preference

Reading Preference	Frequency
Biography (1)	_____
Novels (2)	_____
History (3)	_____
Science (4)	_____
Science fiction (5)	_____

TABLE 2.3

Grouped Frequency Distribution of IQ's Based on an Interval Width of 5

Interval	Midpoint	f
145–149	147	1
140–144	142	0
135–139	137	1
130–134	132	2
125–129	127	4
120–124	122	3
115–119	117	1
110–114	112	4
105–109	107	3
100–104	102	3
95–99	97	3

TABLE 2.4

Grouped Frequency Distribution for Ages of 25 Third Grade Students ($i = 3$ Months)

Class Interval		Midpoint	f	cf	c%
Apparent Limits	Real Limits				
108–110	107.5–110.5	109	1	25	100
105–107	104.5–107.5	106	1	24	96
102–104	101.5–104.5	103	3	23	92
99–101	98.5–101.5	100	5	20	80
96–98	95.5–98.5	97	5	15	60
93–95	92.5–95.5	94	3	10	40
90–92	89.5–92.5	91	2	7	28
87–89	86.5–89.5	88	4	5	20
84–86	83.5–86.5	85	1	1	4

6. What is the percentile rank of the following ages?

(a) 88 months is in the __15__ _/12_ percentile.

(b) 94 months is in the __34__ _38_ percentile.

(c) 104 months is in the __89.99__ percentile.

7. What age corresponds to each of the following percentiles?

(a) 25th _____ 91.38

(b) 50th __97.00__

(c) 75th __100.75__

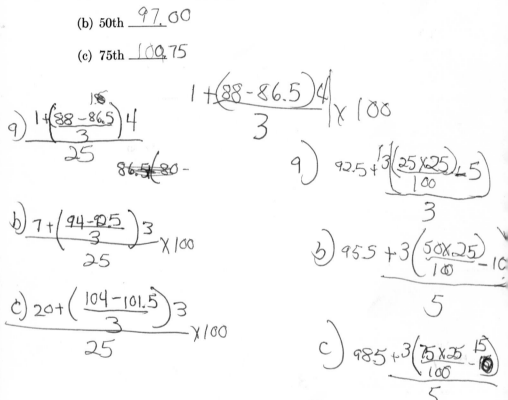

$$6) \frac{1 + \left(\frac{88 - 86.5}{3}\right)4}{25}$$

$$86.5 \le 80 -$$

$$\frac{1 + \left(\frac{88 - 86.5}{3}\right)4}{3} \times 100$$

$$b) \frac{7 + \left(\frac{94 - 92.5}{3}\right)3}{25} \times 100$$

$$c) \frac{20 + \left(\frac{104 - 101.5}{3}\right)3}{25} \times 100$$

$$a) \frac{92.5 + 3\left(\frac{25 \times 25}{100} - 5\right)}{3}$$

$$b) \frac{95.5 + 3\left(\frac{50 \times 25}{10} - 10\right)}{5}$$

$$c) \frac{98.5 + 3\left(\frac{75 \times 25}{100} - 15\right)}{5}$$

Formulas

Interval scale transformation

$X' = bX + a$

Ratio scale transformation

$X' = bX$

Class intervals

$i = $ Range/Number of intervals

Midpoint $= (i - 1)/2 + $ Lower limit of each interval

$NCI = $ Range/i

Lower real limit $= $ Apparent lower limit $- (1/2)$ (unit of measurement)

Upper real limit $= $ Apparent upper limit $+ (1/2)$ (unit of measurement)

Percentiles

Percentage $= f/N \times 100$

$$PR\ (X) = \frac{cf_{ll} + \left(\dfrac{X - X_{ll}}{i}\right)f_i}{N} \times 100$$

$$X = X_{ll} + \frac{i\left(\dfrac{PR \times N}{100} - cf_{ll}\right)}{f_i}$$

freq.

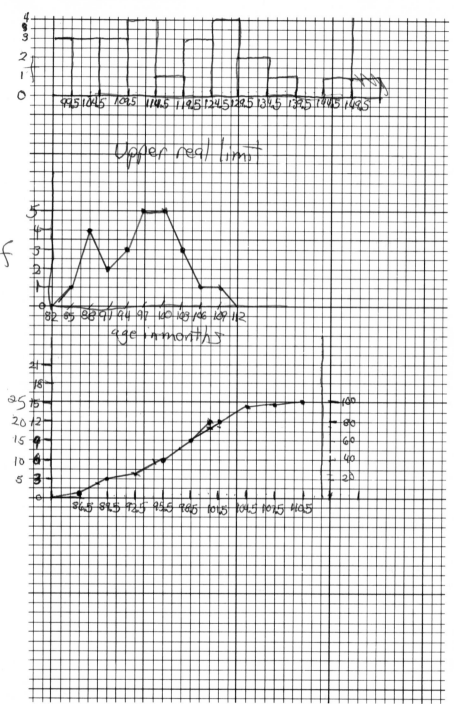

Upper real limit

f

age in months

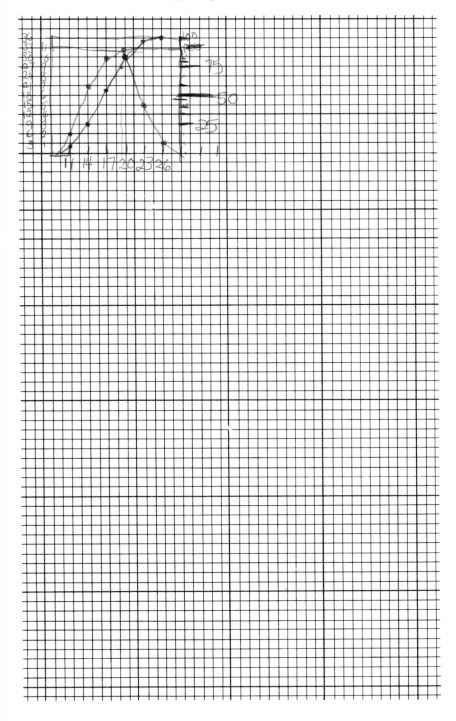

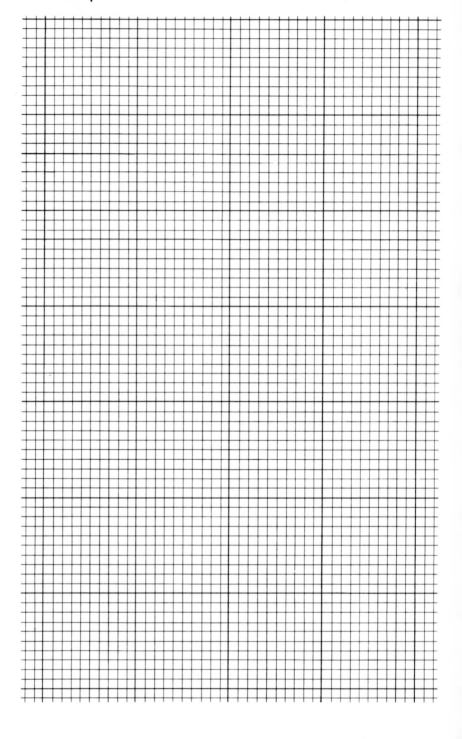

CHAPTER 3

Measures of Central Tendency and Variability

A. Conceptual Questions

1. Each of the following statements or questions refers to either the mode, median, or mean. Indicate the measure of central tendency most appropriate in each context.

(a) This statistic corresponds to the 50th percentile. _____

(b) A major disadvantage of this statistic is that it does not use every number in the distribution. _____

(c) A major disadvantage of this statistic is that it is affected by extreme scores. _____

(d) In a symmetric bimodal distribution the arithmetic mean is equal to the _____.

(e) Ms. Rosofsky wishes to implement a behavior modification system with her students. In order to make the program effective she has asked each student to submit the name of his or her favorite candy. Which measure of central tendency should she use to decide which candy to buy? _____

(f) Mr. Van Praag, a very eccentric billionaire, arranges the paintings in his priceless art collection in order of their realism. When speaking of the typical painting in his collection, which measure of central tendency should he use? _____

(g) Which measure of central tendency should be used when describing the typical height of hockey players in the United States? _____

(h) Which measure of central tendency should the government use to report most accurately the typical annual income for the residents of Newark, Delaware? _____

(i) Suppose it was advantageous for a certain public relations firm to inflate, without perjury, the typical annual income for a New York City resident. Which measure of central tendency should the firm calculate? _____

2. Indicate whether each of the following statements is true or false.

_____(a) The range is a more stable measure of variability than the interquartile range.

_____(b) The median is less influenced by chance than the mode because the median takes into account the entire distribution.

_____(c) The standard deviation is the square of the variance.

_____(d) The symbol for the standard deviation of a sample is s^2.

_____(e) The symbol for the population variance is σ^2.

_____(f) If the data of an experiment are measured in feet, then the standard deviation is reported as feet squared.

3. Insert "equal to" $(=)$, "less than" $(<)$, or "greater than" $(>)$ in each blank to make the following statements true.

(a) In a negatively skewed distribution the mean ____ the median ____ the mode.

(b) If a positive constant is added to each score of a normal distribution, the mean ____ the median ____ the mode.

(c) When each score in a normal distribution is multiplied by 5 the mean _____ the median _____ the mode.

(d) In a positively skewed distribution the mean _____ the median _____ the mode.

(e) In a normal distribution the mean _____ the median _____ the mode.

(f) When each datum in a normal distribution is multiplied by 0.5 the mean _____ the median _____ the mode.

B. Problems

1. Feeling that some students were daydreaming, Ms. Ehrenreich decided to give her math class a surprise quiz. The results of this test are reported in Table 3.1. Based on these data, answer the following questions.

   (a) What is the mode of this distribution? _____

   (b) If you were to group the scores by two's, what would the modal interval of the distribution be? What would the mode be?

_____

_____

   (c) What is the median of this (ungrouped) distribution?

_____

   (d) What is the mean of this (ungrouped) distribution?

_____

   (e) How many students had grades equal to or greater than the mean?

_____

   (f) What is the range of the distribution? _____

   (g) What is the interquartile range of this distribution?

_____

TABLE 3.1

Scores of 50 Students on a 10-Question True-False Quiz

Score	f	Score	f
10	4	5	2
9	12	4	1
8	10	3	2
7	9	2	2
6	7	1	1

(h) Calculate s^2 (to three decimal places).

_____

(i) Calculate the standard deviation of this distribution.

_____

(j) Suppose Ms. Ehrenreich decided to pass only those students who attained scores equal to or greater than a measure of central tendency. Which statistic would pass more students—the mode or the median?

_____

2. IQ scores for 50 high school seniors are reported in Table 3.2. Use these data to complete the following problems.

(a) Use the space provided in Table 3.3 to make a grouped frequency distribution, with interval width, i, of 3.

_____

(b) What is the mode of the grouped frequency distribution?

_____

(c) What is the median of the grouped frequency distribution?

_____

(d) What is the mean of the grouped frequency distribution?

_____

TABLE 3.2
IQ Scores of Fifty High School Seniors

101	96	124	105	102	103	98	111	109	99
104	126	120	105	97	115	112	103	100	108
119	100	101	119	110	106	97	99	113	127
108	125	105	115	107	112	122	95	113	124
99	104	126	103	112	120	104	108	105	116

TABLE 3.3
Grouped Frequency Distribution for a Set of 50 IQ Scores

Apparent Limits	Real Limits	Midpoint (X_m)	cf	fX_m	X_m^2	fX_m^2
128–130						
125–127						
122–124						
119–121						
116–118						
113–115						
110–112						
107–109						
104–106						
101–103						
98–100						
95–97						

(e) What is the range of the grouped frequency distribution?

_____

(f) What is the interquartile range of the grouped frequency distribution?

_____

(g) What is the standard deviation of the grouped frequency distribution?

_____

(h) What is the variance of the grouped frequency distribution?

_____

3. Two researchers, each working in a different laboratory, measured the pecking behavior of pigeons during exposure to loud music. Discovering that their methods were identical, they decided to pool their data and publish their results jointly. Table 3.4 shows the results of each of the two experiments. Using these data:
(a) Calculate the combined mean ($\bar{X}_{comb}$).
(b) Calculate the combined variance (s^2_{comb}).
(c) Calculate the combined standard deviation (s_{comb}).

_____

_____

_____

_____

_____

TABLE 3.4
Data from Two Independent Experiments on Key Pecking Behavior in Pigeons

Data from Group I	Data from Group II
$N_1 = 15$	$N_2 = 30$
$\bar{X}_1 = 14.5$	$\bar{X}_2 = 12.2$
$s^2_1 = 4.41$	$s^2_2 = 8.41$
$s_1 = 2.1$	$s_2 = 2.9$

Formulas

Measures of central tendency

Median (ungrouped) = $(N + 1)/2$

Median (grouped) = $X_{ll} + \dfrac{i(N/2 - cf_{ll})}{f_i}$

Mean (ungrouped) = $\bar{X} = \dfrac{\Sigma X}{N}$

Mean (ungrouped) = $\bar{X} = \dfrac{\Sigma fX}{N}$

Mean (grouped) = $\bar{X} = \dfrac{\Sigma fX_m}{N}$

Measures of variability

Range = Largest value − Smallest value + (1 × Unit of measurement)

Interquartile range = $IQR = Q_3 - Q_1$

Variance (definition) = $s^2 = \dfrac{\Sigma x^2}{N} = \dfrac{\Sigma(X - \bar{X})^2}{N}$

Standard deviation (definition) = $s = \sqrt{\dfrac{\Sigma x^2}{N}}$

Variance (ungrouped) = $s^2 = \dfrac{\Sigma X^2}{N} - \left(\dfrac{\Sigma X}{N}\right)^2 = \dfrac{\Sigma X^2}{N} - \bar{X}^2$

Standard deviation (ungrouped) = $s = \sqrt{\dfrac{\Sigma X^2}{N} - \bar{X}^2}$

Variance (grouped) = $s^2 = \dfrac{\Sigma fX_m^2}{N} - \bar{X}^2$

Standard deviation (grouped) = $s = \sqrt{\dfrac{\Sigma fX_m^2}{N} - \bar{X}^2}$

Measures for combined samples

Mean = $\bar{X}_{comb} = \dfrac{N_1\bar{X}_1 + N_2\bar{X}_2}{N_1 + N_2}$

Variance = $s^2_{comb} = \dfrac{N_1(s_1^2 + \bar{X}_1^2) + N_2(s_2^2 + \bar{X}_2^2)}{N_1 + N_2} - \bar{X}^2_{comb}$

scatterplot for #2 in text

Correlation: Measures of Relationship Between Two Variables

A. Conceptual Questions

1. Indicate whether each of the following statements is true or false.

_____ (a) We can tell the quantitative relationship between two variables, X and Y, by looking at a scatter plot.

_____ (b) A scatter plot can usually tell us whether the correlation is negative or positive, linear or curvilinear.

_____ (c) A Pearson product moment correlation coefficient measures only the linear relationship between two variables.

_____ (d) In order to use the Spearman rho, variables measured on an interval or ratio scale must be converted to ranks.

_____ (e) Data are always converted to standard or z scores when making a scatter plot.

_____ (f) Data are always converted to standard or z scores before calculating a Pearson r.

_____ (g) A Pearson r equal to $+1.0$ shows a stronger relationship between two variables than a correlation of -1.0.

_____ (h) A high positive correlation was found between math and chemistry averages for eleventh graders attending the Reeves boarding school. This correlation will probably decrease if all students with an IQ of less than 115 are eliminated from the sample.

_____ (i) A correlation coefficient of $+0.46$ shows a greater relationship between variables than a correlation coefficient of -0.78.

_____ (j) A high correlation between the amount of candy eaten by 100 kindergarten students and the amount of cavities they got during that year proves that eating candy causes tooth decay.

2. The data collected from each of the five experiments described below are presented in Figure 4.1. Using both the descriptions and the graphed data, answer the following questions for each experiment.

(1) Do the two variables appear to be correlated? If yes, how would you describe the form of the relationship? (positive or negative)

(2) What is the appropriate measure of correlation? (Pearson r or Spearman rho).

(3) If a correlation were indeed found in such an experiment, does it seem likely that the two variables constitute a cause and effect relationship? If so, indicate which variable is the cause and which the effect.

(a) Interested in studying age-related skills, Ms. Bowles and her associates administered a series of mathematics aptitude and achievement tests to 500 subjects ranging in age from 8 to 25.

(1) _____

(2) _____

(3) _____

(b) Mr. Rosenthal, a high school football coach, wished to refute the claim that the best football players are "dumb jocks." To this end, he ranked the football skills of his 50 varsity players (assigning 1 to the best player) and then compared each athlete's rank and scholastic average.

(1) _____

(2) _____

(3) _____

(c) An elementary school teacher, wanting to impress students with the importance of studying, compared each student's test score with the average number of hours spent studying.

(1) _____

(2) _____

(3) _____

(d) The public library administrators were concerned about the decreasing number of books taken out each month. Using monthly records accumulated over the past 5 years, they compared the number of hours spent each month reading books for entertainment and watching television.

(1) _____

(2) _____

(3) _____

(e) A park commissioner compared the temperature for every non-rainy Sunday during the summer to his judgment of park attendance. (Ratings of attendance were on a seven-point scale ranging from 7, very crowded; to 1, almost empty.)

(1) _____

(2) _____

(3) _____

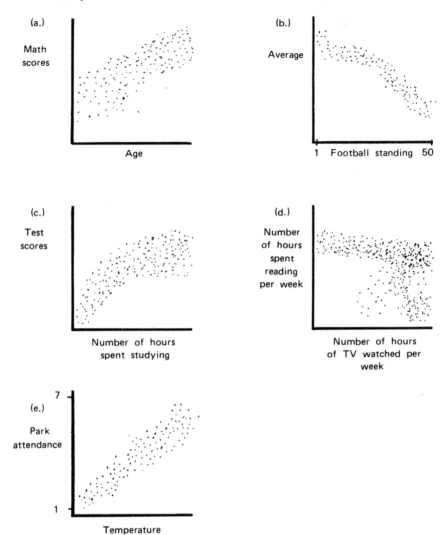

Fig. 4.1 Data collected in five hypothetical experiments

B. Problems

1. A hypothetical distribution consists of the following 8 scores: 25, 20, 29, 32, 11, 34, 16, and 13. Calculate the z scores for these data, and demonstrate numerically the following properties of standard or z scores. (Use the space provided in Table 4.1 to organize this distribution.)

TABLE 4.1

Hypothetical Data to Calculate z Scores and Demonstrate Some Properties of z Scores[a]

X	$x = X - \overline{X}$	$z = \dfrac{x}{s}$	z^2
25			
20			
29			
32			
11			
34			
16			
13			
$\Sigma X =$ _____	$\Sigma x =$ _____	$\Sigma z =$ _____	$\Sigma z^2 =$ _____

[a] (Note: round s to two decimal places in computing z scores.)

(a) Demonstrate that the mean of the z scores in a distribution is equal to zero. That is, $\bar{z} = 0$.

_____

_____

_____

(b) Show that the variance and standard deviation of a set of z scores equal 1.0. That is, $s_z^2 = s_z = 1.0$.

_____

_____

_____

(c) Demonstrate that the sum of the squared z scores is equal to N, the number of z scores in the sample. That is, $\Sigma z^2 = N$.

_____

_____

_____

2. The producer of a news show was extremely displeased with the meteorologist on the eleven o'clock news who predicts the weather each evening for the following day. His weather predictions seemed totally unrelated to the weather conditions. In order to lend more strength to his opinion, the producer collected the following information. He randomly selected 15 rainy days during the past 4 months and compared the amount of rainfall to the precipitation probability given the previous night. These data are reported in Table 4.2. Using this information and the space provided in Table 4.3, compute the means, variances, and standard deviations of the two sets of scores and compute the Pearson r using the raw score formula.

(a) $\bar{X} = $ _____

$\bar{Y} = $ _____

$s_x^2 = $ _____

$s_x = $ _____

$s_y^2 = $ _____

$s_y = $ _____

(b) $r \; = $ _____

TABLE 4.2

Data on the Precipitation Probability and the Amount of Rainfall

Day	Precipitation Probability, X (%)	Rainfall, Y (tenths of inches)	Day	Precipitation Probability, X (%)	Rainfall, Y (tenths of inches)
1	90	9	9	90	7
2	40	7	10	10	1
3	20	5	11	40	4
4	30	5	12	10	2
5	80	1	13	50	3
6	60	2	14	80	7
7	70	8	15	40	1
8	20	3			

TABLE 4.3

Data on the Precipitation Probability and the Amount of Rainfall

Day	X	Y	X^2	Y^2	XY
1					
2					
3					
4					
5					
6					
7					
8					
9					
10					
11					
12					
13					
14					
15					

$\Sigma X =$ _____ $\Sigma Y =$ _____ $\Sigma X^2 =$ _____ $\Sigma Y^2 =$ _____ $\Sigma XY =$ _____

3. Mr. Hayden, a horse breeder, was interested in the relationship between the rank of a sire and the performance of his offspring. After choosing nine famous race horses, he asked a colleague to rank them on desirability as a sire based on performance and stud fees. He then calculated the percentage of races won by the best colt of each sire when the colt was a 2-year-old. Table 4.4 presents the data Mr. Hayden collected.

(a) Using Table 4.4 rank the colts and compute a Spearman rho on the ranks. (Note: A rank of 1 should be given to the colt winning the most races.) rho = _____

TABLE 4.4

Ranks of Sires and Percentage of Races Won by Their Colts in 1 Year

Sire/Colt	Sire's Rank (X)	% of Races Won by Colt	Colt's Rank Y)	$D = X - Y$	D^2
A	2	78			
B	5	42			
C	1	44			
D	7	30			
E	9	10			
F	3	41			
G	8	36			
H	6	25			
I	4	68			
				$\Sigma D =$ ____	$\Sigma D^2 =$ ____

Formulas

Standard scores

$$z_x = \frac{X - \bar{X}}{s_x} = \frac{x}{s_x}$$

Pearson product correlation coefficient

Pearson r (definition) $= r = \dfrac{\Sigma z_x z_y}{N}$

Pearson r (deviation scores) $=$

$$r = \frac{\Sigma xy}{N s_x s_y} = \frac{\Sigma xy}{N \sqrt{\left(\dfrac{\Sigma x^2}{N}\right)\left(\dfrac{\Sigma y^2}{N}\right)}} = \frac{\Sigma xy}{N \sqrt{\dfrac{\Sigma x^2 \Sigma y^2}{N^2}}} = \frac{\Sigma xy}{\sqrt{\Sigma x^2 \Sigma y^2}}$$

Pearson r (raw scores) $= r = \dfrac{\Sigma XY - \dfrac{(\Sigma X)(\Sigma Y)}{N}}{\sqrt{\left[\Sigma X^2 - \dfrac{(\Sigma X)^2}{N}\right]\left[\Sigma Y^2 - \dfrac{(\Sigma Y)^2}{N}\right]}}$

or $\qquad r = \dfrac{\dfrac{\Sigma XY}{N} - \bar{X}\bar{Y}}{\sqrt{\left(\dfrac{\Sigma X^2}{N} - \bar{X}^2\right)\left(\dfrac{\Sigma Y^2}{N} - \bar{Y}^2\right)}}$

Spearman rho

$$r_{\text{rho}} = 1.0 - \frac{6\Sigma D^2}{N(N^2 - 1)}$$

CHAPTER 5

Linear Regression: Predicting One Variable from Another

A. Conceptual Questions

1. Fill in the blanks below with the word or words which will make each statement true.

(a) The variable we always wish to predict is the _____ variable.

(b) The slope of the least squares regression equation when both scores are expressed as z scores is _____.

(c) Solving the equation $Y = 4X + 2$ for X we get $X =$ _____.

(d) When we predict X from Y the _____ (horizontal, vertical) squared deviations are minimized.

(e) The proportion of variance accounted for by the linear regression equation is equal to _____.

(f) One of the assumptions underlying the use of X to predict Y _____ (is, is not) that X either causes or has some effect on Y.

(g) In the equation $Y = 7X + 2$, as X increases by 1 Y increases by
_____.

(h) The _____ variable is the predictor variable.

(i) The "least squares" criterion refers to the fact that we _____
_____ of the data from the prediction (regression) line.

(j) The definitional formula for predicting $\hat{z}_y$ from z_x is $\hat{z}_y =$ _____
_____ z_x.

(k) The best estimate of Y is the mean $(\bar{Y})$ when _____.

(l) When we predict Y from X the _____ (horizontal, vertical) squared deviations are minimized.

(m) The square root of the variance around the regression line is the
_____.

(n) The better the regression line fits the data, the _____
(higher, lower) the variance of the estimate $(s^2_{\text{est } y})$ will be.

(o) In the equation $Y = bX + a$ the y intercept (the point at which the line crosses the ordinate) is equal to _____.

2. For each of the variables below, indicate which is the predictor variable, which is the dependent variable, and whether there is a causal relationship between the predictor and dependent variables.

(a) The length of time it takes to read a word and the number of letters in the word

Predictor variable: _____

Dependent variable: _____

(b) $\hat{z}_x = rz_y$

Predictor variable: _____

Dependent variable: _____

_____

(c) Personality inventory and diagnosis of mental disturbances

Predictor variable: _____

Dependent variable: _____

_____

(d) Aptitude test and achievement test

Predictor variable: _____

Dependent variable: _____

_____

(e) Resume of job experience and success at a job

Predictor variable: _____

Dependent variable: _____

_____

(f) $X = bY + a$

Predictor variable: _____

Dependent variable: _____

_____

(g) Distance to be traveled and number of gallons of gas needed.

Predictor variable: _____

Dependent variable: _____

_____

(h) SAT (Scholastic Aptitude Test) scores and high school grades

Predictor variable: _____

Dependent variable: _____

_____

(i) SAT (Scholastic Aptitude Test) scores and college grade point average

Predictor variable: _____

Dependent variable: _____

_____

B. Problems

1. In each of the linear equations of Table 5.1 solve for Y (to two decimal places) when $X = -5, -1, -1/2, 0$ and 3 (using the space provided in the table). Then plot these equations on the graph paper provided at the end of the chapter.

Table 5.1

Use for Solving Linear Equations

Equation	X	Y	X	Y	X	Y	X	Y	X	Y
(a) $Y = X/10 + 6$	−5	____	−1	____	−½	____	0	____	3	____
(b) $3Y = 2X - 7$	−5	____	−1	____	−½	____	0	____	3	____
(c) $4Y = 3X$	−5	____	−1	____	−½	____	0	____	3	____
(d) $Y = X + 2$	−5	____	−1	____	−½	____	0	____	3	____
(e) $Y = 0.5X + 1.6$	−5	____	−1	____	−½	____	0	____	3	____

2. For each equation presented in Question 1, indicate the values of b_y and a_y. Then solve the equations in terms of X and indicate the values of b_x and a_x.

(a) $b_y =$ _____ $a_y =$ _____

   $b_x =$ _____ $a_x =$ _____

(b) $b_y =$ _____ $a_y =$ _____

   $b_x =$ _____ $a_x =$ _____

(c) $b_y =$ _____ $a_y =$ _____

   $b_x =$ _____ $a_x =$ _____

(d) $b_y =$ _____ $a_y =$ _____

   $b_x =$ _____ $a_x =$ _____

(e) $b_y =$ _____ $a_y =$ _____

   $b_x =$ _____ $a_x =$ _____

3. What is the predicted z score for Y, $\hat{z}_y$, if we know that the standard

score of X, z_x, equals 1.23 and that 25 % of the variance is accounted for by the correlation coefficient (r) relating X to Y?

---

4. Using the following data: $\bar{X} = 95$, $s_x^2 = 4$, $\bar{Y} = 123$, $s_y = 5$, and $r^2 = 0.64$

(a) Formulate the linear regression equation that would be necessary to predict X from Y.

(b) Formulate the linear regression equation that would be used to predict Y from X.

(c) If X equals 90, what is the predicted value of Y?

(d) If Y equals 138, what is the predicted value of X?

_____

_____

(e) Plot both regression equations on the graph paper provided at the end of the chapter.

5. Dr. Morrsarian, a physics professor, was interested in how beneficial or detrimental one student could be to his or her lab partner. He randomly paired his 18 students at the first lab meeting and then compared the final lab grades for the two partners. These grades are presented in Table 5.2.

TABLE 5.2
Final Grades Collected from Dr. Morrsarian's Physics Class

Pair	X	Y	X^2	Y^2	XY	$\hat{X}$	$\hat{Y}$
1	63	59	____	____	____	____	____
2	72	75	____	____	____	____	____
3	51	48	____	____	____	____	____
4	86	88	____	____	____	____	____
5	28	30	____	____	____	____	____
6	52	60	____	____	____	____	____
7	79	88	____	____	____	____	____
8	63	59	____	____	____	____	____
9	54	55	____	____	____	____	____

$\Sigma X =$ ___ $\Sigma Y =$ ___ $\Sigma X^2 =$ ___ $\Sigma Y^2 =$ ___ $\Sigma XY =$ ___

(a) Using Table 5.2 compute the quantities required to formulate the regression equation necessary to predict the grade of the X member of each lab pair from the Y member. (Use the raw score formulas.)

_____

_____

(b) Using these data formulate the regression equation necessary to predict the grade of the Y member of the lab team from that of the X member.

_____

_____

(c) Plot the raw data and the two linear equations on the same axes. (Use the graph paper provided at the end of the chapter.)

Formulas

Linear equations

$$Y = bX + a$$

$$X = (1/b)Y + (-a/b)$$

Regression equations—predicting Y from X

$$\hat{z}_y = rz_x$$

$$\hat{Y} = b_y X - a_y$$

$$\hat{Y} = r\left(\frac{s_y}{s_x}\right) X - r\left(\frac{s_y}{s_x}\right) \bar{X} + \bar{Y}$$

Alternative computing formulas—predicting Y from X

$$b_y = \frac{N\Sigma XY - (\Sigma X)(\Sigma Y)}{N\Sigma X^2 - (\Sigma X)^2}$$

$$a_y = \frac{(\Sigma X^2)(\Sigma Y) - (\Sigma XY)(\Sigma X)}{N\Sigma X^2 - (\Sigma X)^2}$$

Regression equations—predicting X from Y

$$\hat{z}_x = rz_y$$

$$\hat{X} = b_x Y - a_x$$

$$\hat{X} = r\left(\frac{s_x}{s_y}\right) Y - r\left(\frac{s_x}{s_y}\right) \bar{Y} + \bar{X}$$

Alternative computing formulas—predicting X from Y

$$b_x = \frac{N\Sigma XY - (\Sigma X)(\Sigma Y)}{N\Sigma Y^2 - (\Sigma Y)^2}$$

$$a_x = \frac{(\Sigma Y^2)(\Sigma X) - (\Sigma XY)(\Sigma Y)}{N\Sigma Y^2 - (\Sigma Y)^2}$$

Variance

$r^2 = $ the proportion of variance accounted for

$1 - r^2 = $ the proportion of variance not accounted for

$s_{\text{est } y}^2 = $ the variance of the estimate of Y

$$= \frac{\Sigma(Y - \hat{Y})^2}{N}$$

$$= s_y^2(1 - r^2)$$

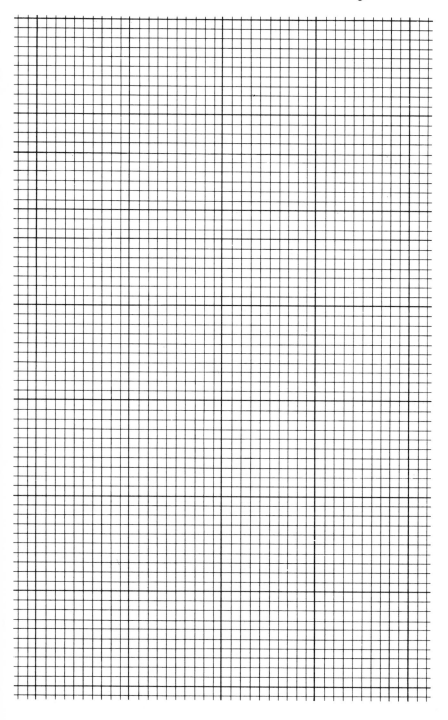

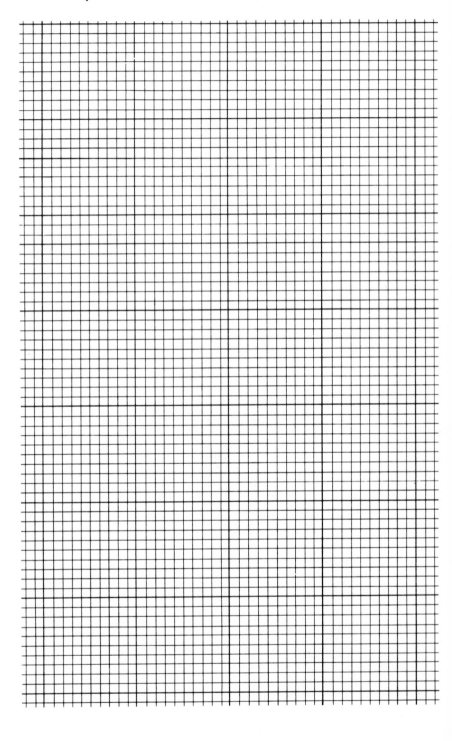

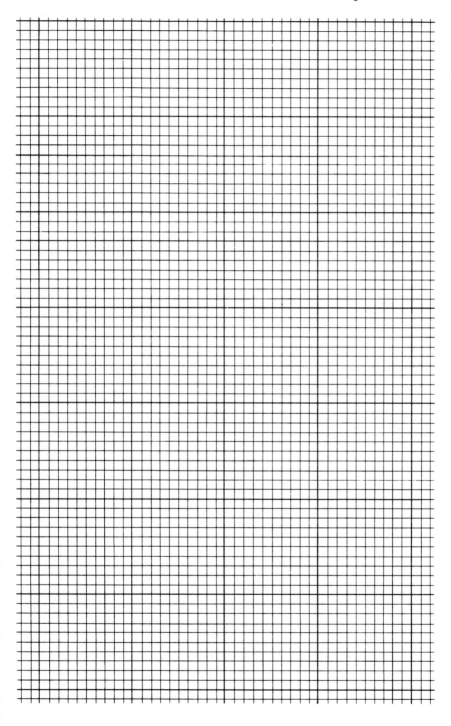

CHAPTER 6

Probability and Its Relationship to Statistics

A. Conceptual Questions

1. In each statement below one or more words have been omitted. Fill in each blank with the appropriate word or words.

(a) To calculate the probability that two events will both occur (A *and* B) one would use the _____ mult. _____ rule.

(b) _____ $p\left(\dfrac{A}{B}\right)$ _____ is the number of outcomes favoring A when B has occurred divided by the total number of possible outcomes.

(c) _____ sample space _____ is the total set of all equally likely outcomes.

(d) By using the _____ or _____ rule, one could calculate the probability that either one of two events (A *or* B) will occur.

(e) _____ $P(A)$ _____ is the number of events favorable to A divided by the total number of possible events.

(f) If two events are _____ mutually exclusive _____, the occurrence of one precludes the occurrence of the other.

(g) All elements in the sample space must be _____ equally likely _____ and _____ denumerable _____.

54

2. Each statement or question below is followed by four choices. Choose the one that best completes the statement or answers the question and place its number in the blank on the left.

____(a) If two events are mutually exclusive and exhaustive, what is the probability that on the fifth trial either one of them will occur?
- (1) 1
- (2) 1/5
- (3) 1/10
- (4) Cannot say without more information about the outcomes on the first four trials.

____(b) If two events are _____ they are sampled with replacement.
- (1) Mutually exclusive
- (2) Mutually exhaustive
- (3) Independent
- (4) Nonindependent

____(c) If two events are _____ they are sampled without replacement.
- (1) Mutually exclusive
- (2) Mutually exhaustive
- (3) Independent
- (4) Nonindependent

____(d) The probability that an event will occur is _____.
- (1) Always greater than 1
- (2) Always between 0 and 1
- (3) Equal to 1/2, if there are two possible events
- (4) There is not enough information given to answer this question.

____(e) The gambler's fallacy _____.
- (1) Refers to the fact that gamblers are destined to lose
- (2) Assumes that chance events in a series are not independent
- (3) Assumes that chance events in a series are mutually exclusive
- (4) None of the above

3. Indicate whether each equation or description below refers to *r*-tuplets, permutations, arrangements, or combinations.

(a) ___*perm*___ = $n!$

(b) ___Arrang___ is a proper subset of the number of distinguishable events in a particular order where no event is repeated.

(c) ___r tuplets___ $= n_1 \times n_2 \times \cdots \times n_r$

(d) ___Arrang___ $= n!/(n - r)!$

(e) ___Comb___ is the number of distinguishable groups of a particular size without regard to order.

(f) _____ would be used to calculate the number of groups
of three children (each from a different grade) which could be formed
from 20 first-graders, 25 second-graders, and 22 third-graders.

(g) _____ $= n!/r!(n - r)!$

(h) _____ = the number of combinations multiplied by the
number of permutations of each combination.

B. Problems

(Note: Express all probabilities as fractions or products of fractions.)

1. Suppose a monkey were seated at a special typewriter which contained exactly 8 keys—A, E, G, I, L, M, N and T. (1) What is the probability that the monkey would type out each of the following names? (2) What is the probability that at least one of five monkeys, each at his or her own typewriter, would type out each of the following names? (Assume that each of the 8 letters is equally likely to be hit.)

(a) LIAM

(1) $\left(\dfrac{L}{8}\right)^4$ _____

(2) $1 - \left[\left(1 - \dfrac{1}{8}\right)^4\right]^5$ _____

(b) GLENNA

(1) $\dfrac{1}{8}^6$ _____

(2) _____

(c) TIM

(1) $\left(\dfrac{1}{8}\right)^3$ _____

(2) _____

2. What is the probability that two or more people will be born under the same sign of the zodiac if there are three people in a room? (Assume that one twelfth of the population was born under each sign of the zodiac.)

3. What is the probability of each of the following events when drawing cards from a regular deck of 52 playing cards?

(a) Drawing three spades in a row (without replacement)

$$\frac{1}{4} \quad \frac{12}{51} \quad \frac{11}{50}$$

(b) Drawing any ace or the 2 of diamonds

$$2 \left(\frac{4}{52} \times \frac{1}{52} \right.$$

(c) Drawing three hearts and then two spades (with replacement)

$$\frac{13}{52} \times \frac{13}{52} \times \frac{13}{52} \times \frac{13}{52} \times \frac{13}{52}$$

(d) Drawing the ace, king, queen, and jack of the same suit in that order (without replacement)

(e) Drawing all 4 aces (with replacement)

_____

4. How many five-person committees can be formed from a group of 10 men and 5 women such that there are

(a) Three women and two men on every committee

$$\left(\frac{5}{3}\right) \times \frac{10}{2} = 18 \times 45 = 450$$

(b) Two women and three men on every committee

$$\frac{5}{2} \times \frac{10}{3} = 10 \times 120 = 1200$$

(c) Five men on each committee

$$\frac{10}{5} = 252$$

5. Mr. Briggs is running an experiment to test the effects of trigram construction on reading time. He wishes to use the vowels a and i and the consonants b, c, d, and g.

(a) How many CVC (consonant-vowel-consonant) trigrams can be constructed if no consonant is repeated within a trigram?

$4 \times 2 \times 3$

(b) How many CVC trigrams can be constructed if the consonants can be repeated within a trigram?

$4 \times 2 \times 4$

(c) If after a brief exposure to the stimulus the subject merely has to tell which vowel—a or i—was used, what correction for guessing should Mr. Briggs employ?

number correct   numb. wrong

(d) Suppose he decides to use CVCV quadragrams—how many stimulus items can he construct with these letters if neither vowels nor consonants are repeated?

$4 \times 2 \times 3 \times 1 = 24$

(e) How many CVCV quadragrams can be constructed if letters can be repeated?

$4 \times 2 \times 4 \times 2 = 64$

6. What is the probability that with two dice each of the following sums will be rolled? Give the odds against each event's occurring.

(a) two ___ $\frac{1}{36}$ _____

(b) three ___ $\frac{2}{36}$ _____

(c) six ___ $\frac{5}{36}$ _____

(d) seven _____

(e) eleven _____

7. Unable to decide which of her two children should receive the extra cupcake, Ms. Lane told them she had chosen a number between 1 and 10, and that the child who guessed correctly would receive the cupcake. Numbers 3, 6, and 2 were guessed and none of them proved correct.

(a) What is the probability that a four guessed next will be correct?

$\frac{1}{7}$ _____

(b) If the four was not correct, what is the probability that a five or a seven will be correct on the next (5th) trial? ___ $\frac{1}{3}$ _____

8. Interested in whether or not the ears function independently, Dr. Green conducted the following experiment. A particular tone, A, at a particular intensity was detected by the right ear 46 % of the time and by the left ear 42 % of the time. Another tone, B, was detected by the right ear 53 % of the time and by the left ear 48 % of the time. Using this information, answer the following questions.

(a) Suppose the two ears function independently. What is the probability that a binaural presentation (presentation to both ears) of tone A will be detected?_____

(b) What is the probability that a binaural presentation of tone B will be detected if the ears function independently? _____

(c) If tone A is presented to the right ear and tone B is presented to the left ear, what is the probability that if the ears function independently a stimulus will be detected? _____

Formulas

Probability—simple and compound events

$$P(A) = \frac{\text{Number of possible outcomes favoring } A}{\text{Total number of possible outcomes}}$$

$$P(A/B) = \frac{\begin{array}{c}\text{Number of possible outcomes favoring } A \\ \text{when } B \text{ has occurred}\end{array}}{\text{Total number of possible outcomes}}$$

$P(A/B) = P(A)$, when A and B are independent events

$P(A \text{ and } B) = P(A) \times P(B)$, when A and B are independent events

$P(A \text{ and } B) = P(A) \times P(B/A)$

$\qquad\qquad = P(A/B) \times P(B)$, when A and B are not independent events

$P(A \text{ or } B) = P(A) + P(B)$, when A and B are mutually exclusive events

$P(A \text{ or } B \text{ or both}) = P(A) + P(B) - P(A \text{ and } B)$, when A and B are nonmutually exclusive events

$b{:}a$ = the odds against event A, when $P(A) = \dfrac{a}{a+b}$

Number of outcomes

r-Tuplets: $N_r = n_1 \times n_2 \times n_3 \times \cdots \times n_r$

r-Tuplets: $N_r = n^r$, when the number of each type of event is the same

Permutations: $P_n = n!$

Arrangements: $A_r^n = n \times (n-1) \times (n-2) \times \cdots \times (n-r+1)$

$$= \frac{n!}{(n-r)!}$$

Combinations: $C_r^n = \dbinom{n}{r} = \dfrac{n!}{r!\,(n-r)!}$

CHAPTER 7

An Introduction to Experimental Design

A. Conceptual Questions

1. In each sentence below fill in the blank with the word or words which will make the sentence true.

(a) The _____ variable represents the behavior sampled in an experiment.

(b) The _____ variable is manipulated by the experimenter.

(c) Experimental results (data) are evaluated by _____.

(d) When deciding on the appropriate analysis it is important to know the scale of measurement of the _____ variable.

(e) A Latin square will yield _____ permutations of five conditions.

(f) In a Latin square of six conditions each condition would appear in each position _____ time(s).

(g) When right-handed subjects are assigned to one experimental condition and left-handed subjects are assigned to a second condition, the independent variable (handedness) is said to be _____ (natural, artificial).

(h) It is advisable to use ABBA with only half the subjects and _____ with the other half.

(i) Sample statistics for nominal data are either _____ or _____.

(j) When trials are arranged so that the average position of any one condition is about equal to the average position of any other condition, the sequence is _____.

(k) When the dependent variable is measured on a(n) _____ scale, the sample statistic will most likely be the median.

(l) All members of a population have an equal probability of being picked for a sample when _____ sampling techniques are used.

(m) When taking a public opinion poll, one is most likely to use _____ sampling methods when picking subjects.

(n) Sequences of trials are counterbalanced when it _____ (is, is not) important whether or not subjects can anticipate the type of event.

2. Each of the following questions can be answered by one of four choices given below. Choose the most appropriate answer and place its number in the space provided to the left of each question. The four choices are (1) exactly one, (2) one or more, (3) exactly two, and (4) two or more.

_____(a) How many independent variables are appropriate for an experiment analyzed with a one-way analysis of variance?

_____(b) How many levels of each independent variable are appropriate for an experiment analyzed by a one-way analysis of variance?

_____(c) How many dependent variables are appropriate for an experiment analyzed by a one-way analysis of variance?

_____(d) How many independent variables are appropriate for an experiment analyzed by a two-way analysis of variance?

_____(e) How many levels of each independent variable are appropriate for an experiment analyzed by a two-way analysis of variance?

_____(f) How many dependent variables are appropriate for an experiment analyzed by a two-way analysis of variance?

3. Indicate whether each of the following statements is true or false by placing a "T" or "F" to the left of each question.

_____(a) Stimuli which are difficult for the subject to distinguish are usually randomized.

_____(b) In choosing the appropriate statistical test, a competent experimenter takes into account whether or not the independent variable is natural or artificial.

_____(c) The various conditions for a particular independent variable can be manipulated quantitatively but not qualitatively.

_____(d) To statistically analyze the results of an experiment, the dependent variable must be on an interval or ratio scale.

_____(e) A completely randomized two-way factorial experiment with three levels of one variable and two levels of the other variable can be considered either a 2 × 3 design or a 3 × 2 design.

_____(f) The median can be used as a test statistic for interval or ratio data.

_____(g) The t test is a specific case of the analysis of variance.

_____(h) When interested in what an organism can do, the method used in choosing the sample is not critical.

_____(i) Whether stimulus items are randomly chosen or controlled is usually not critical.

_____(j) In a Latin square, each condition follows every other condition an equal number of times.

4. Following each statement below are four choices. Select the most appropriate word or phrase to complete each statement and indicate its number in the space provided to the left of each statement.

_____(a) In a 3 × 5 mixed factorial design where the between-subjects variable has three levels, each subject participates in _____ conditions.
(1) Two
(2) Three
(3) Five
(4) Fifteen

_____(b) The two- in a two-way ANOVA refers to the fact that there are _____.
(1) Two dependent variables
(2) Two variables: one dependent and one independent
(3) Two independent variables
(4) None of the above

_____(c) Each subject in a completely randomized 2 × 3 factorial experiment will participate in _____ conditions.
(1) One
(2) Two
(3) Three
(4) Six

_____(d) In a 3 × 4 within-subjects (repeated measures) factorial experiment each subject participates in _____ conditions.
(1) One
(2) Two
(3) Three
(4) Twelve

_____(e) It is necessary to control for order of trial blocks _____ subjects.
(1) Within
(2) Between
(3) Neither
(4) Both

___(f) In order to counterbalance order of presentation of trial blocks within subjects, an experimenter might _____.
(1) Use a Latin square
(2) Use the ABBA method
(3) Both (1) and (2)
(4) Neither (1) nor (2)

_____(g) To guard against subjects' anticipation of stimuli, an experimenter should _____.

   (1) Counterbalance trials
   (2) Try to deceive the subject
   (3) Counterbalance trial blocks
   (4) Randomize the sequence of stimuli

_____(h) In choosing the appropriate sample statistic a critical factor is

   _____.

   (1) The scale of measurement of the dependent variable
   (2) The number of levels of the independent variable
   (3) The number of independent variables
   (4) All of the above

B. Problems

1. Briefly answer each of the following questions in the space provided.

(a) In what kind of experiment can either a t test or a one-way analysis of variance be used?

_____   _____

_____

(b) Why is a within-subjects design more sensitive than a between-subjects design?

_____

_____

(c) When would an experimenter choose a between-subjects design instead of a within-subjects design?

_____   _____

_____

(d) Why is the method of choosing a sample important?

_____

_____

(e) What is the justification for using the data gathered from college students (who represent a highly specialized segment of the population) to learn about the population at large?

_____

_____

(f) When and why is it desirable to counterbalance trials?

_____

_____

(g) Name two methods of randomizing repeated stimuli.

_____

_____

(h) When would it be preferable to counterbalance blocks of trials instead of individual trials?

_____

_____

2. In each one-factor experiment below choose whether the appropriate analysis is an independent groups t test, a matched-pairs t test, a one-way analysis of variance, completely randomized, or a one-way repeated measures analysis of variance. Indicate your choice in the space provided after each experiment.

(a) Visual and acoustic sensitivity are measured on a ratio scale for each of 10 subjects.

_____

(b) IQ scores of husbands and wives are measured for 15 couples.

_____

(c) Comparing 10 male and 10 female executives on IQ scores.

_____

(d) Fifteen college students were each measured on her or his reaction time (speed of responding) when responding to high, medium, and low frequency words.

_____

(e) Achievement test scores of students taught calculus by either an experienced teacher, a new teacher, or a more advanced student.

_____

(f) Measuring the IQ scores of women working as clerks, secretaries, and executives.

_____   _____

(g) Measuring the science aptitude of men who have either below average, average, or superior intelligence ratings.

_____

(h) Testing the maze-running time of rats reared in either a neutral or enriched environment.

_____

(i) Measuring the weight of orphanage-reared and home-reared 15-year-olds.

_____

(j) Measuring the time needed for subjects to judge as different two stimuli which differ on either one, two, three, or four dimensions, when each subject sees all stimuli.

_____

3. Each of the following two-factor experiments can be analyzed with either a random, mixed, or repeated measures ANOVA. For each experiment described below indicate (1) the two independent variables, (2) the number of levels of each, (3) whether the independent variables are artificial or natural, (4) whether each variable is within-subjects or between-subjects, and (5) the appropriate ANOVA. Indicate your answers in the space provided after each experiment.

(a) Ms. Bernice Hauser, a reading specialist, examined the reading comprehension of students from below-average, normal, and above-average reading groups when each student was given both high- and low-interest reading materials.

(1) _____   _____

(2) _____

(3) _____

(4) _____

(5) _____

(b) Dr. Richard Di Rocco treated 40 rats with either a high or low dosage of a stimulant prior to training them on complicated mazes. After waiting one week, 10 rats from each group were given the same dosage received during training, while the remaining 20 rats were not given another dose. The rats were then tested on the previously learned mazes. The scores on this test constituted the dependent variable.

(1) _____

(2) _____

(3) _____

(4) _____

(5) _____

(c) Every year each student attending the Paul Stuart High School for Boys is tested on his math achievement and English achievement. The school's administration wants to study one particular class of 25 boys over the 4-year period each boy attends high school.

(1) _____

(2) _____

(3) _____

(4) _____

(5) _____

(d) Investigators have become interested in the relationship of both zodiac sign and aggressiveness to the annual salary of middle-aged males. After personality inventories were administered, subjects were designated as either aggressive or nonaggressive and sorted according to zodiac sign. Subjects' annual incomes were then analyzed.

(1) _____

(2) _____

(3) _____

(4) _____

(5) _____

(e) Sixty subjects participated in an experiment designed to evaluate the effects of both incentive and task difficulty on performance. Subjects were assigned to one of three incentive groups receiving either 1, 10, or 25 cents for each correct answer on a series of verbal tasks. Each subject participated in tasks of high, medium, and low difficulty.

(1) _____

(2) _____

(3) _____

(4) _____

(5) _____

4. In each of the following experiments state the optimum method of choosing (1) the subjects (random sampling, controlled sampling, or method not important), and (2) the stimuli. Indicate your answers in the space provided after each experiment.

(a) Testing the effect of high, medium, and low frequency words on reading speed.

(1) _____

(2) _____

(b) Previewing TV and radio commercials to predict how the population reacts to different commercials.

(1) _____

(2) _____

(c) Testing the effect of specialized training on learning different tactile discriminations.

(1) _____

(2) _____

(d) Predicting whether sex will influence voting on political issues.

(1) _____

(2) _____

(e) Investigating the general knowledge of the inhabitants of a particular country.

(1) _____

(2) _____

5. Construct a standard Latin square for an experiment with 7 conditions (T, U, V, W, X, Y, and Z). (Use the grid below.)

(a) Is this the only Latin square which can be constructed for these 7 conditions?

_____

(b) Is a Latin square a between-subjects control or a within-subjects control? _____

(c) Does a Latin square cover all possible (nonrepeating) permutations of the stimulus conditions? _____

(d) Why or why not? _____

_____

CHAPTER 8

Theoretical Frequency Distributions: The Binomial and Normal Distributions

A. Conceptual Questions

1. Match each distribution named in column A with the appropriate definition in column B. Indicate your choice by placing the number of the definition in the blank to the left of the name.

A	B
3 (a) ____ Sampling distribution	(1) The elements in this distribution can take on an infinite number of values.
5 (b) ____ Discrete distribution	(2) The distribution of values obtained from a subset of the population.
1 4 (c) ____ Continuous distribution	(3) The distribution of all possible values of the test statistic.
4 ✱ (d) ____ Population distribution	(4) The (often theoretical) distribution of the values of a dependent variable which include all the members of a group.
2 (e) ____ Sample distribution	(5) All the values of this distribution are integers.

2. Fill in the missing word or words which will make each statement below true.

(a) Trials of binary independent events are known as _____ _Bernoulli_ _____ trials.

(b) There are _____ terms in a binomial expansion because the desired event may happen 0 times.

(c) In a binomial distribution, the two events _____ (must, need not) have equal probabilities of occurring.

(d) In a binomial distribution, the two events _____ (must, need not) be independent.

(e) A binomial distribution is completely described by the two parameters _____ and _____.

(f) A normal distribution is completely described by the two parameters _____ and _____.

(g) The _____ distribution is a continuous approximation of the _____ distribution.

(h) In a normal distribution the proportion of the distribution lying above the mean is _____.

(i) A _____ distribution describes the probability that one of two independent events occurred with each possible frequency out of N opportunities.

(j) The probability of a z score of 2.00 equals _____.

(k) The proportion of successes is equal to the frequency of successes divided by _____.

(l) The _____ is always symmetric and unimodal.

(m) As the probability of event A deviates from 1/2, the binomial distribution becomes _____ (more, less) skewed and the standard deviation _____ (increases, decreases).

B. Problems

1. Expand the binomial for $p = 1/6$ and $N = 5$ as would be done in computing the probability of obtaining 5, 4, $\cdots$, 0 sixes out of five throws of a die.

_____

_____

_____

_____

2. Mr. Epps lectures in an introductory psychology course which contains 600 men and 400 women. Write the binomial expansion which expresses the probability of obtaining 4, 3, 2, 1, or 0 men in a randomly chosen group of 4 students. Make a histogram of these probabilities using the graph paper provided at the end of the chapter. (Note: Assume that students are chosen *with* replacement so that the binomial probabilities will be appropriate.)

_____

_____

_____

_____

3. Suppose a fair die is tossed 5 times and a success is defined as the tossing of a 1 or a 2.

(a) What is the probability of a success?

_____

(b) What is the probability that a 1 or a 2 occurs exactly three times?

_____

(c) What is the probability that a 1 or a 2 never occurs?

_____

(d) What is the probability that a 1 or a 2 occurs at least once?

_____

(e) What is the probability that a 1 or a 2 occurs exactly five times? (That is, all five tosses consist of a 1 or a 2.)

_____

4. Seventy-five percent of the freshman class at a particular university graduate in four years. (Note: In the following questions, assume sampling with replacement.)

(a) What is the probability that in a group of 6 students none will graduate?

_____

_____

(b) What is the probability that in a group of 6 students exactly 4 will graduate?

_____

_____

(c) What is the probability that at least 3 out of 6 students will graduate?

_____

_____

(d) If there are 1,000 students in the entering class, how many students would be expected to graduate in 4 years?

_____

_____

(e) Assume there are 1,000 students in every freshman class over the infinite future. Calculate the mean and standard deviation of the distribution of graduating seniors.

_____

_____

5. On an English exam the mean score was 78 and the standard deviation was 12. Calculate the z scores for each of the following grades.

(a) 92_____

(b) 58_____

(c) 62_____

(d) 75_____

(e) 85_____

6. The average height of basketball players is 6'3" (i.e., 75 inches) with a standard deviation of 2.5 inches. What height in inches corresponds to each of the following z scores?

(a) +2.5 _____

(b) −1.3 _____

(c) +0.5 _____

(d) +1.8 _____

(e) −2.6 _____

7. Find the area under the normal curve for each of the following (use (Table C.1).

(a) between $z = 0.5$ and $z = 1.6$

_____

(b) above $z = -0.75$

_____

(c) for $z = 2.5$

_____

(d) between $z = -2.6$ and $z = +0.85$

_____

(e) below $z = +1.3$

_____

8. Two thousand high school seniors took a history exam. The mean grade was 68, the standard deviation was 10, and the distribution of scores was normal.

(a) How many students obtained at least a 70 and thus passed the exam?

_____

_____

(b) How many students received a grade of at least 85 and passed with honors?

_____

_____

(c) If students receiving grades between 50 and 70 were allowed to take the exam over, how many new exams would be needed?

_____

_____

(d) What score is at the 90th percentile?

_____

_____

(e) What score is at the 45th percentile?

_____

_____

Formulas

Binomial distribution

$$p + q = 1$$

$$(p + q)^N = \binom{N}{N} p^N q^0 + \binom{N}{N-1} p^{N-1} q^1 + \binom{N}{N-2} p^{N-2} q^2$$

$$+ \cdots + \binom{N}{r} p^r q^{N-r} + \cdots + \binom{N}{0} p^0 q^N$$

$$P(r \text{ out of } N \text{ successes}) = \binom{N}{r} p^r q^{N-r}$$

$$\mu_r = Np$$

$$\sigma_r = \sqrt{Npq}$$

$$\mu_P = p$$

$$\sigma_P = \sqrt{\frac{pq}{N}}$$

Normal distribution

$$z = \frac{X - \mu}{\sigma}$$

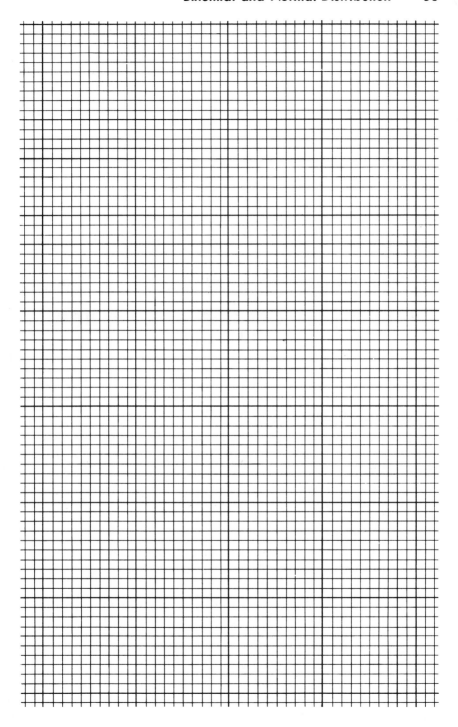

CHAPTER 9

The Logic of Statistical Influence: Hypothesis Testing and Estimation

A. Conceptual Questions

1. Each statement below refers to either the alternative hypothesis (H_1) or the null hypothesis (H_0). Indicate the appropriate hypothesis in the spaces provided.

(a) The __H_1__ hypothesis is tested indirectly.

H_0 (b) An experimenter would probably want to accept the _____ hypothesis when seeking to prove that data generated by a theoretical model are indistinguishable from human behavior.

H_0 (c) The _____ hypothesis states an exact relationship between population parameters.

H_0 (d) If there were no effect of the experimental manipulation we would accept the _____ hypothesis.

H_1 (e) The _____ hypothesis is diffuse.

86

(f) The _____ hypothesis of an experiment might be that the variance of the experimental group equals the variance of the control group ($\sigma_E^2 = \sigma_C^2$).

(g) A possible _____ hypothesis is: the mean of the treated group is less than or equal to the mean of the control group ($\mu_T \leq \mu_C$).

(h) The _____ hypothesis might state that the standard deviation of the voting practices of registered Republicans is smaller than that of registered Democrats ($\sigma_R < \sigma_D$).

(i) The _____ hypothesis is accepted when the test statistic falls into the rejection range.

(j) A two-tail test is used when the _____ hypothesis is not directional.

(k) An experimenter would probably want to accept the _____ hypothesis if her aim were to show that two groups were well matched.

2. In the spaces provided, write in the word or words which best complete the following paragraph.

When comparing two population parameters we ask the following question: Could a difference as large as that which was obtained between population parameters be due to (a)? If the answer is yes then we can accept the (b) hypothesis and fail to accept the (c) hypothesis. If the answer is no then we will (d) the alternative hypothesis and (e) the null hypothesis.

(a) _____ chance _____

(b) _____ null _____

(c) _____ alt _____

(d) _____ acc _____

(e) _____ rej _____

3. Decide whether each of the following statements is true or false. Indicate your answer in the space provided to the left of each statement.

_(a) When the power of a statistical test is maximized, the probability of incorrectly rejecting the null hypothesis is also maximized.

_(b) The larger the absolute difference between H_0 and the true value of H_1, the more powerful the test.

_(c) A statistic which is significant at the 0.001 level is always significant at the 0.05 level.

_(d) It is more likely that a point estimate will be correct if the corresponding interval estimate is small.

_(e) A biased point estimate cannot be changed into an unbiased point estimate.

_(f) The null hypothesis, as its name implies, must be a hypothesis of no difference between population parameters.

_(g) In order to calculate the probability of committing a Type I error we must first assume that a particular value of H_1 is true.

_(h) We can assume that the mean of the sampling distribution ($\bar{X}$) equals the population mean (μ) if the sample size, N, is very large.

_(i) The point estimate is not always the best estimate of a population parameter.

4. In the spaces provided indicate which of the following statements refer to Type I errors and which refer to Type II errors.

_(a) This error results from falsely rejecting a true H_0.

_(b) The probability of making this error is equal to the area under the rejection region when the null hypothesis is true.

_(c) The probability of making this type of error is not generally known.

_(d) The probability of making this type of error is called beta (β).

_(e) The probability of making this type of error is known.

_____ (f) This error leads to incorrectly accepting a false alternative hypothesis.

_____ (g) As the probability of making this type of error increases, the power decreases.

_____ (h) The probability of making this type of error is called alpha (α).

5. Complete each statement below with the appropriate word or phrase.

(a) The range within which a population parameter lies with a specified probability is the _____ int est _____.

(b) _____ hyp test _____ requires that we divide all of the possible states of the world into two mutually exclusive and exhaustive states.

(c) Hypothesis testing assesses whether the effects observed in an experiment are due to _____ chance _____ or _____ ind var _____ _____.

(d) We are interested in the effects of experimental manipulation on the _____ dep var _____ variable.

(e) With a directional alternative hypothesis, a _____ 1 tailed _____ test is used.

(f) When interested only in treatments which have large effects, one would use a _____ small _____ sample size.

(g) As the value of α is increased, the power of a test is _____ dec _____.

(h) Population _____ parameter _____ are estimated from sample _____ statistics _____.

(i) As the sample size increases, the standard deviation of the sampling distribution _____ dec _____.

(j) The _____ SE _____ of the mean depends on the standard deviation of the population (σ) and the sample size (N).

(k) An extreme value in either tail of the sampling distribution will reject a nondirectional _____ null _____ hypothesis.

(l) The standard deviation of the sampling distribution is the _____
    _____S.E.,_____ .

(m) The _____norma l_____ distribution is a good approximation for the binomial distribution.

(n) When N _____lnc_____ , the sampling distribution of sample means approaches a normal distribution.

(o) When the standard deviation of the population (σ) is estimated, the sampling distribution of means follows a _____t dist_____ .

(p) According to the _central limit th_ the sampling distribution of sample means drawn from a population of unknown form will approach a normal distribution as the sample size (N) increases.

6. Choose the word or words which best complete the following statements. Indicate your answer in the space provided to the left of each statement.

_4_ _____ (a) The sampling distribution is defined as the distribution of all possible values of a test statistic when _____.
    (1) the population is normal
    (2) the test statistic is extreme
    (3) the alternative hypothesis is true
    (4) the null hypothesis is true

_2_ _____ (b) We evaluate the validity of the _____ by evaluating the value of the _____.
    (1) test statistic/null hypothesis
    (2) null hypothesis/test statistic
    (3) dependent variable/independent variable
    (4) population/sample

_2_ _____ (c) The power function is the graph of the power of the test for every possible _____.
    (1) value of H_0
    (2) value of H_1
    (3) significance level
    (4) sample size

_l_ _____ (d) Which of the following is least useful when choosing a test statistic?

    (1) the sample size
    (2) the population parameters of interest
    (3) the number of levels of the independent variable
    (4) the nature of the dependent variable

_____ (e) In order to evaluate the test statistic we must refer to
    _____.

    (1) the alternative hypothesis
    (2) the sampling distribution
    (3) the population distribution
    (4) all of the above

_____ (f) A parametric test is _____ than a nonparametric test.
    (1) more powerful
    (2) just as powerful
    (3) less powerful
    (4) cannot be determined without knowledge of the particular
    experiment

_____ (g) The area under the rejection region is equal to _____.
    (1) the significance level
    (2) the probability of making a Type I error
    (3) the probability of obtaining a test statistic in that area
    when the null hypothesis is true
    (4) all of the above

_____ (h) To calculate an interval estimate, the experimenter must
    know the sampling distribution of _____.
    (1) the population
    (2) the point estimate
    (3) the sample
    (4) the subjects

_____ (i) An unbiased statistic is _____.
    (1) not consistently greater than or less than the population
    value
    (2) never greater than or less than the population value
    (3) s^2
    (4) constantly overestimating or underestimating the popu-
    lation parameter

_____ (j) As the sample gets larger the interval estimate _____.
(1) stays the same

(2) becomes larger
(3) becomes smaller
(4) becomes more important

_____ (k) The range within which a parameter will lie with a certain probability is indicated by the _____.
(1) rejection range
(2) confidence limits
(3) level of significance
(4) power of the test

_____ (l) We can assume a normal sampling distribution of means when the sample size, N, is small in which of the following cases?
(1) when the population distribution is normal and the population standard deviation is known
(2) when the population standard deviation is estimated and the population is normal
(3) when the population distribution follows a t distribution
(4) none of the above

_____ (m) Which of the following statements does *not* apply to the t distribution? It is _____ .
(1) symmetric
(2) used when the population variance is estimated
(3) independent of the number of observations
(4) unimodal

_____ (n) The form of the sampling distribution of the sample means depends on _____.
(1) the form of the population distribution
(2) N, the sample size
(3) whether σ is estimated or known
(4) all of the above

B. Problems

1. For each experimental situation described below, state (1) the null hypothesis, (2) the alternative hypothesis, and (3) whether it is directional or nondirectional.

(a) Testing whether a die is fair by tossing it 60 times and observing the number of times a one comes up.

(1) _____

(2) _____

(3) _____

(b) Testing whether sex is a predictor of manual dexterity.

(1) _____

(2) _____

(3) _____

(c) Testing the notion that cats are smarter than dogs.

(1) _____

(2) _____

(3) _____

(d) Testing whether a certain drug reduces anxiety.

(1) _____

(2) _____

(3) _____

(e) Testing whether children who watch educational television programs have above average IQ scores.

(1) _____

(2) _____

(3) _____

2. Briefly answer each of the following questions.

(a) Why are hypotheses never tested for inequality between two conditions?

_____

_____

(b) In psychology, we usually do *not* test for a non-zero difference between conditions. Why?

_____

_____

(c) What does dividing the state of the world into two mutually exclusive and exhaustive states mean?

_____

_____

(d) Why do we divide the world into two such states when hypothesis testing?

_____

_____

(e) Evaluate and explain the following statement: For the same level of significance, a one-tailed test requires a smaller difference between two sample means.

_____

_____

(f) An experimenter reported that the level of significance of a particular test statistic is 0.001. What does the number 0.001 represent?

_____

_____

(g) Why must a specific parameter value for H_1 be assumed in order to calculate the power $(1 - \beta)$ of a test?

_____

_____

(h) Explain the relationship between the directionality of the alternative hypothesis and the power of the test.

_____

_____

(i) What is the theoretical distinction between accepting the null hypothesis and failing to reject the null hypothesis?

_____

_____

(j) What is the purpose of statistical inference?

_____

_____

(k) To obtain a sampling distribution one could either draw repeated samples of a particular size or compute the theoretical probability. Which method is more desirable and why?

_____

_____

Formulas

Normal sampling distribution for r occurrences out of N

$$\mu_r = Np$$

$$\sigma_r = \sqrt{Npq}$$

$$z_r = \frac{r - \mu_r}{\sigma_r}$$

Normal sampling distribution for proportions

$$\mu_P = p$$

$$\sigma_P = \sqrt{\frac{pq}{N}}$$

$$z_P = \frac{P - \mu_P}{\sigma_P}$$

Measures of sample variance and standard deviation

$$s^2 = \frac{\Sigma x^2}{N}$$

$$s = \sqrt{\frac{\Sigma x^2}{N}}$$

Point estimates of population variance and standard deviation

$$\hat{s}^2 = \frac{\Sigma x^2}{N - 1}$$

$$\hat{s} = \sqrt{\frac{\Sigma x^2}{N - 1}}$$

Confidence limits for point estimates

$$95\% \text{ confidence limit} = S \pm z_{0.025}(SE)$$

$$99\% \text{ confidence limit} = S \pm z_{0.005}(SE)$$

Standard error of the mean

$$s_{\bar{x}} = \frac{\hat{s}}{\sqrt{N}} = \frac{s}{\sqrt{N - 1}}$$

CHAPTER 10

Comparing a Sample Mean with a Population Mean or Comparing Two Sample Means: The z and t Tests

A. Conceptual Questions

1. Choose the word or words which will make each sentence true. Indicate your choice by filling in the blank space in each statement.

(a) The confidence limits obtained with a z test give the maximum and minimum values within which the _population_ mean lies with a specified probability.

(b) When σ is _known_ _____ the sampling distribution of the mean is normal.

(c) Choosing a statistical test depends on the form of the _sampling distribution_ _____.

(d) The average difference between two sample means when the null hypothesis is true equals _0_.

(e) The standard deviation of the distribution of the differences between two sample means depends on the _pop. stan. devs._ and the _degrees of corr_.

98

null (f) When σ is known, a normal sampling distribution can be used to test whether the mean is equal to a hypothetical value specified by the _____ hypothesis.

(g) The _degrees of free dom_ indicates the number of values in a distribution which can be freely chosen once a particular statistic for that distribution is known.

(h) The _homogeneity_ assumption of the t distribution states that both samples are drawn from populations with equal standard deviations.

(i) The t test is said to be _robust_ because deviations from its underlying assumptions do not produce large effects with samples of equal size.

(j) If the sample mean falls in the _rejection region_ of its sampling distribution the null hypothesis is rejected.

2. Choose the word or phrase in parentheses which will make each statement true.

(a) Because the normal distribution is _____ (unimodal, symmetric) we use the same value to compute both the upper and lower confidence limits.

(b) A _one_ (z, t) test must be used when the population scores are assumed to be normally distributed and the population standard deviation is estimated.

(c) A _____ (within, between) subjects design helps control for large individual differences among subjects.

(d) A _____ (z, t) test is used when $\hat{s}$ is used as the value of the population standard deviation.

(e) As the positive correlation between scores increases, the standard deviation of the difference between the two sample means will _____ (increase, decrease) and, thus, the corresponding t value will _____ (increase, decrease).

(f) When the population standard deviation _____ (is, is not) known the sampling distribution is normal.

(g) The t distribution _____ (does, does not) depend on the sample size.

(h) The z distribution _____ (does, does not) depend on the sample size.

(i) One of the assumptions underlying the t test is that each of the two samples is drawn from a _____ (normal, t) distribution.

(j) A larger area of the distribution will lie above a particular _____ (t, z) score than the identical _____ (t, z) score.

(k) As the sample size _____ (increases, decreases) the critical value for the t distribution will approach the critical value for the normal distribution.

3. Choose the phrase which best completes each statement and place its number in the space provided.

_____ (a) z tests are not usually performed because:
  (1) An experimenter rarely knows enough about a population to hypothesize a specific value for its standard deviation.
  (2) The population standard deviation is usually known.
  (3) We can usually assume that the population distribution is normal.
  (4) All of the above.

_____ (b) In which of the following experiments would you be most likely to use a z test?
  (1) Comparing the maze learning times of rats reared in isolation to the learning times of rats reared in groups.
  (2) Comparing the height of politicians to the mean height of the general population.
  (3) Comparing the IQ scores of first-born children to the IQ scores of their younger siblings.
  (4) All of the above.

_____ (c) When using a t test, if two samples of different sizes yield identical descriptive statistics:

  (1) The results of both samples will be equally significant.
  (2) The smaller sample will produce more significant results.
  (3) The larger sample will produce more significant results.
  (4) It is impossible to tell without knowing the level of significance obtained with each sample.

L____ (d) Which of the following statements is *not* true for both the
normal and t distributions?
(1) The distributions vary with sample size.
(2) The distributions are unimodal.
(3) The distributions are symmetric.
(4) The underlying populations from which the samples are
drawn have normal distributions.

4. Indicate whether each of the following statements is true or false in the
space provided.

T ____ (a) The t distribution is a family of distributions each associated
with different degrees of freedom.

F ____ (b) If it is necessary to compute interval estimates a z test must
be used.

T ____ (c) Critical z scores are independent of the degrees of freedom.

f ____ (d) When using a t test to compare two means from independent
samples, one must know the sampling distribution of differences between the two sample means and not the sampling
distribution of the mean.

F ____ (e) Each subject must participate in both experimental conditions to justify the use of a matched t test.

T ____ (f) The average difference score is identical to the difference between the two sample means.

t ____ (g) The mean of a normal sampling distribution of sample means
equals the population mean.

F ____ (h) The standard error of the sampling distribution of sample
means equals the population standard deviation.

F ____ (i) When the difference between two means is large enough to
reject the null hypothesis with a two-tailed test, then the
null hypothesis can always be rejected by a one-tailed test.

B. Problems

1. Mr. Miller teaches art classes in an affluent suburban high school. Much to his chagrin, many of his colleagues assume that those students who are interested and excel in art are not as intelligent as their fellow students. Mr. Miller decided to put this claim to rest once and for all. From the school records he obtained the IQ scores of his 25 senior students and found that the mean IQ for this class was 114.

Assuming the population mean, μ, is 100 and the standard deviation, σ, is 15, answer the following questions.

$$z = \frac{\bar{X} - \mu_0}{\sigma_{\bar{x}}} \qquad \frac{114 - 100}{\frac{\sigma}{\sqrt{25}}}$$

(a) Is the sample mean significantly different from the population mean? At what level?

$$\frac{4}{15} \qquad \overline{.93} \qquad .0918$$

$$4.6$$

(b) What are the 95 % confidence limits for these data?

$$\frac{6\cancel{0}}{\frac{\sqrt{N}}{15\cancel{}}} \atop \frac{}{5}$$

$$114 \pm \cancel{.025}\ 1.96 \times \cancel{2.03}$$
$$5.88$$

$$108.12 - 119.88$$

(c) What are the 99 % confidence limits for these data?

After doing this experiment, Mr. Miller proudly displayed these results to his fellow teachers. One of his colleagues, Ms. Binkoff, raised the following objection. It was already known that the students of this school were brighter than the population average and thus Mr. Miller's art students should be compared to the rest of the students in this school and not to the general population.

Mr. Miller thought this objection valid. Thus he obtained the average IQ for this rather specialized population of students, $\mu = 110$, but he was unable to obtain the population standard deviation, σ. Instead he calculated the sample variance, $s^2 = 121$.

(d) Using this information, decide whether the sample mean is significantly different from the population mean.

$$\sqrt{s^2_{x_1} + s_{x_2}^2 - 2rs_{x_1}s_{x_2}}$$

$$\sqrt{121 + 121 - 2}$$

$t = $ _____ df = _____ $p < $ _____

(e) What are the 95 % confidence limits for these data?

_____

_____

(f) Mr. Miller combined his 24 juniors with the 25 seniors already in the sample of art students. Suppose this new sample yielded identical statistics. Is the sample mean significantly different from the population mean?

_____

_____

$t = $ _____ df = _____ $p < $ _____

(g) What are the 95 % confidence limits for these data?

_____

_____

2. Dr. Karen Paul investigated the effect of unintentional learning on recognition memory. (Unintentional learning, as its name implies, refers to the acquisition of knowledge without the intent to do so.) Each subject was given several paragraphs and instructed to read them as clearly and expressively as possible. This was followed by the presentation of a series of words which the subject was told to remember. Half of the words in the study session had also appeared in the paragraphs previously read by the subjects. Following this presentation a distractor task was given to prevent rehearsal, and then subjects were given a list containing all the studied words intermixed with an equal number of words which had not appeared in either the paragraphs or the study phase. Words were controlled for both frequency and word length. Recognition scores on words presented in both the paragraph and the study list were compared to words presented in the study list alone. It was hoped that this would indicate whether unintentional learning affected recognition memory. These data are reported in Table 10.1.

TABLE 10.1

Recognition Scores for Testing the Effect of Unintentional Learning

Subject Number	(X_1) Words Presentedin Paragraph and Study List	(X_2) Words Presented Only in Study List	$D = X_1 - X_2$	D^2
1	98	94	_____	_____
2	93	80	_____	_____
3	87	85	_____	_____
4	94	83	_____	_____
5	86	83	_____	_____
6	75	76	_____	_____
7	92	84	_____	_____
8	81	75	_____	_____
9	95	88	_____	_____
10	72	63	_____	_____
11	65	70	_____	_____
12	84	75	_____	_____

$\Sigma X_1 = $ _____ $\Sigma X_2 = $ _____ $\Sigma D = $ _____ $\Sigma D^2 = $ _____

$\bar{X}_1 = $ _____ $\bar{X}_2 = $ _____ $\bar{D} = $ _____

$s_D{}^2 = \dfrac{\Sigma D^2}{N} - \bar{D}^2 = $ _____

(a) State the experimental and null hypotheses.

H_1: _____

H_0: _____

(b) Using the space provided in Table 10.1, calculate the quantities shown.

(c) Calculate the t ratio, using the direct difference method. Is the t ratio significant? At what level?

_____

_____

$t =$ _____   df $=$ _____ $p <$ _____

(d) Suppose Dr. Paul had hypothesized that recognition memory would be better with unintentional learning. State the null and experimental hypotheses.

H_0: _____

H_1: _____

(e) Is the t ratio significant? At what level?

_____

_____

$t =$ _____ $p <$ _____

(f) Based on this study, what can you conclude about unintentional learning?

_____

_____

3. The Palmer-Axelrod research firm was commissioned to investigate whether a small amount of marijuana influences logical thought processes as measured by achievement scores on a mathematics aptitude test. They recruited 50 high school teachers, each of whom was tested both immediately after smoking a small amount of marijuana and either the preceding or the following day. A summary of the data they collected is presented in Table 10.2.

TABLE 10.2

Data from Study Examining the Influence of Marijuana on Math Aptitude Scores

With Marijuana	Without Marijuana
$\bar{X}_1 = 594$	$\bar{X}_2 = 610$
$s_1 = 53$	$s_2 = 72$
$r = 0.42$	

$$s_{\bar{X}_1 - \bar{X}_2} = \sqrt{s_{\bar{X}_1}^2 + s_{\bar{X}_2}^2 - 2rs_{\bar{X}_1}s_{\bar{X}_2}} = \underline{\hspace{4cm}}$$

$$t = \frac{\bar{X}_1 - \bar{X}_2}{s_{\bar{X}_1 - \bar{X}_2}} = \underline{\hspace{4cm}}$$

(a) State the experimental and null hypotheses.

H_1: _____

H_0: _____

(b) Use Table 10.2 to calculate the t ratio and degrees of freedom.

$t =$ _____

$df =$ _____

(c) Is the t ratio significant? At what level?

_____

_____

$p <$ _____

(d) What can you conclude about these data?

_____

_____

4. After expending considerable time and money in the previous study (problem 3), they decided to do a *post hoc* analysis of these data. Now instead of dividing the test scores into groups based on marijuana consumption they divided them based only on the order in which the two tests had been taken. (Many studies demonstrate improvement of performance with repeated tests.) These new summary statistics are presented in Table 10.3.

TABLE 10.3
Post Hoc Analysis of Math Aptitude Data

Test Taken First	Test Taken Second
$\bar{X}_1 = 551$	$\bar{X}_2 = 653$
$s_1 = 37$	$s_2 = 32$
$r = 0.72$	

$$s_{\bar{X}_1 - \bar{X}_2} = \sqrt{s_{\bar{X}_1}^2 + s_{\bar{X}_2}^2 - 2rs_{\bar{X}_1}s_{\bar{X}_2}} = \underline{\qquad\qquad}$$

$$t = \frac{\bar{X}_1 - \bar{X}_2}{s_{\bar{X}_1 - \bar{X}_2}} = \underline{\qquad\qquad}$$

(a) State the null and experimental hypotheses.

H_0: _____

H_1: _____

(b) Use Table 10.3 to calculate the t ratio and the degrees of freedom.

$t =$ _____

$df =$ _____

(c) Is the t ratio significant? At what level?

_____

$p <$ _____

(d) What can you conclude about these data based on this analysis and the previous one?

_____

_____

_____

5. Many investigators have been able to demonstrate a left cerebral hemisphere superiority for verbal materials in normal adults. These experiments typically compare the latency of responding to a stimulus presented exclusively to the left hemisphere with the response latency to a stimulus presented to the right hemisphere. It is reasoned that a short response time indicates superior processing abilities, and thus one hopes to find shorter latencies for presentations of verbal materials to the left cerebral hemisphere. As her senior thesis, Alice Rosofsky decided to compare laterality effects in adults to laterality effects in prepubertal children in an effort to determine whether these laterality effects develop before or after puberty. She tested 15 adults and 15 children using visually presented words. The scoring method took into account only correct responses and yielded scores ranging from 0 (no lateralization) to 31 (good lateralization). These data are reported in Table 10.4.

TABLE 10.4
Data from Laterality Study of Children and Adults

Subject Number	Adults (X_1)	X_1^2	Children (X_2)	X_2^2
1	25	_____	5	_____
2	10	_____	11	_____
3	28	_____	15	_____
4	5	_____	9	_____
5	20	_____	7	_____
6	19	_____	13	_____
7	18	_____	23	_____
8	0	_____	8	_____
9	23	_____	12	_____
10	25	_____	7	_____
11	31	_____	10	_____
12	18	_____	11	_____
13	15	_____	21	_____
14	3	_____	20	_____
15	20	_____	13	_____

$$\Sigma X_1 = \underline{\quad} \quad \Sigma X_1^2 = \underline{\quad} \quad \Sigma X_2 = \underline{\quad} \quad \Sigma X_2^2 = \underline{\quad}$$

$$\bar{X}_1 = \underline{\quad\quad} \qquad\qquad \bar{X}_2 = \underline{\quad\quad}$$

$$s_1^2 = \frac{\Sigma X_1^2}{N_1} - \bar{X}_1^2 = \underline{\quad\quad} \qquad s_2^2 = \frac{\Sigma X_2^2}{N_2} - \bar{X}_2^2 = \underline{\quad\quad}$$

$$s_{\bar{X}_1 - \bar{X}_2} = \underline{\quad\quad}$$

(a) What are the experimental and null hypotheses?

H_0: _____

H_1: _____

(b) Using the space provided in Table 10.4 calculate the t ratio.

$t =$ _____

df $=$ _____

(c) Is the t ratio significant? At what level?

_____

_____

$p <$ _____

(d) What can Ms. Rosofsky conclude from this study?

_____

_____

6. Upon reviewing this experiment (problem 5), Ms. Rosofsky's advisor pointed out a serious flaw in the experimental design. The left hemisphere superiority can be clearly shown only for right-handed individuals. Ms. Rosofsky had failed to take this into account when collecting her data. Fortunately she was able to contact 14 of the 15 adults and all of the children. After testing her subjects for their handedness, she discarded the following left-handed adult subjects: 4, 8, and 14; and the one left-handed child, 7. In addition she discarded adult subject 6 because she could not recontact him.

TABLE 10.5

Abridged Data from Laterality Study of Children and Adults

Subject Number	Adults (X_1)	X_1^2	Subject Number	Children (X_2)	X_2^2
1	————	————	1	————	————
2	————	————	2	————	————
3	————	————	3	————	————
5	————	————	4	————	————
7	————	————	5	————	————
9	————	————	6	————	————
10	————	————	8	————	————
11	————	————	9	————	————
12	————	————	10	————	————
13	————	————	11	————	————
15	————	————	12	————	————
			13	————	————
			14	————	————
			15	————	————

$$\Sigma X_1 = \text{\_\_\_\_\_} \quad \Sigma X_1^2 = \text{\_\_\_\_\_}$$

$$\bar{X}_1 = \text{\_\_\_\_\_}$$

$$s_1^2 = \frac{\Sigma X_1^2}{N_1} - \bar{X}_1^2 = \text{\_\_\_\_\_}$$

$$\Sigma X_2 = \text{\_\_\_\_\_} \quad \Sigma X_2^2 = \text{\_\_\_\_\_}$$

$$\bar{X}_2 = \text{\_\_\_\_\_}$$

$$s_2^2 = \frac{\Sigma X_2^2}{N_2} - \bar{X}_2^2 = \text{\_\_\_\_\_}$$

$$s_{\bar{X}_1 - \bar{X}_2} = \text{\_\_\_\_\_}$$

(a) Using these abridged data and the space provided in Table 10.5 calculate the t ratio.

$t = $ _____

$df = $ _____

(b) Is the t ratio significant? At what level?

_____

_____

$p < $ _____

(c) What can you conclude as the result of this and the previous experiment?

_____

_____

_____

Formulas

Hypothesis testing when the population variance is known

—Testing the difference between a sample mean $(\bar{X})$ and population mean (μ)

$$z = \frac{\bar{X} - \mu}{\sigma_{\bar{x}}} = \frac{\bar{X} - \mu}{\sigma/\sqrt{N}}$$

—Testing the difference between two independent sample means; $N_1 = N_2 = N$

$$z = \frac{\bar{X}_1 - \bar{X}_2}{\sigma_{\bar{x}_1 - \bar{x}_2}} = \frac{\bar{X}_1 - \bar{X}_2}{\sqrt{\dfrac{\sigma_1^2 + \sigma_2^2}{N}}}$$

—Testing the difference between two independent sample means; $N_1 \neq N_2$

$$z = \frac{\bar{X}_1 - \bar{X}_2}{\sigma_{\bar{x}_1 - \bar{x}_2}} = \frac{\bar{X}_1 - \bar{X}_2}{\sqrt{\dfrac{\sigma_1^2}{N_1} + \dfrac{\sigma_2^2}{N_2}}}$$

—Testing the difference between two correlated sample means; $N_1 = N_2$

$$z = \frac{\bar{X}_1 - \bar{X}_2}{\sigma_{\bar{x}_1 - \bar{x}_2}} = \frac{\bar{X}_1 - \bar{X}_2}{\sqrt{\sigma_{\bar{x}_1}^2 + \sigma_{\bar{x}_2}^2 - 2r\sigma_{\bar{x}_1}\sigma_{\bar{x}_2}}}$$

—Confidence limits

95% limits $= \bar{X} \pm 1.96\sigma_{\bar{x}}$

99% limits $= \bar{X} \pm 2.58\sigma_{\bar{x}}$

Hypothesis testing when the population variance is *not* known

—Testing the difference between a sample mean $(\bar{X})$ and population mean (μ)

$$t = \frac{\bar{X} - \mu}{s_{\bar{x}}}$$

$$s_{\bar{x}} = \frac{\hat{s}}{\sqrt{N}} = \frac{s}{\sqrt{N-1}}$$

$$df = N - 1$$

—Testing the difference between two independent sample means; $N_1 = N_2 = N$

$$t = \frac{\bar{X}_1 - \bar{X}_2}{s_{\bar{x}_1 - \bar{x}_2}}$$

$$s_{\bar{x}_1 - \bar{x}_2} = \sqrt{\frac{\hat{s}_1^2 + \hat{s}_2^2}{N}} = \sqrt{\frac{s_1^2 + s_2^2}{N - 1}}$$

$$df = 2N - 2$$

—Testing the difference between two independent sample means; $N_1 \neq N_2$

$$t = \frac{\bar{X}_1 - \bar{X}_2}{s_{\bar{x}_1 - \bar{x}_2}}$$

$$s_{\bar{x}_1 - \bar{x}_2} = \sqrt{\frac{N_1 s_1^2 + N_2 s_2^2}{N_1 + N_2 - 2}\left(\frac{1}{N_1} + \frac{1}{N_2}\right)}$$

$$df = N_1 + N_2 - 2$$

—Testing the difference between two correlated means; $N_1 = N_2 = N$

$$t = \frac{\bar{X}_1 - \bar{X}_2}{s_{\bar{x}_1 - \bar{x}_2}}$$

$$s_{\bar{x}_1 - \bar{x}_2} = \sqrt{s_{\bar{x}_1}^2 + s_{\bar{x}_2}^2 - 2r s_{\bar{x}_1} s_{\bar{x}_2}}$$

$$t = \frac{\bar{D}}{s_{\bar{D}}} = \frac{\bar{X}_1 - \bar{X}_2}{s_{\bar{D}}}$$

$$s_{\bar{D}} = \sqrt{\frac{\hat{s}_D^2}{N}} = \sqrt{\frac{s_D^2}{N - 1}}$$

$$df = N - 1$$

—Confidence limits

$$95\% \text{ limits} = \bar{X} \pm t_{0.025} s_{\bar{x}}$$

$$99\% \text{ limits} = \bar{X} \pm t_{0.005} s_{\bar{x}}$$

Comparing Two Sample Variances or More Than Two Sample Means: The F test and Analysis of Variance

A. Conceptual questions

1. In each sentence below there is a blank followed by several choices. Choose the most appropriate word or words to complete each statement.

(a) The F ratio has _____ (only one, two, five) different degrees of freedom associated with it.

(b) The F ratios form a distribution which _____ (is, is not) symmetric.

(c) The F ratio is _____ (always, sometimes, never) negative.

(d) When used for a one-tailed test (directional hypothesis), the significance level for the F ratio _____ (is, is not) halved.

(e) The Sitman and Dubrofsky educational testing service recently conducted a study in which they collected IQ scores from two groups of students hypothesized to differ in mean IQ. When using the F test to show that the variances of the two groups come from the same population, they hope to _____ (accept, reject) the null hypothesis.

116

(f) The F ratio is computed by dividing the _____ (larger, smaller) sample variance by the _____ (larger, smaller) sample variance.

(g) If the alternative hypothesis is true, the variance among group means is _____ (greater, less) than the variance within scores in each group.

(h) The assumptions underlying the analysis of variance _____ (must, need not) be strictly fulfilled to use the test.

2. After each question below are four possible answers. Indicate the number representing the best answer for each question.

_____(a) Mr. Miller wished to ascertain whether the error rates of two separate experimental conditions were drawn from two populations with equal variances. For condition one, there were 35 error rates which had a standard deviation ($\hat{s}$) of 2.5, while condition two contained 38 error rates with a variance ($\hat{s}^2$) of 4. The F ratio equals:
   (1) 4/2.5
   (2) 16/6.25
   (3) 6.25/4
   (4) 2.5/2

_____(b) To test the assumption of homogeneity of variance one would use:
   (1) F test
   (2) analysis of variance
   (3) t test
   (4) There is no way to test this assumption.

_____(c) A one-way analysis of variance (ANOVA) is used when:
   (1) testing for homogeneity of variance
   (2) population scores are skewed
   (3) there are two or more independent variables
   (4) there is only one independent variable

_____(d) Ms. Lane differentially fed two groups of rats from the same population. She then tested the stamina of each group. What test should she use to compare these two means:
(1) analysis of variance
(2) t test

(3) either (1) or (2)
(4) neither (1) nor (2)

_____(e) In order to use the analysis of variance, two assumptions must be met. The first assumption is that of homogeneity of variance. What other assumption underlies this test?
(1) There is a difference among means.
(2) The population scores are normally distributed.
(3) The samples are drawn from populations with the same mean.
(4) A t test is inappropriate.

_____(f) When might a researcher use a nonparametric test?
(1) When there are three or more independent variables.
(2) When the alternative hypothesis is nondirectional.
(3) When homogeneity of variance cannot be demonstrated.
(4) When population scores are normally distributed.

B. Problems

1. Political researchers Bradford and Davis are interested in the effect of the Watergate political scandal on voting practices. They postulated that registered Republicans would show greater conformity in their support of the official party candidates and platforms before the scandal than after it. These investigators devised a system of evaluating and quantifying the voting records of two randomly selected groups of registered Republicans: one from 1968 and the other from 1976. They hypothesized that the group voting in 1968 would show less variability than those voting in 1976. Using the data in Table 11.1, answer the following questions.

TABLE 11.1
Data Showing Voting Records of Two Groups of Registered Republicans

1968 Voting Record	1976 Voting Record
$\bar{X}_{68} = 1285$	$\bar{X}_{76} = 1283$
$s_{68}^2 = 182$	$s_{76}^2 = 573$
$N_{68} = 30$	$N_{76} = 25$

(a) Calculate the degrees of freedom (df) of each group.

df_{68} = _____ df_{76} = _____

(b) Calculate the estimated variance ($\hat{s}^2$) of each group.

$\hat{s}_{68}^2$ = _____

$\hat{s}_{76}^2$ = _____

(c) Calculate the appropriate F ratio.

F = _____

(d) What is the minimum F ratio necessary for significance at the 0.01 level?

$F \geq$ _____

(e) If the hypothesis being tested were directional, what would be the level of significance for an F ratio ≥ 1.91?

_____

(f) Should Bradford and Davis accept or reject their experimental hypothesis?

_____

2. The Fox Fertilizer Factory claims to have developed two chemicals which, when used together, increase the yield of peach trees. Before marketing this mixture, they must determine the optimal proportion of each substance. To do this they randomly assigned each of Mr. Ross's 25 best peach trees to one of five groups. The groups numbered 1 to 5 consisted of 10%, 20%, 30%, 40%, or 50% of chemical A (and thus, 90%, 80%, 70%, 60%, or 50% of chemical B, respectively). At harvest time Mr. Ross recorded the number of marketable peaches from each tree. The data he collected are presented in Table 11.2.

TABLE 11.2

Number of Marketable Peaches for Each Fertilizer Mixture

Mixture group				
1	2	3	4	5
(10% A)	(20% A)	(30% A)	(40% A)	(50% A)
120	160	95	92	115
130	172	89	78	101
98	143	113	116	111
100	162	120	85	94
115	99	106	130	115

Sums _____ _____ _____ _____ _____

$\bar{A}_1 =$ _____ $\bar{A}_2 =$ _____ $\bar{A}_3 =$ _____ $\bar{A}_4 =$ _____ $\bar{A}_5 =$ _____

$s =$ _____, $a =$ _____, $N =$ _____

$T =$ _____

$TS =$ _____

$C =$ _____

$SS_{tot} =$ _____

$SS_A =$ _____

$SS_{err} =$ _____

(a) Using these data, graph the mean of each group on the graph paper provided at the end of the chapter.

(b) With the information provided, perform a one-way analysis of variance. Use Table 11.3 to organize your findings.

(c) Is there a significant difference among means?

_____

(d) If so, which concentration would you recommend? Why?

_____

TABLE 11.3
Summary of ANOVA Calculations

Source of variance	SS	df	MS	F	p
A (Main Effect)					
Error (Within Groups)					
Total					

Additional work space:

3. Dr. Pondey posits that intelligence is influenced by birth order. To test this notion, he collected the IQ scores of the 31 students in his class who belong to families with exactly three children. (He was careful to use families where all three children are natural siblings raised together by their biological parents.) The data he collected are presented in Table 11.4.

TABLE 11.4

IQs of Dr. Pondey's Students Grouped by Birth Order

Oldest Child	Middle Child	Youngest Child
116	126	121
123	98	110
111	124	126
105	121	120
128	106	97
140	142	114
99	138	131
123	112	123
107	128	108
	107	119
	123	
	119	

Sums $\underline{1052}$ $\underline{1444}$ $\underline{1169}$

$\bar{A}_1 = \underline{116.88}$ $\bar{A}_2 = \underline{120.33}$ $\bar{A}_3 = \underline{116.9}$

$s_1 = $ _____, $s_2 = $ _____, $s_3 = $ _____, $a = $ _____, $N = $ _____

$T = $ _____

$TS = $ _____

$C = $ _____

$SS_{tot} = $ _____

$SS_A = $ _____

$SS_{err} = $ _____

(a) Using these data, graph the mean of each group on the graph paper provided at the end of the chapter.

(b) With the information provided, perform a one-way analysis of variance. Use Table 11.5 to organize your findings.

(c) Is there a significant difference among means?

TABLE 11.5
Summary Table for One-Way Analyses of Variance Calculations

Source of Variance	SS	df	MS	F	p
A (Main Effect)					
Error (Within Groups)					
Total					

Additional work space:

4. Dr. Palmer, observing the results of the previous experiment, decided to replicate the study using the IQs of siblings. He was able to obtain the IQ scores of each child in 10 families containing exactly three children. The data he collected are reported in Table 11.6.

TABLE 11.6
IQs of Dr. Palmer's Subjects Grouped by Birth Order

Family	Oldest Child	Middle Child	Youngest Child	S sums
1	130	135	131	_____
2	124	126	109	_____
3	110	108	115	_____
4	108	122	110	_____
5	115	111	107	_____
6	117	121	111	_____
7	100	107	98	_____
8	120	132	115	_____
9	119	128	130	_____
10	130	135	135	_____
Sums	_1173_	_1225_	_1161_	
	$\bar{A}_1 = $ _117.3_	$\bar{A}_2 = $ _122.5_	$\bar{A}_3 = $ _116.1_	

$s = $ _____, $a = $ _____, $N = $ _____

$T = $ _____

$TS = $ _____

$C = $ _____

$SS_{tot} = $ _____

$SS_A = $ _____

$SS_S = $ _____

$SS_{A \times S} = $ _____

(a) Using these data, graph the mean of each group on the graph paper provided at the end of the chapter.

(b) With the information provided, perform a one-way analysis of variance. Use Table 11.7 to organize your findings.

TABLE 11.7
Summary of One-Way ANOVA Calculations

Source of Variance	SS	df	MS	F	p
A (Main Effect)					
S (Subjects)					
A × S (Error)					
Total					

Additional work space:

(c) Is there a significant difference among means?

_____

(d) What can we conclude from Dr. Pondey's and Dr. Palmer's experiments?

_____

Formulas

F distribution

$$F = \frac{\hat{s}_L^2}{\hat{s}_S^2}$$

$$\text{df} = N_L - 1, \qquad N_S - 1$$

One-way analysis of variance—general formula

$$F = \frac{\text{MS}_{\text{bet}}}{\text{MS}_{\text{with}}}$$

One-way analysis of variance—completely randomized

$$T = \sum_{i=1}^{s} \sum_{j=1}^{a} X_{ij}$$

$$TS = \sum_{i=1}^{s} \sum_{j=1}^{a} X_{ij}^2$$

$$C = \frac{T^2}{N}$$

$$\text{SS}_{\text{tot}} = TS - C$$

$$\text{SS}_A = \sum_{i=1}^{a} \frac{A_i^2}{s_i} - C$$

$$\text{SS}_{\text{err}} = \text{SS}_{\text{tot}} - \text{SS}_A$$

$$F = \frac{\text{SS}_A/(a - 1)}{\text{SS}_{\text{err}}/(N - a)} = \frac{\text{MS}_A}{\text{MS}_{\text{err}}}$$

$$\text{df} = (a - 1), (N - a)$$

One-way analysis of variance—repeated measures

$$T = A_1 + A_2 + A_3 + \cdots + A_a$$

$$TS = \sum_{i=1}^{s} \sum_{j=1}^{a} X_{ij}^2$$

$$C = \frac{T^2}{N}$$

$$\text{SS}_{\text{tot}} = TS - C$$

$$\text{SS}_A = \sum_{i=1}^{a} \frac{A_i^2}{s} - C$$

$$\text{SS}_S = \sum_{j=1}^{s} \frac{S_j^2}{a} - C$$

$$\text{SS}_{A \times S} = \text{SS}_{\text{tot}} - \text{SS}_A - \text{SS}_S$$

$$F_A = \frac{\text{SS}_A/(a - 1)}{\text{SS}_{A \times S}/(a - 1)(s - 1)} = \frac{\text{MS}_A}{\text{MS}_{A \times S}}$$

$$\text{df} = (a - 1), (a - 1)(s - 1)$$

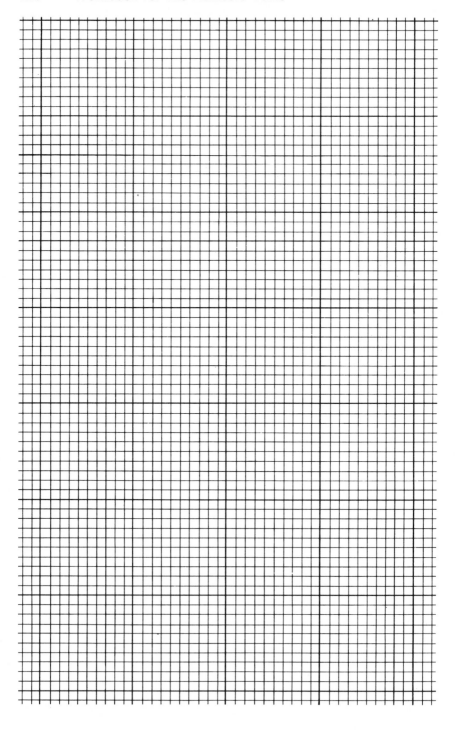

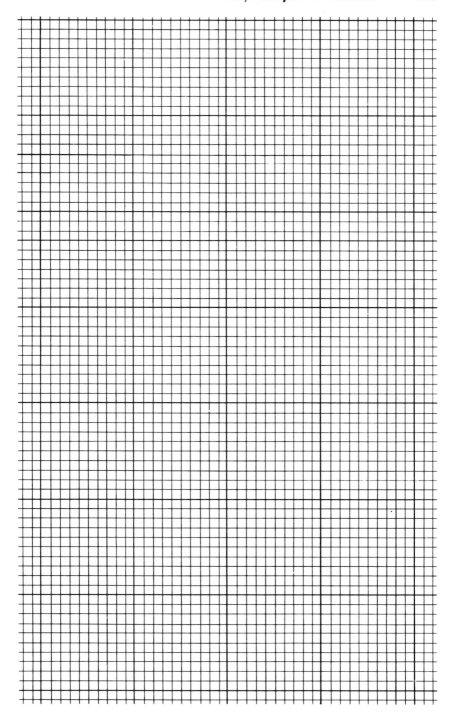

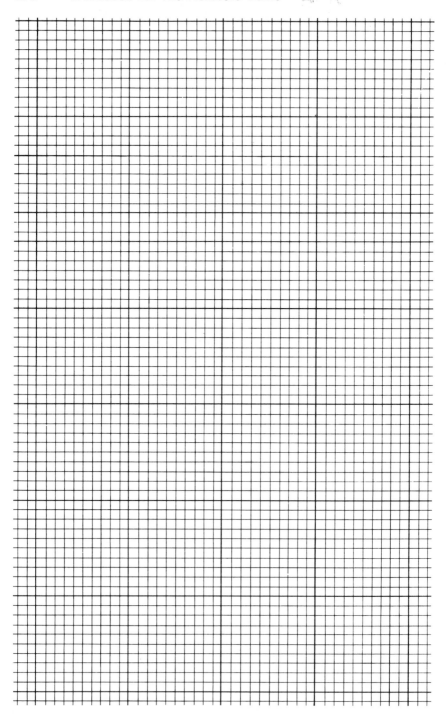

CHAPTER 12

Two-Way Analysis of Variance

A. Conceptual questions

1. Following each statement are four words or phrases. Place the number corresponding to the most appropriate choice in the space before each letter.

_____(a) If a 2 × 3 ANOVA is performed, _____ F ratios will   ３
    be obtained.
    (1) one
    (2) two
    (3) three
    (4) six

_____(b) The design for a particular experiment is denoted as a 4 ×
    (2 × 6) design. Each subject is required to participate in   ２
    _____ condition(s).
    (1) one
    (2) two
    (3) six
    (4) twelve

_____(c) The design in the preceding question _____.   １
    (1) is a mixed design
    (2) has repeated measures on both factors
    (3) is completely randomized
    (4) is a three-way ANOVA

131

_____(d) In an experiment using an $A \times (B \times S)$ design _____. |
  (1) A and B are independent factors.
  (2) every subject participates in every experimental condition
  (3) both A and B use the same error term when performing the appropriate ANOVA
  (4) all of the above

_____(e) In order to test intuitions about data from an experiment with an $(A \times B \times S)$ design, a competent experimenter would _____.   3
  (1) calculate and examine the mean for each condition
  (2) perform a three-way ANOVA
  (3) perform a two-way ANOVA
  (4) graph the means

_____(f) When calculating F ratios in an $A \times (B \times S)$ design _____. 4
  (1) the same error term is used when calculating F_A, F_B, and $F_{A \times B}$
  (2) one error term is used for F_A and F_B, and a second error term is used for $F_{A \times B}$
  (3) three different error terms are used
  (4) one error term is used for F_A and a second error term is used for F_B and $F_{A \times B}$

  3

_____(g) In order to use an ANOVA, the dependent variable (data) must belong to the _____ scale(s) of measurement.
  (a) nominal, ordinal, interval, or ratio
  (2) ordinal, interval, or ratio
  (3) interval or ratio
  (4) only the ratio

2. In the space provided, indicate whether each of the following statements is true or false.

  F

_____(a) In an $A \times B$ design, proving that both factor A and B factor are significant implies that there will be a significant interaction between A and B.

  T

_____(b) If the means from a 2×2 ANOVA are graphed, the factor represented by two separate functions is known as the parameter of the graph.

_____(c) The parameter of the graph is plotted along the abscissa (x axis).

_____(d) If no interaction is obtained when performing a 2×2 ANOVA the slopes of the two functions will be equal.

_____(e) Knowing F_A is significant gives some information about the significance of $F_{A \times B}$.

_____(f) The crossover effect is independent of any interaction effect.

3. In each statement below fill in the blank with the appropriate word or words.

(a) The _____ is the test statistic calculated when performing an analysis of variance.

(b) In a 3×4 analysis of variance _____ independent factors are manipulated.

(c) In an $(A \times B \times S)$ design _____ error terms are used.

(d) If an experimenter manipulates two levels of one variable and five levels of a second variable, the appropriate analysis would be a _____ ANOVA. (Assume both factors are completely randomized.)

(e) In an experiment with a completely randomized 2×3 design each subject participates in exactly _____ of the _____ possible combinations of factors A and B.

(f) A design denoted as a $(2 \times 3 \times 10)$ design requires that each of _____ subjects participate in _____ number of conditions.

(g) A graphic display of data _____ (can, cannot) tell us whether the experimental results are quantitatively significant.

(h) A graphic display of data _____ (can, cannot) tell us what experimental results are qualitatively present.

4. For each graph below, indicate in the space provided whether factor A, factor B, and the interaction between factors A and B are likely to be significant (sig.) or nonsignificant (n.s.).

yes
no

(a)

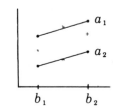

A _____

B _____

A × B   N O _____

(b)

n A

ho

yes

A _____

B _____

A × B _____

(c)

A _____

yes   A _____

No   B _____

yes   A × B _____

(d)

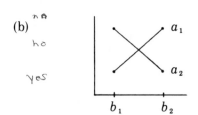

No   A _____

yes   B _____

Ivo   A × B _____

(e)

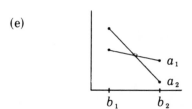

no   A _____

yes   B _____

ye   A × B _____

(f)

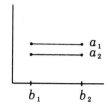

no ~~yes~~ A _____

no B _____

NO $A \times B$ _____

(g)

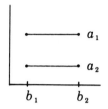

yes A _____

no B _____

no $A \times B$ _____

(h)

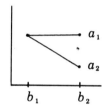

yes A _____

no B _____

yes $A \times B$ _____

B. Problems

1. The K & M Lane Drug Company tested the effects of a new antidepressant drug on the depressive symptoms of male and female schizophrenic patients. After each patient was first tested with one form of a reliable affective states inventory, the test drug was administered and the patients were retested with a second form of the same inventory. (On this test a high score indicates a highly depressed state.) Table 12.1 contains the data collected from the 6 male and 6 female patients.

TABLE 12.1
Data from the Affective States Inventory of Depressed Patients

Drug Condition (Factor B)	Sex (Factor A)	
	Male (a_1)	Female (a_2)
Before Drug (b_1)	72	83
	84	79
	63	80
	75	62
	69	91
	81	71
With Drug (b_2)	62	71
	73	80
	62	68
	65	54
	50	73
	72	62

(a) Is this an example of a completely randomized design, a mixed design, or a design with repeated measures on both factors? (Check this answer before proceeding.)

_____

(b) Using the space provided in Table 12.2, calculate the mean of each condition.

$\overline{A_1B_1}$ = _____ $\overline{A_2B_1}$ = _____

$\overline{A_1B_2}$ = _____ $\overline{A_2B_2}$ = _____

TABLE 12.2
Work Table for ANOVA (Problem 1)

Drug Condition (Factor B)	Sex (Factor A)	
	Male ($a1$)	Female (a_2)

Before Drug (b_1)

$A_1B_1 =$ _____	$A_2B_1 =$ _____	
$\overline{A_1B_1} =$ _____	$\overline{A_2B_1} =$ _____	$B_1 =$ _____

With Drug (b_2)

$A_1B_2 =$ _____	$A_2B_2 =$ _____	$B_2 =$ _____
$\overline{A_1B_2} =$ _____	$\overline{A_2B_2} =$ _____	
$A_1 =$ _____	$A_2 =$ _____	$T =$ _____
		$TS =$ _____

AS matrix

$A_1S_1 =$ _____	$A_2S_1 =$ _____
$A_1S_2 =$ _____	$A_2S_2 =$ _____
$A_1S_3 =$ _____	$A_2S_3 =$ _____
$A_1S_4 =$ _____	$A_2S_4 =$ _____
$A_1S_5 =$ _____	$A_2S_5 =$ _____
$A_1S_6 =$ _____	$A_2S_6 =$ _____

(c) On the paper provided at the end of this chapter, make two separate graphs of these means. In the first use sex as the parameter and in the second use drug condition as the parameter of the graph.

(d) Based on these graphs, what can you intuit about the qualitative properties of these data?

(e) Using the space provided in Tables 12.2 and 12.3, calculate and report the appropriate ANOVA.

(f) What are the significant findings of this research? (Include significance level.) What can be concluded about the use of this drug?

_____

_____

_____

TABLE 12.3
Summary Table for ANOVA (Problem 1)

Source of variance	SS	df	MS	F	p
A (sex)	___	___	___	___	___
S/A	___	___	___		
B (drug condition)	___	___	___	___	___
A × B	___	___	___	___	___
B × S/A	___	___	___		
Total	___	___			

Additional work space:

2. Hamlin & Levow, Inc., developed programmed learners to teach Spanish, French, and Italian to third-grade children. To assess their value they compared the language achievement of students being taught in groups of four by a highly rated teacher to the achievement of students using this programmed learner. Twenty-four third-graders of average intelligence and with no knowledge of any foreign language were chosen for this study. Each child was randomly assigned to one of three foreign languages (Spanish, French, or Italian) and one of two learning methods (programmed or teacher instructed). Each student studied the assigned foreign language by the prescribed method for 2 hours a week during a 20-week period. At the end of this time achievement tests were administered to each child. Table 12.4 shows the scores of these tests.

TABLE 12.4

Scores of 24 Third-Grades on Foreign Language Achievement Tests

Instruction condition (Factor B)	Language (Factor A)		
	Spanish (a_1)	French (a_2)	Italian (a_3)
Programmed (b_1)	72	69	63
	83	66	72
	96	78	78
	79	64	59
Teacher Instruction (b_2)	83	96	89
	95	87	93
	89	93	86
	98	86	95

(a) Which type of ANOVA should Hamlin & Levow, Inc., perform on the data? (Check this answer before proceeding.)

_____

(b) Using the space provided in Table 12.5 calculate the mean of each condition.

$\overline{A_1B_1}$ = _____ $\overline{A_2B_1}$ = _____ $\overline{A_3B_1}$ = _____

$\overline{A_1B_2}$ = _____ $\overline{A_2B_2}$ = _____ $\overline{A_3B_2}$ = _____

TABLE 12.5

Work Table for ANOVA (Problem 2)

Instruction Condition (Factor B)	Language (Factor A)		
	Spanish (a_1)	French (a_2)	Italian ($a_.$)

Programmed (b_1)

————   ————   ————

————   ————   ————

————   ————   ————

————   ————   ————

————   ————   ————

$A_1B_1 =$ ——— $A_2B_1 =$ ——— $A_3B_1 =$ ——— $B_1 =$ ———

$\overline{A_1B_1} =$ ——— $\overline{A_2B_1} =$ ——— $\overline{A_3B_1} =$ ———

Teacher In-structed (b_2)

————   ————   ————

————   ————   ————

————   ————   ————

————   ————   ————

$A_1B_2 =$ ——— $A_2B_2 =$ ——— $A_3B_2 =$ ——— $B_2 =$ ———

$\overline{A_1B_2} =$ ——— $\overline{A_2B_2} =$ ——— $\overline{A_3B_2} =$ ———

$A_1 =$ ——— $A_2 =$ ——— $A_3 =$ ——— $T =$ ———

$TS =$ ———

(c) On the paper provided at the end of this chapter, graph these means using Instruction Condition (Factor B) as the parameter of the graph.

(d) Based on this graph, what can you intuit about the qualitative properties of these data?

_____

_____

_____

(e) Using the space provided in Tables 12.5 and 12.6, calculate and report the appropriate ANOVA.

(f) What are the significant findings of this research? (Include level of significance.) What can be concluded about the use of this method in teaching these languages?

_____

_____

_____

_____

TABLE 12.6
Summary Table for ANOVA (Problem 2)

Source of Variance	SS	df	MS	F	p
A (Language)	____	____	____	____	____
B (Instruction)	____	____	____	____	____
A × B	____	____	____	____	____
Error	____	____	____		
Total	____	____			

Additional work space:

3. Dr. Deborah Helen wished to examine the effect of different presentation rates on recall of high and low frequency words. She constructed lists each consisting of 5 high and 5 low frequency words in a random order. No word appeared on more than one list. Half of her eight subjects were exposed to the first four lists at a fast presentation rate and the remaining four lists at a slow presentation rate. The other four subjects received the slow presentation condition first. Immediately following the presentation of each list subjects were given a short distractor task to prevent rehearsal. Then each subject was required to write down as many words as possible without regard to their presentation order. The percentage of correctly recalled words for each subject was calculated according to frequency group and presentation rate. These data are reported in Table 12.7.

(a) Which type of experimental design is this problem an example of? (Check this answer before proceeding.)

TABLE 12.7
Percentage of Correctly Recalled Words

Frequency (Factor B)	Presentation Rate (Factor A)	
	Slow (a_1)	Fast (a_2)
Low (b_1)	75	60
	70	60
	75	55
	60	50
	60	45
	60	50
	70	55
	75	85
High (b_2)	95	80
	85	70
	90	80
	90	75
	85	70
	75	65
	80	65
	90	80

TABLE 12.8
Work Table for ANOVA (*Problem 3*)

Frequency (Factor B)	Presentation Rate (Factor A)		
	Slow (a_1)	Fast (a_2)	BS matrix
Low (b_1)	———	———	$B_1S_1 =$ ———
	———	———	$B_1S_2 =$ ———
	———	———	$B_1S_3 =$ ———
	———	———	$B_1S_4 =$ ———
	———	———	$B_1S_5 =$ ———
	———	———	$B_1S_6 =$ ———
	———	———	$B_1S_7 =$ ———
	———	———	$B_1S_8 =$ ——— $B_1 =$ ———
	$A_1B_1 =$ ———	$A_2B_1 =$ ———	
	$\overline{A_1B_1} =$ ———	$\overline{A_2B_1} =$ ———	
High (b_2)	———	———	$B_2S_1 =$ ———
	———	———	$B_2S_2 =$ ———
	———	———	$B_2S_3 =$ ———
	———	———	$B_2S_4 =$ ———
	———	———	$B_2S_5 =$ ———
	———	———	$B_2S_6 =$ ———
	———	———	$B_2S_7 =$ ———
	———	———	$B_2S_8 =$ ———
	$A_1B_2 =$ ———	$A_2B_2 =$ ———	$B_2 =$ ———
	$\overline{A_1B_2} =$ ———	$\overline{A_2B_2} =$ ———	
	$A_1 =$ ———	$A_2 =$ ———	$T =$ ———
			$TS =$ ———

	AS matrix		S matrix
	$A_1S_1 =$ ———	$A_2S_1 =$ ———	$S_1 =$ ———
	$A_1S_2 =$ ———	$A_2S_2 =$ ———	$S_2 =$ ———
	$A_1S_3 =$ ———	$A_2S_3 =$ ———	$S_3 =$ ———
	$A_1S_4 =$ ———	$A_2S_4 =$ ———	$S_4 =$ ———
	$A_1S_5 =$ ———	$A_2S_5 =$ ———	$S_5 =$ ———
	$A_1S_6 =$ ———	$A_2S_6 =$ ———	$S_6 =$ ———
	$A_1S_7 =$ ———	$A_2S_7 =$ ———	$S_7 =$ ———
	$A_1S_8 =$ ———	$A_2S_8 =$ ———	$S_8 =$ ———

(b) Using the space provided in Table 12.8, calculate the mean of each condition.

$\overline{A_1B_1}$ = _____ $\overline{A_2B_1}$ = _____

$\overline{A_1B_2}$ = _____ $\overline{A_2B_2}$ = _____

(c) On the paper provided at the end of this chapter, graph these means using word frequency (Factor B) as the parameter of the graph.

(d) Based on this graph, what can you intuit about the qualitative properties of these data?

_____

_____

_____

(e) Using the space provided in Tables 12.8 and 12.9, calculate and report the appropriate ANOVA.

(f) What are the significant finds of this research? (Include level of significance.) What can be concluded about the recall of high and low frequency words at different presentation rates?

_____

_____

_____

_____

TABLE 12.9
Summary Table for ANOVA (*Problem 3*)

Source of Variance	SS	df	MS	F	p
A (presentation rate)	————	————	————	————	————
S	————	————	————		
A × S	————	————	————		
B (frequency)	————	————	————	————	————
B × S	————	————	————		
A × B	————	————	————	————	————
A × B × S	————	————	————		
Total	————	————			

Additional work space:

Additional Work space

Formulas

Two-way analysis of variance—completely randomized: $A \times B$

$$C = T^2/N$$

$$\text{SS}_{\text{tot}} = TS - C$$

$$\text{SS}_A = \sum \frac{A^2}{bs} - C$$

$$\text{SS}_B = \sum \frac{B^2}{as} - C$$

$$\text{SS}_{A \times B} = \sum \frac{AB^2}{s} - C - \text{SS}_A - \text{SS}_B$$

$$\text{SS}_{\text{err}} = \text{SS}_{\text{tot}} - \text{SS}_A - \text{SS}_B - \text{SS}_{A \times B}$$

$$F_A = \frac{\text{SS}_A/(a-1)}{\text{SS}_{\text{err}}/ab(s-1)} = \frac{\text{MS}_A}{\text{MS}_{\text{err}}} \; ; \text{df} = a - 1, ab(s-1)$$

$$F_B = \frac{\text{SS}_B/(b-1)}{\text{SS}_{\text{err}}/ab(s-1)} = \frac{\text{MS}_B}{\text{MS}_{\text{err}}} \; ; \text{df} = b - 1, ab(s-1)$$

$$F_{A \times B} = \frac{\text{SS}_{A \times B}/(a-1)(b-1)}{\text{SS}_{\text{err}}/ab(s-1)} = \frac{\text{MS}_{A \times B}}{\text{MS}_{\text{err}}}; \text{df} = (a-1)(b-1), ab(s-1)$$

Two-way analysis of variance—repeated measures: $(A \times B \times S)$

$$C = T^2/N$$

$$\text{SS}_{\text{tot}} = TS - C$$

$$\text{SS}_A = \sum \frac{A^2}{bs} - C$$

$$\text{SS}_B = \sum \frac{B^2}{as} - C$$

$$\text{SS}_S = \sum \frac{S^2}{ab} - C$$

$$\text{SS}_{A \times B} = \sum \frac{AB^2}{s} - \text{SS}_A - \text{SS}_B - C$$

$$\text{SS}_{A \times S} = \sum \frac{AS^2}{b} - \text{SS}_A - \text{SS}_S - C$$

$$\text{SS}_{B \times S} = \sum \frac{BS^2}{a} - \text{SS}_B - \text{SS}_S - C$$

$$SS_{A \times B \times S} = SS_{tot} - SS_A - SS_B - SS_S - SS_{A \times B} - SS_{A \times S} - SS_{B \times S}$$

$$F_A = \frac{SS_A/(a-1)}{SS_{A \times S}/(a-1)(s-1)} = \frac{MS_A}{MS_{A \times S}}; df = a - 1, (a-1)(s-1)$$

$$F_B = \frac{SS_B/(b-1)}{SS_{B \times S}/(b-1)(s-1)} = \frac{MS_B}{MS_{B \times S}}; df = b - 1, (b-1)(s-1)$$

$$F_{A \times B} = \frac{SS_{A \times B}/(a-1)(b-1)}{SS_{A \times B \times S}/(a-1)(b-1)(s-1)} = \frac{MS_{A \times B}}{MS_{A \times B \times S}};$$

$$df = (a-1)(b-1), (a-1)(b-1)(s-1)$$

Two-way analysis of variance—mixed: $A \times (B \times S)$

$$C = T^2/N$$

$$SS_{tot} = TS - C$$

$$SS_A = \sum \frac{A^2}{bs} - C$$

$$SS_B = \sum \frac{B^2}{as} - C$$

$$SS_{A \times B} = \sum \frac{AB^2}{s} - SS_A - SS_B - C$$

$$SS_{S/A} = \sum \frac{AS^2}{b} - SS_A - C$$

$$SS_{B \times S/A} = SS_{tot} - SS_A - SS_B - SS_{A \times B} - SS_{S/A}$$

$$F_A = \frac{SS_A/(a-1)}{SS_{S/A}/a(s-1)} = \frac{MS_A}{MS_{S/A}}; df = (a-1), a(s-1)$$

$$F_B = \frac{SS_B/(b-1)}{SS_{B \times S/A}/a(b-1)(s-1)} = \frac{MS_B}{MS_{B \times S/A}}; df = (b-1), a(b-1)(s-1)$$

$$F_{A \times B} = \frac{SS_{A \times B}/(a-1)(b-1)}{SS_{B \times S/A}/a(b-1)(s-1)} = \frac{MS_{A \times B}}{MS_{B \times S/A}};$$

$$df = (a-1)(b-1), a(b-1)(s-1)$$

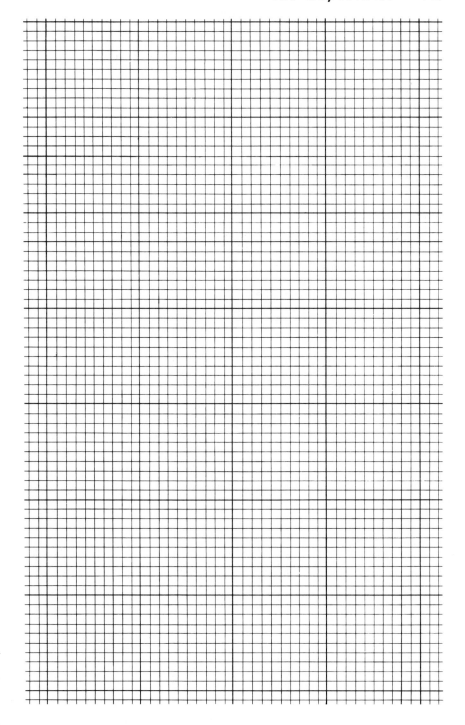

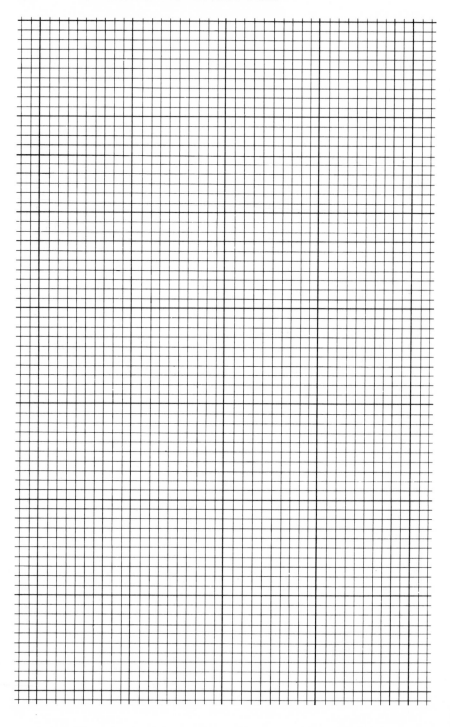

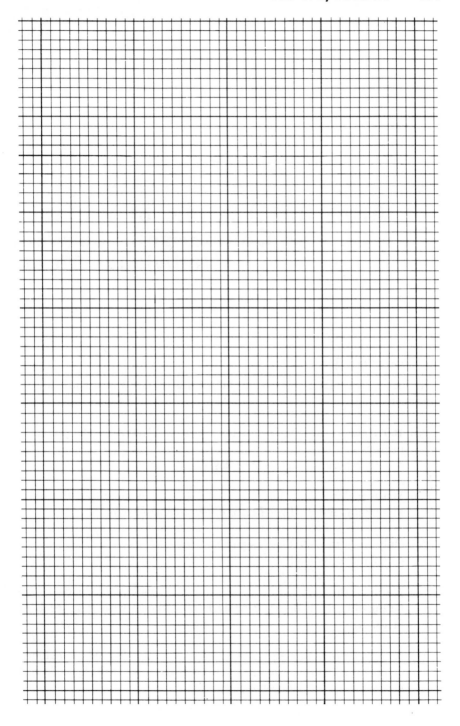

CHAPTER 13

After the Analysis of Variance: Comparisons between Individual Means

A. Conceptual questions

1. Fill in each blank below with the word or phrase which will make each statement true.

(a) If F_A and F_B are significant for a 2×2 ANOVA, a planned comparison _____ (is, is not) used to find out exactly where the significance lies.

(b) When making a _____ comparison, the probability of making a Type I error must be controlled for.

(c) Only when the ANOVA is significant can _____ comparisons be made.

(d) No more than _____ planned comparisons are permissible for a one-way analysis of variance with four levels of factor A.

(e) A comparison among _____ is a planned comparison which examines one independent variable collapsed across the second independent variable.

(f) A _____ comparison compares means of one independent variable at a particular level of the other independent variable.

(g) A _____ analysis is frequently used with a 2 × 2 factorial design to determine the exact nature of a significant interaction.

(h) _____ tests compare all possible pairs of means.

(i) As the number of comparisons increases, the probability of incorrectly _____ the null hypothesis increases.

(j) With the _____ test, the difference between means which is required to obtain significance increases as the difference between ranks increases.

(k) The Tukey test _____ (can, cannot) yield significant results if the results of the ANOVA are not significant.

(l) Another name for the _____ test is the Honestly Significant Difference (HSD) test.

2. Choose the answer that best completes each statement. Indicate your choice by placing the appropriate number in the space provided.

_____ (a) It is not necessary that the over-all ANOVA be significant when deciding to:
(1) perform a planned comparison
(2) perform a post hoc comparison
(3) perform either a planned or a post hoc comparison
(4) perform neither a planned nor a post hoc comparison

_____ (b) Which of the following comparisons among $\bar{A}_1$, $\bar{A}_2$, and $\bar{A}_3$ are nonorthognal?
(1) $\bar{A}_1 > \bar{A}_2$; $\bar{A}_3 > \bar{A}_2$
(2) $\bar{A}_1 < \bar{A}_2$; $\bar{A}_1 < \bar{A}_3$
(3) both
(4) neither

_____ (c) An experiment with a 3 × 4 factorial design was conducted. The researcher, interested in whether the three levels of *A* differed from each other on one particular level of *B* should:
(1) perform a 3 × 4 ANOVA
(2) perform a simple main effects analysis
(3) perform a marginal means analysis
(4) perform a trend analysis

_____ (d) How many comparisons can be made with the data from an experiment which manipulates 5 levels of one variable?
(1) 2
(2) 4
(3) 5
(4) 10

_____ (e) How many post hoc comparisons can be made with the data from a one-factor experiment with 10 levels?
(1) 5
(2) 10
(3) 25
(4) 45

3. Decide whether each of the following is true or false. Indicate your choice by placing the appropriate letter to the left of each statement.

_____ (a) Orthogonal comparisons are mutually independent, planned comparisons.

_____ (b) When performing a simple main effects analysis on a mixed design, the same error term is used regardless of which independent variable is fixed.

_____ (c) Planned comparisons test all possible pairs of means.

_____ (d) The more conservative post hoc tests require a larger difference between means to obtain significance.

_____ (e) The Newman-Keuls test is more conservative than the Tukey test.

_____ (f) Both the Newman-Keuls test and the Tukey test use the same test statistic.

_____ (g) A pair of means which is significantly different according to the Tukey test will always be significantly different according to the Newman-Keuls test.

B. Problems

1. Dr. Douglas Ohman's experimental psychology class investigated the effect of meaningfulness and pronounceability on the recognition thresholds of trigrams (three-letter stimuli). They used four types of stimuli: (1) trigrams which are neither meaningful nor pronounceable (e.g., BSP), (2) trigrams which are meaningful but not pronounceable (e.g., JFK), (3) trigrams which are not meaningful, but are pronounceable (e.g., TEM), and (4) trigrams which are both meaningful and pronounceable (e.g., TAR). Forty trigrams (ten of each type) were randomly mixed and individually presented (via a tachistoscope) to six subjects. The average minimum exposure time (TRT) necessary for each subject to correctly report each type of stimulus was recorded. The sums and averages for each type of trigram are reported in Table 13.1.

TABLE 13.1
Recognition Threshold Data for Four Types of Trigrams

	A_1 (e.g., BSP)	A_2 (e.g., JFK)	A_3 (e.g., TEM)	A_4 (e.g., TAR)
Sums	557	442	478	398
Means	$\bar{A}_1 =$ 92.84	$\bar{A}_2 =$ 73.67	$\bar{A}_3 =$ 79.67	$\bar{A}_4 =$ 66
	$s =$ _____	$a =$ _____	$N =$ _____	
	$SS_A =$ 2265.792	$MS_A =$ 755.2639	$df_A =$ _____	
	$MS_{err} =$ 93.870	$df_{err} =$ _____		

Complete the information in the table based on the above description and answer the following questions.

(a) Using the paper provided at the end of the chapter, graph these means.

(b) What is the maximum number of comparisons among means which may be computed from these data?

_____

(c) Fill out the blanks in Table 13.1 and then perform the following planned comparisons.

(d) Is there a significant difference between the thresholds of trigrams which are meaningful and nonpronounceable (A_2) and those which are nonmeaningful and pronounceable (A_3)?

_____

_____

_____

_____

$F' = $ _____ df = _____, _____ $p < $ _____

(e) Is there a significant difference between the combined thresholds of trigrams which are either meaningful or pronounceable but not both ($A_2 + A_3$) and the thresholds of trigrams which are both meaningful and pronounceable (A_4)?

_____

_____

_____

_____

$F' = $ _____ df = _____, _____ $p < $ _____

(f) Is there a significant difference between the threshold of trigrams which are neither meaningful nor pronounceable (A_1) and the combined threshold of trigrams which are either meaningful or pronounceable or both ($A_2 + A_3 + A_4$)?

_____

_____

_____

_____

$F' = $ _____ $df = $ _____, _____ $p < $ _____

(g) State in words the findings of these analyses.

_____

_____

_____

_____

2. Dr. Blackman investigated the effect of different training procedures on the ability of two strains of mice to learn new mazes. Mice either (1) were trained on mazes similar to the ones they would be tested on (compatible condition), (2) were trained on mazes dissimilar to the ones they would be tested on (incompatible condition), or (3) received no prior training (control). She used thirty mice, half bred for inferior ability to learn mazes and half bred for superior ability to learn mazes. Five "bright" mice and five "dull" mice were in each training condition. Following the training session each mouse was placed in a test maze and the running time was recorded. The sums and averages of the running times for each condition are reported in Table 13.2. Complete the information in this table using the above description and answer the following questions.

TABLE 13.2

Maze Running Times for Mice in Dr. Blackman's Experiment (in Seconds)

Mouse Type (Factor B)	Control(a_1)	Training Condition (Factor A)		Marginal Sums for B
		Compatible (a_2)	Incompatible (a_3)	
Bright (b_1)	$A_1B_1 = 163$	$A_2B_1 = 97$	$A_3B_1 = 217$	
	$\overline{A_1B_1} = 32.6$	$\overline{A_2B_1} = 19.4$	$\overline{A_3B_1} = 43.4$	_____
Dull (b_2)	$A_1B_2 = 355$	$A_2B_2 = 302$	$A_3B_2 = 506$	
	$\overline{A_1B_2} = 71$	$\overline{A_2B_2} = 60.4$	$\overline{A_3B_2} = 101.2$	_____
Marginal Sums for A	_____	_____	_____	

$$a = \text{_____} \qquad b = \text{_____} \qquad s = \text{_____}$$

$$\text{SS}_{err} = 2976.00 \quad \text{MS}_{err} = \text{_____} \quad df = \text{_____}$$

(a) Using the paper provided at the end of this chapter, graph the means of these data.

(b) Are "bright" mice (b_1) differentially affected by the training condition?

_____

_____

$$F'_{A \text{ at } b_1} = \text{_____} df = \text{\_\_\_\_}, \text{\_\_\_\_} \ p < \text{_____}$$

(c) Is there a significant difference between training ($a_2 + a_3$) and no training (a_1)?

_____

_____

_____

_____

$F' = $ _____ df = _____, _____ $p <$ _____

(d) Is there a significant difference between compatible training (a_2) and incompatible training (a_3)?

_____

_____

_____

_____

$F'_A = $ _____ df = _____, _____ $p <$ _____

(e) Are "dull" mice (b_2) differentially affected by the training condition?

_____

_____

_____

_____

$F'_{A \text{ at } b_2} = $ _____ df = _____, _____ $p <$ _____

(f) Is there a significant difference between "bright" mice (b_1) and "dull" mice (b_2)?

_____

_____

_____

_____

$F'_B =$ _____ df = _____, _____ $p <$ _____

(g) Are "dull" mice (b_2) significantly worse than "bright" mice (b_1) with no training (a_1)?

_____

_____

_____

_____

$F'_{B \text{ at } a_1} =$ _____ df = _____, _____ $p <$ _____

(h) Which of the above analyses are marginal means comparisons and which simple main effects comparisons?

Marginal means comparisons: _____

Simple main effects comparisons: _____

(i) Describe, in words, the results of these analyses.

_____

_____

_____

_____

3. A new drug has recently been developed to help hyperactive children function in a school setting. After it had been used successfully for two years the distributors, Tex-Joffee Corp., wished to compare the behavior of children taking another drug widely used for this purpose during the past fifteen years. They also wished to investigate and compare the cumulative effect of taking each of these two drugs.

Students at a particular residential school are given a battery of behavioral tests, including one for hyperactivity, every three months. The Tex-Joffee Corp. was able to compile hyperactivity scores for five children taking the new drug and five children taking the old drug at both three months and twelve months after medication was begun. These ten children were similar with respect to age, degree of hyperactivity before medication, and intelligence. The sums and averages of behavioral scores are reported in Table 13.3. (High scores mean low hyperactivity.) Complete the information in this table and answer the following questions.

TABLE 13.3

Behavioral Scores For Hyperactive Children

Time on Drug at Testing (Factor B)	Type of Drug Taken (Factor A)	
	Old Drug (a_1)	New Drug (a_2)
3 Months (b_1)	$A_1B_1 = 48$	$A_2B_1 = 97$
	$\overline{A_1B_1} = 9.6$	$\overline{A_2B_1} = 19.4$
12 Months (b_2)	$A_1B_2 = 61$	$A_2B_2 = 63$
	$\overline{A_1B_2} = 12.2$	$\overline{A_2B_2} = 12.6$

$a = $ _____ $b = $ _____ $s = $ _____

$SS_{S/A} = 155.8$ $df_{S/A} = $ _____

$SS_{B \times S/A} = 3.5$ $df_{B \times S/A} = $ _____

$MS_{S/B \text{ at } a_i} = $ _____

$MS_{S/A \text{ at } b_i} = $ _____

(a) Using the paper provided at the end of the chapter, graph these means.

(b) Is there a significant difference between the old drug (a_1) and the new drug (a_2) at the twelve-month testing (b_2)?

_____

_____

_____

_____

$F'_{A \text{ at } b_2} =$ _____ df = _____, _____ $p <$ _____

(c) Is there a significant difference between the old drug (a_1) and the new drug (a_2) at the three-month testing (b_1)?

_____

_____

_____

_____

$F'_{A \text{ at } b_1} =$ _____ df = _____, _____ $p <$ _____

(d) Is there a significant difference between the three month (b_1) and the twelve month (b_2) behavioral measures for those students taking the old drug (a_1)?

_____

_____

_____

_____

$F'_{B \text{ at } a_1} =$ _____ df = _____, _____ $p <$ _____

(e) Is there a significant difference between the three month (b_1) and twelve month (b_2) behavioral measures for those students taking the new drug (a_2)?

_____

_____

_____

_____

$F'_{B \text{ at } a_2} =$ _____ df = _____, _____ $p <$ _____

(f) How would you describe the results of these analyses?

_____

_____

_____

_____

4. Dr. Ellis Levinson tested six 4-, 6-, 8-, 10-, 12-, 14-, 16-, and 20-year-olds on their ability to learn foreign languages. Analyzing the data with a one-way ANOVA, he found out only that age is a highly significant variable. The data he collected are shown in Table 13.4. (High scores indicate a high aptitude for foreign languages.) Complete the information in this table and do the following:

TABLE 13.4

Scores on a Foreign Language Aptitude Examination

				Age of Subject (Factor A)				
	4	6	8	10	12	14	16	20
Sums	93	100	95	60	36	24	74	86
Means	15.5	16.67	15.83	10.00	6.00	4.00	12.33	14.33
Rank	——	——	——	——	——	——	——	——

$s = $ _____ $a = $ _____ $N = $ _____

$SS_A = 659.96$ $MS_A = 94.28$ $df_A = $ _____

$SS_{err} = 130.00$ $MS_{err} = 3.25$ $df_{err} = $ _____

$F = 94.28/3.25 = 29.01$ $df = $ _____, _____ $p < $ _____

			Reordered Sums by Rank				
A_1	A_2	A_3	A_4	A_5	A_6	A_7	A_8
——	——	——	——	——	——	——	——

(a) Reorder the sums by rank in the space provided at the bottom of Table 13.4.

(b) Compute the differences between all pairs of sums and place them in the appropriate spaces in Table 13.5.

(c) Calculate the critical differences necessary for significance under the Newman-Keuls test for each of the following rank differences (r).

$r = 2;$ $CD_{0.05} = $ _____ $CD_{0.01} = $ _____

$r = 6;$ $CD_{0.05} = $ _____ $CD_{0.01} = $ _____

$r = 4;$ $CD_{0.05} = $ _____ $CD_{0.01} = $ _____

TABLE 13.5
Matrix of Differences

	A_1	A_2	A_3	A_4	A_5	A_6	A_7	A_8	
A_1	—	—	—	—	—	—	—	—	$r = 8$
A_2		—	—	—	—	—	—	—	$r = 7$
A_3			—	—	—	—	—	—	$r = 6$
A_4				—	—	—	—	—	$r = 5$
A_5					—	—	—	—	$r = 4$
A_6						—	—	—	$r = 3$
A_7							—	—	$r = 2$
A_8									

(d) Calculate the critical differences necessary for significance under the Tukey test for each of the following rank differences (r).

$r = 3$; $CD_{0.05} = $ _____ $CD_{0.01} = $ _____

$r = 5$; $CD_{0.05} = $ _____ $CD_{0.01} = $ _____

$r = 8$; $CD_{0.05} = $ _____ $CD_{0.01} = $ _____

(e) Circle each difference in Table 13.5 which is significant under the Newman-Keuls test at the 0.01 level.

(f) Put an X through each difference in Table 13.5 which is significant under the Newman-Keuls test but not significant under the Tukey test at the 0.01 level.

(g) What can Dr. Levinson conclude from these analyses?

_____

_____

_____

_____

Formulas

Planned comparisons—two single means

$$SS_{A'} = \frac{A_1^2}{s} + \frac{A_2^2}{s} - C$$

$$C = \frac{(A_1 + A_2)^2}{2s}$$

Planned comparisons—average of two means with a single mean

$$SS_{A'} = \frac{(A_1 + A_2)^2}{2s} + \frac{A_3^2}{s} - C$$

$$C = \frac{(A_1 + A_2 + A_3)^2}{3s}$$

Planned comparisons—number of comparisons permissible

Number of permissible comparisons = df of the numerator of the F ratio

= number of conditions − 1

Planned comparisons—two-way ANOVA error terms

—Completely randomized designs

$$MS_{err}$$

—Repeated on both factors

$$MS_{A \times B \times S}$$

—Mixed designs

$$MS_{S/B \text{ at } a_i} = MS_{B \times S/A}$$

$$df_{S/B \text{ at } a_i} = a(b - 1)(s - 1)$$

$$MS_{S/A \text{ at } b_i} = \frac{SS_{S/A} + SS_{B \times S/A}}{df_{S/A} + df_{B \times S/A}}$$

$$df_{S/A \text{ at } b_i} = a(s - 1)$$

Post hoc tests—number of comparisons

Number of permissible comparisons $= \dfrac{n(n - 1)}{2}$

Post hoc tests—Newman-Keuls test and Tukey test

$$r = j - i + 1$$

$$j > i$$

$$q_r = \frac{A_{i+r-1} - A_i}{\sqrt{sMS_{err}}}$$

$$CD_{0.05} = q_{r,0.05} \sqrt{sMS_{err}}$$

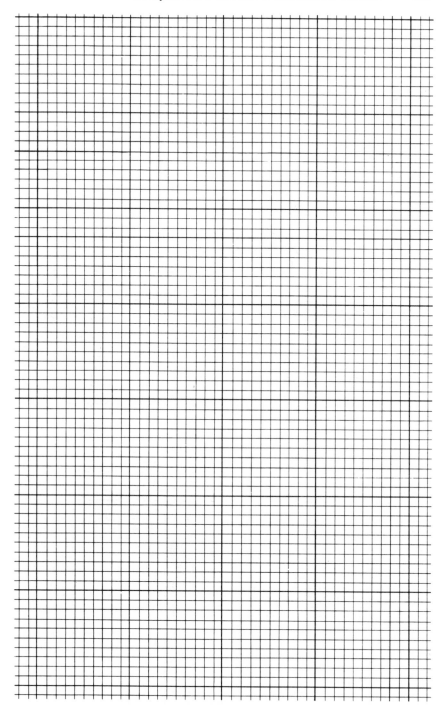

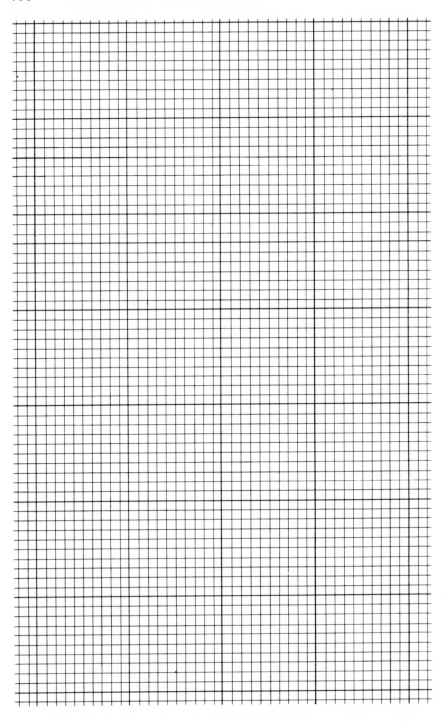

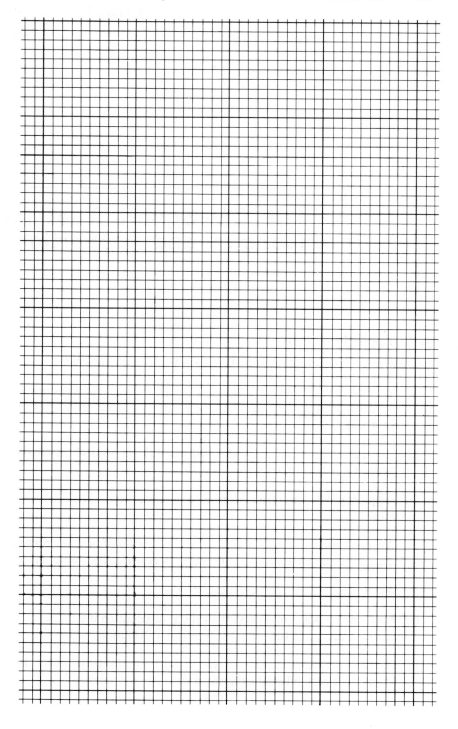

The Chi-Square Test for Frequencies and Proportions

A. Conceptual questions

1. Fill in the word or phrase which best completes each statement.

means (a) In order to compute _____ as measures of central tendency, data must be quantitative and on an interval or ratio scale.

Frequencies (b) _____ are used when the dependent variable is measured on a nominal scale.

categorical (c) Frequency data are often referred to as _____ data.

correction for continuity (d) One must use a _____ when df = 1 in order to _____ (increase, decrease) the value of χ^2.

df = 1 (e) When _____ $z^2 = \chi^2$.

continuous approximation (f) For a small number of observations the χ^2 distribution is a _____ _____ to the correct theoretical distribution.

(g) It _____ (is, is not) correct to combine different trials and different subjects in the same χ^2 analysis.

(h) The normal test is usually used with _____ *proportions*
when the degrees of freedom are equal to _____ . *1*

2. Choose the number corresponding to the word or phrase which best completes each statement.

_____ (a) The degrees of freedom for a 2×2 chi square distribution *4*
are equal to:
(1) 1
(2) 2
(3) 4
(4) It depends on the number of observations.

_____ (b) The sum of the expected frequencies in a chi square must
equal:
(1) 1
(2) the sum of the observed frequencies
(3) the number of subjects
(4) all of the above

_____ (c) The sum of the observed proportions must equal:
(1) 1
(2) the sum of the expected proportions
(3) the sum of the observed frequencies divided by the sum
of the expected frequencies
(4) all of the above

_____ (d) When computing the chi square test statistic one should
avoid:
(1) degrees of freedom equal to 1
(2) an expected frequency equal to 3
(3) an observed frequency equal to 1
(4) all of the above

_____ (e) If we know that $\chi^2 = 4$ then:
(1) $z = 4$
(2) $z = 2$
(3) $z = 16$
(4) impossible to tell with this information

3. Indicate whether each of the following statements is true or false.

_____ (a) Both the normal and χ^2 tests are continuous approximations to the exact probabilities associated with theoretical frequencies.

_____ (b) As the degrees of freedom increase the skewness of the chi square distribution also increases.

_____ (c) If data is categorized along only one dimension the degrees of freedom equal one.

_____ (d) A correction for continuity is never done when one has more than two sample frequencies along a single dimension.

_____ (e) One would use a normal test instead of χ^2 when combining different subjects and different trials within the same analysis.

B. Problems

1. Dr. Kate Turley spent five years working in several primitive villages. In the course of her work she treated patients with an extremely rare disease. Of the 40 afflicted adults, 14 were female. Intrigued by the observation that more males than females had contracted this disease, she wished to determine the likelihood that this affliction is sex-linked to males.

(a) State the null and experimental hypotheses.

H_0: _____

H_1: _____

TABLE 14.1

Observed and Expected Frequencies of Males and Females Contracting this Disease

	Sex Male	Female	
f_o	26	14	_____
f_e	20	20	_____

(b) Use the information given above and Table 14.1 to determine whether or not this disease is sex-linked to males.

$\chi^2 =$ _____ df = _____ $p <$ _____

(c) Dr. Peters, working in a nearby village, diagnosed 10 more cases of this disease—7 males and 3 females. Combine the data from both doctors and convert the frequencies to proportions. Report these proportions in Table 14.2.

TABLE 14.2

Observed and Expected Proportions of Males and Females Contracting this Disease

	Sex Male	Female	
p_o	_____	_____	1.00
p_e	_____	_____	1.00

(d) Using the information in Table 14.2 retest the hypothesis that this disease is more sex-linked to males.

$\chi^2 =$ _____   df = _____ $p <$ _____

2. A leading university recently conferred 2,000 bachelor's degrees on women and 3,000 on men. Degrees in the humanities were received by 1,100 of the women and 1,400 of the men; the remaining graduates were awarded degrees in the sciences.

(a) Use the information above to complete the proportions in Table 14.3. (Remember the sum of the observed proportions must equal the sum of the expected proportions.)

TABLE 14.3

Observed and Expected Proportions of Men and Women Receiving Undergraduate Degrees in Either the Humanities or the Sciences

			Sex of Graduate		
			Female	Male	
	Humanities	p_o			0.50
Area		p_e	0.20	0.30	
of					
Study	Sciences	p_o			0.50
		p_e	0.20	0.30	
			0.40	0.60	1.00

(b) Evaluate the statement that an individual's sex is significantly related to his or her chosen field of study.

$\chi^2 =$ _____   df = _____ $p <$ _____

(c) Using the normal test for comparing two proportions, determine whether the proportion of women receiving degrees in the humanities is significantly different from the proportion of men receiving such degrees.

$z =$ _____ $p <$ _____

3. The Glenna-Liam research firm was commissioned by a leading ice cream manufacturer to determine whether grade school children prefer vanilla, chocolate, or vanilla fudge ice cream. They asked 500 children to rank these three flavors. A week later each child was given a taste of each and then asked for a rating. Only the data from children who reported the same flavor at both interviews were used. The preferred flavors of 480 children are reported in Table 14.4.

TABLE 14.4

Observed and Expected Frequencies of Children's Ice Cream Preferences

	Vanilla	Chocolate	Vanilla Fudge	
f_o	183	212	85	450
f_e				

(a) Complete Table 14.4.

(b) Use this information to determine whether children show a preference for one particular flavor of ice cream.

$\chi^2 = $ _____   df $= $ _____ $p < $ _____

4. Dr. Mathew Shechtman, a leading authority on tooth decay, has developed a new treatment which he claims can significantly reduce the number of cavities children will get in a 12-month period. He obtained permission to use his treatment with half of his 70 patients under 13. At the end of one year he classified each child as having had either a small, moderate, or large number of cavities. The results from his classification of children by treatment group and amount of cavities are recorded in Table 14.5.

TABLE 14.5

Observed and Expected Frequencies of the Amount of Cavities Children Got with and without Dr. Shechtman's Treatment

		Few	Moderate	Many	
			Number of Cavities		
(With treatment)	f_o	14	17	4	35
	f_e				
(Without treatment)	f_o	5	9	21	35
	f_e				
		19	26	25	70

(a) What are the null and experimental hypotheses?

H_0: _____

H_1: _____

(b) Using the information in Table 14.3, evaluate the success of Dr. Shechtman's new dental treatment.

$\chi^2 = $ _____ df = _____ $p < $ _____

(c) What would you conclude about Dr. Shechtman's new treatment?

_____

_____

_____

_____

5. Despite the prevalence of such time-honored᾽ phrases as "you can't tell a book by its cover," people's actions sometimes seem to be based on the appearance of the person they are interacting with. Dr. Martin Sharon, a leading social psychologist, wished to assess the influence of appearance of college-aged experimenters on the helpfulness of middle-aged subjects. One male and one female experimenter went to suburban shopping centers randomly asking middle-aged patrons for either a dime in exchange for two nickels or for two nickels in exchange for a dime. Each experimenter made his or her request of 20 subjects when dressed in a conservative manner (e.g., a suit or dress) and 20 subjects when dressed in a freaky manner (e.g., jeans, beads, etc.). Experimenters were unaware of the purpose of this study and were well-mannered at all times. Each subject was classified according to the experimental condition (i.e., dress and sex of the interviewer) and whether he or she was willing to make the requested exchange. The results of this study are shown in Table 14.6.

TABLE 14.6

Observed and Expected Frequencies of the Relationship between Appearance of Experimenter and Behavior of Subject

		Conservative Male	Conservative Female	Freaky Male	Freaky Female	
Willing to give change	f_o	15	17	4	6	—
	f_e					
Unwilling to give change	f_o	5	3	16	14	—
	f_e					
		20	20	20	20	80

Subject's Behavior (row label)

(a) Using the above information, complete Table 14.6. (Remember the sum of the expected frequencies must equal the sum of the observed frequencies.)

(b) Is there a relationship between the appearance of the experimenter and the behavior of the subject?

$\chi^2 =$ _____ df = _____ $p <$ _____

(c) Describe the results of this study.

_____

_____

_____

_____

Formulas

Chi-square distribution

—Theoretical definition

$$\chi^2 = \Sigma z^2$$

—General formulas—frequencies and proportions

$$\chi^2 = \sum_{i=1}^{k} \frac{(f_o - f_e)^2}{f_e}$$

$$\chi^2 = N \sum_{i=1}^{k} \frac{(p_o - p_e)^2}{p_e}$$

—Simplified computing formulas—frequencies and proportions (one-way χ^2)

$$\chi^2 = \Sigma \frac{f_o^2}{f_e} - N$$

$$\chi^2 = N \Sigma \frac{p_o^2}{p_e} - N$$

—Simplified computing formula—$2 \times 2 \; \chi^2$

$$\chi^2 = \frac{N(|bc - ad| - N/2)^2}{(a + b)(a + c)(b + d)(c + d)}$$

—Correction for continuity (df = 1)—frequencies and proportions

$$\chi^2 = \Sigma \frac{(|f_o - f_e| - \frac{1}{2})^2}{f_e}$$

$$\chi^2 = N \Sigma \frac{(|p_o - p_e| - 1/(2N))^2}{p_e}$$

—Degrees of freedom—comparisons along one dimension

$$df = k - 1$$

—Degrees of freedom—comparisons along two dimensions

$$df = (k - 1)(r - 1)$$

—expected frequency for a cell in a two-way classification χ^2

$$f_e = \frac{f_r \times f_c}{N}$$

Normal distribution

$$\mu_P = p$$

$$\sigma_P = \sqrt{\frac{pq}{N}}$$

Normal test

—Comparing a single sample proportion with a theoretical or expected proportion

$$z = \frac{P - \mu_P}{\sigma_P} = \frac{P - p}{\sqrt{\dfrac{pq}{N}}}$$

—Comparing a single sample proportion with a theoretical or expected proportion—with the correction for continuity

$$z = \frac{|P - p| - 1/(2N)}{\sqrt{\dfrac{pq}{N}}}$$

—Comparing two sample proportions

$$z = \frac{P_1 - P_2}{\sigma_{P_1-P_2}}$$

$$\sigma_{P_1-P_2} = \sqrt{pq\left(\frac{1}{N_1} + \frac{1}{N_2}\right)}$$

$$p = \frac{N_1 P_1 + N_2 P_2}{N_1 + N_2}$$

$$q = 1 - p$$

—Comparing two sample proportions—correction for continuity

$$z = \frac{|P_1 - P_2| - \dfrac{N_1 + N_2}{2N_1 N_2}}{\sigma_{P_1-P_2}}$$

CHAPTER 15

Tests on Ranked Data:
Some Nonparametric Methods

A. Conceptual questions

1. Fill in each blank below with the word or words which best complete each sentence.

(a) _____ tests do not make assumptions about the form of the population distributions or their variances.

(b) Parametric tests assume that the population distributions are _____ and that the population variances are _____.

(c) _____ tests use interval or ratio information about data.

(d) The arc sine transformation can be used to transform the dependent variable of _____ and permit the use of a parametric test.

(e) Using the same data, a parametric test is _____ (more, less) likely to yield significance than a nonparametric test.

(f) The measure of central tendency tested in nonparametric tests is the _____.

(g) The Mann-Whitney U test is _____ (more, less) powerful than the median test.

(h) The Wilcoxon signed rank test is _____ (more, less) powerful than the sign test.

(i) When the normal test is used instead of a sign test for one sample, a _____ must be used.

2. Choose the number corresponding to the phrase which best completes each statement. Indicate your answer in the space provided.

_____ (a) The power of a statistical test increases as:
 (1) the quantity of information used increases
 (2) the probability of incorrectly rejecting the null hypothesis increases
 (3) the probability of not detecting the experimental effect decreases
 (4) all of the above

_____ (b) When N is small the sign test is based on the:
 (1) binomial distribution
 (2) normal distribution
 (3) chi square distribution
 (4) none of the above because the sign test is nonparametric

_____ (c) The median test is based on the:
 (1) binomial distribution
 (2) normal distribution
 (3) chi square distribution
 (4) none of the above, because the median test is nonparametric

_____ (d) When the dependent variable is the number correct computed from a finite number of trials:
 (1) the range of scores is from 0 to 1
 (2) assumptions of normality and homogeneity are violated
 (3) the variance and shape of the distribution are equal everywhere in the range
 (4) all of the above

_____ (e) If the dependent variable is the probability correct computed on a finite number of trials, then as the mean approaches 0 or 1 the:

(1) distribution becomes more skewed and the variance decreases

(2) distribution becomes more skewed and the variance increases

(3) distribution becomes less skewed and the variance decreases

(4) distribution becomes less skewed and the variance increases

3. Indicate whether each of the following statements is true or false.

_____ (a) When performing a matched t test, deviations from normality and homogeneity are not critical.

_____ (b) Parametric tests are easier to compute and therefore more desirable than nonparametric tests.

_____ (c) There is no nonparametric method of investigating the interaction of two independent variables.

_____ (d) If the dependent variable is measured on a ratio scale a nonparametric test cannot be used.

_____ (e) Nonparametric tests are more powerful than parametric tests because they are not bound by population assumptions.

B. Problems

1. Pearne University's experimental psychology graduate program requires prospective students to submit Miller Analogy Test (MAT) scores. Of the 14 students accepted by this program in 1975, 11 achieved MAT scores above the national median for first-year experimental psychology graduate students.

(a) Which test is appropriate for determining whether students accepted into this program are significantly different from other first-year students? (Check this answer before proceeding.)

_____

(b) Do the students accepted to Pearne University have significantly different MAT scores?

_____

_____

(c) Evaluate the hypothesis that students accepted by Pearne University are not only different but that they are in fact superior to other students.

_____

_____

_____

(d) Between 1968 and 1975, 48 of the 76 students who entered the graduate program at Pearne University had MAT scores which were above the median score for first-year graduate students. Use a normal test to determine whether Pearne University students have significantly higher MAT scores than other students.

_____

_____

_____

2. Some professors at Pearne University feel that MAT scores bear no relationship to a student's ability to do graduate work. Since only 68 % of the students who enter Pearne's graduate program receive their doctorates, these professors decided to compare the MAT scores of students who have dropped out of the program to those who have received their Ph.D.'s. From the departmental records they collected the MAT scores of students who entered the graduate program between 1968 and 1970 and then classified them nto graduates and non-graduates. Table 15.1 presents these data.

(a) Which parametric test would be used to determine whether these two samples are drawn from populations with significantly different means?

_____

TABLE 15.1

MAT Scores of Experimental Psychology Graduate Students Entering Pearne University Between 1968 and 1970

Graduates		Dropouts	
MAT score	Rank	MAT score	Rank
53	—————	85	—————
40	—————	72	—————
61	—————	92	—————
59	—————	93	—————
78	—————	67	—————
87	—————	60	—————
48	—————	53	—————
74	—————	63	—————
60	—————	78	—————
39	—————	82	—————
		98	—————
		70	—————
		89	—————
		52	—————

(b) Which two nonparametric tests would be appropriate to evaluate the hypothesis that students who complete graduate school have higher MAT scores than those who drop out of graduate school? (Check this answer before doing the following computations.)

_____

_____

(c) Use the less stringent of the two tests mentioned above to evaluate the hypothesis that there is a significant difference between the MAT scores of students who do and do not graduate. (Use the appropriate tables to aid your calculations.)

_____

_____

_____

TABLE 15.2

Use with Problem Number 2

		Graduates	Dropouts	
Above the median	f_o			
	f_e	5	7	12
Below the median	f_o			
	f_e	5	7	12
		10	14	

(d) Test the above hypothesis using the more stringent of the two tests. (Use the appropriate tables to aid your calculations.)

_____

_____

_____

3. Many developmental psychologists attribute personality differences to birth order. Firstborn children are posited as more achievement oriented than later-born children. Dr. Lemieux investigated the achievement orientation of siblings as a function of their birth order. He decided to study only families with exactly three children between the ages of 6 and 12. All participating families were evaluated as well-adjusted and middle class. All children were of normal intelligence. No twins or triplets were used in this study. Owing to the possible interaction between achievement orientation and sex, only same sexed siblings were studied and the experiment was run separately for female siblings and male siblings. Using interviews and tests (controlled for age) the children in each family were ranked according to achievement orientation. The data for the female siblings are reported in Table 15.3.

TABLE 15.3
Achievement Orientation Scores for Female Siblings

Family No.	Oldest Child	Middle Child	Youngest Child
1	3	1	2
2	3	2	1
3	2	1	3
4	3	2	1
5	3	2	1
6	3	2	1
7	3	2	1
8	3	1	2
9	1	3	2
10	3	1	2
11	2	1	3

(a) What nonparametric test would you use to determine whether there is a significant difference in the achievement motivation between siblings in different ordinal positions? (Check this answer before proceeding.)

_____

(b) Test Dr. Lemieux's hypothesis that firstborn female siblings will show higher achievement orientation.

_____

_____

_____

TABLE 15.4

Achievement Orientation Scores for Male Siblings

Family No.	Oldest Child	Middle Child	Youngest Child
1	3	2	1
2	3	1	2
3	3	2	1
4	3	2	1
5	2	3	1
6	3	1	2
7	3	1	2
8	3	1	2
9	3	2	1

(c) Using the data from male siblings (Table 15.4), test whether first-born males show stronger achievement orientation than their later-born siblings.

_____

_____

_____

4. The drawings of 27 kindergarten children were analyzed by Dr. Gay Jones, a clinical psychologist, and ranked for evidence of emotional maturity. She then divided the drawings according to the sex of the child to investigate the relative emotional maturity of 5-year-old boys and girls. These ranks are presented in Table 15.5.

TABLE 15.5

Ranks* of the Emotional Maturity of Kindergarten Age Girls and Boys

Boys	Girls
19	5
1	11
11	17.5
20	3
4	22
2	8
21	9
26	11
7	23
14	13
15	24
17.5	16
6	25
	27

* 1 = lowest score.

(a) Which two nonparametric tests are appropriate to test whether these two groups differ in emotional maturity? (Check this answer before proceeding.)

_____

_____

(b) Use the more stringent of the two tests to evaluate the notion that these two groups significantly differ in emotional maturity.

_____

_____

_____

TABLE 15.6

Work Space for Problem 4

		Girls	Boys	
Above the median	f_o			
	f_e	7	6.5	13.5
Below the median	f_o			
	f_e	7	6.5	13.5
		14	13	27

(c) Use the less stringent test to evaluate whether girls show more emotional maturity than boys. (Use the space provided in Table 15.6.)

_____

_____

_____

5. There is much disagreement as to factors which influence nervous disorders in children. Some therapists feel that the presence of a patient's mother is comforting and will therefore reduce nervous symptoms, while others are equally convinced that the mother is somewhat responsible for these disorders and that she will exacerbate these symptoms. Dr. Ronald Rosenthal observed children who, in times of stress, involuntarily twitch while they are with either their mother or a classmate. The number of tics each child showed in each situation is shown in Table 15.7.

TABLE 15.7

Number of Tics for 11 Children in the Presence of the Child's Mother and a Strange Child

Child No.	With Mother	With Child	Difference	Rank	Positive Signed Rank	Negative Signed Rank
1	29	26	_____	_____	_____	_____
2	3	10	_____	_____	_____	_____
3	18	19	_____	_____	_____	_____
4	15	24	_____	_____	_____	_____
5	12	10	_____	_____	_____	_____
6	21	27	_____	_____	_____	_____
7	14	26	_____	_____	_____	_____
8	15	20	_____	_____	_____	_____
9	13	19	_____	_____	_____	_____
10	23	25	_____	_____	_____	_____
11	8	16	_____	_____	_____	_____

(a) Which two nonparametric tests would be appropriate to evaluate the following hypothesis: Children with nervous disorders show less neurotic behavior in the presence of their mothers. (Check this answer before proceeding.)

_____

_____

(b) Using the more stringent of these two tests, evaluate the preceding hypothesis.

_____

_____

_____

(c) Perform the less stringent of these two tests to see if it yields the same conclusions.

_____

_____

_____

6. To stimulate their interest in reading, Ms. Rebecca Philips allows her fourth-grade students to choose their own reading materials. After doing this for several years she began to notice that those students who were most creative seemed to prefer science fiction stories. She tested her 21 students with a standardized creativity test. These scores are grouped by reading preference and presented in Table 15.8. (All children were of average intelligence and reading ability.)

TABLE 15.8

Creativity Scores of Fourth-Graders Grouped by Reading Preference

Biography		Science		Novels		Science Fiction	
Score	Rank	Score	Rank	Score	Rank	Score	Rank
57	———	130	———	95	———	120	———
39	———	54	———	82	———	100	———
72	———	48	———	138	———	140	———
36	———	40	———	40	———	92	———
45	———	91	———	151	———	171	———
141	———						

(a) Which two nonparametric tests are appropriate to evaluate these data? (Check this answer before proceeding.)

_____

_____

(b) Perform the more stringent of these tests to evaluate the hypothesis that children who prefer reading science fiction are more creative than children with other reading preferences.

_____

_____

_____

Formulas

Sign test—single sample ($N \leq 35$)

r = The number of observations above or below the theoretical median, whichever is smaller

N = The total number of observations

Sign test—two matched samples

r = The number of differences between pair members with a plus or minus sign, whichever is smaller

N = The total number of pairs minus the number of tied pairs

Median test—two independent samples

$$\chi^2 = \sum_{i=1}^{4} \frac{(|f_o - f_e| - 0.5)^2}{f_e}$$

$df = 1$

Median test—three or more independent samples

$$\chi^2 = \sum_{i=1}^{2k} \frac{(f_o - f_e)^2}{f_e} \quad \text{where } k = \text{ the number of independent groups}$$

$df = k - 1$

Mann-Whitney U test—two independent samples

T_i = The sum of the ranks of group i

$$T_1 + T_2 = \frac{N(N+1)}{2}$$

$$U_1 = N_1 N_2 + \frac{N_1(N_1 + 1)}{2} - T_1$$

$$U_2 = N_1 N_2 + \frac{N_2(N_2 + 1)}{2} - T_2$$

$$U_1 + U_2 = N_1 N_2$$

$U = U_1$ or U_2, whichever is smaller

Wilcoxon signed ranks test—two matched samples

T = The sum of the ranked differences between pair members associated with either a plus or minus sign, whichever is smaller

$$T_+ + T_- = \frac{N(N+1)}{2}$$

N = The total number of pairs minus the number of tied pairs

Kruskal-Wallis test—three or more independent samples

$$\Sigma T_i = \frac{N(N + 1)}{2}$$

$$H = \frac{12}{N(N + 1)} \sum_{i=1}^{k} \frac{T_i^2}{n_i} - 3(N + 1)$$

df $= k - 1$

Friedman test—three or more matched groups

$$\chi_r^2 = \frac{12}{Nk(k + 1)} \sum^{k} T_i^2 - 3N(k + 1)$$

Normal approximation—single sample ($N > 35$)

$$z = \frac{|r - Np| - 0.5}{\sqrt{Npq}}$$

Normal approximation—two independent samples ($N > 20$)

$$\mu_U = \frac{N_1 N_2}{2}$$

$$\sigma_U = \sqrt{\frac{N_1 N_2 (N_1 + N_2 + 1)}{12}}$$

$$z = \frac{U - \mu_U}{\sigma_U}$$

Transformations of Data, Tests on Correlation Coefficients, and Relationships among Distributions

A. Conceptual questions

1. Choose the word following each blank which best completes the statement.

(a) As the proportion of correct trials (from a fixed number of trials) deviates from 0.5, the distribution becomes _____ (more, less) skewed.

(b) If the true population proportion, p, equals 0.5, the distribution is approximately _____ (skewed, normal).

(c) As the number of correct trials approaches the total number of trials, the distribution variance _____ (increases, decreases).

(d) Using the arc sine transform will _____ (maximize, minimize) the differences among proportions close to 0 and 1.00.

(e) Using the arc sine transform will _____ (maximize, minimize) the differences among proportions close to 0.5.

(f) _____ (Rho, Fisher Z) is used to determine whether two correlation coefficients are significantly different from each other.

2. Indicate whether each of the following statements is true or false.

_____ (a) Parametric tests are appropriate when the dependent variable is the number of correct trials out of a fixed number of trials.

_____ (b) The number of correct items is a linear transform of the proportion of correct items.

_____ (c) The mean of the arc sines is equal to the arc sine of the mean proportions.

_____ (d) Whether or not the correlation coefficient is significantly different from zero is not related to the sign of the coefficient.

_____ (e) Whether or not the correlation coefficient is significantly different from zero does not depend on the number of paired measures.

_____ (f) The sampling distribution is normal whenever the population distribution is normal.

_____ (g) The chi-square distribution was derived by assuming that the dependent variable was normally distributed.

3. Indicate whether each of the following relationships describes the F, t, or χ^2 distribution.

_____ (a) $\displaystyle\sum^{n} z^2$

_____ (b) t^2

_____ (c) $\dfrac{\chi_1^2(n_1)/n_1}{\chi_2^2(n_2)/n_2}$

_____ (d) $\dfrac{z}{\sqrt{\chi^2(n)/n}}$

_____ (e) $\dfrac{\sqrt{x^2(1)/1}}{\sqrt{\chi^2(n)/n}}$

B. Problems

1. Mr. Julius Goldy wished to evaluate the effectiveness of certain spelling drills. He pretested 12 of his third-grade students on 20 sixth-grade level spelling words. He then employed the spelling drills and afterwards retested his students. Four weeks later, with no intervening study, he again tested his students to check whether they had retained the spelling of these words. Table 16.1 reports each student's score on the three spelling tests.

TABLE 16.1

Spelling Scores of Mr. Julius Goldy's Third-Grade Class

Student	Pretest			Test after Instruction			Follow-up Test		
	No. Correct	Propor-tion	$\emptyset$	No. Correct	Propor-tion	$\emptyset$	No. Correct	Propor-tion	$\emptyset$
1	2	___ ___		15	___ ___		14	___ ___	
2	1	___ ___		18	___ ___		12	___ ___	
3	5	___ ___		19	___ ___		19	___ ___	
4	3	___ ___		13	___ ___		10	___ ___	
5	8	___ ___		20	___ ___		18	___ ___	
6	4	___ ___		14	___ ___		15	___ ___	
7	0	___ ___		19	___ ___		19	___ ___	
8	2	___ ___		10	___ ___		5	___ ___	
9	1	___ ___		17	___ ___		12	___ ___	
10	0	___ ___		12	___ ___		12	___ ___	
11	6	___ ___		18	___ ___		17	___ ___	
12	1	___ ___		9	___ ___		7	___ ___	
	$\bar{X}_1 =$ ___ ___			$\bar{X}_2 =$ ___ ___			$\bar{X}_3 =$ ___ ___		

(a) What nonparametric test should be used to evaluate the difference in performance at each testing?

_____

(b) Using the space provided in Table 16.1, calculate the proportion correct for each raw score and perform an arc sine transform on these data. (Note: The arc sine transform of 0 is 0).*

(c) What parametric test can now be used to evaluate the effectiveness of these spelling drills?

_____

* Calculate the mean proportion and mean arc sine transform for each group.

(d) Why would Mr. Julius Goldy prefer to use a parametric test on these data?

_____

_____

(e) Use the pretest data to show that the average arc sine is not equal to the arc sine of the average.

_____

_____

_____

_____

2. The speed-accuracy trade-off is a well known phenomenon. It can be demonstrated that as subjects are forced to work more quickly they begin to make more errors. When conducting a reaction time (RT) experiment, one encourages subjects to work as quickly as possible but without sacrificing accuracy.

Two graduate students, Karen and Michael, co-designed a reaction time experiment and decided they would each run 20 subjects. They compared their results and found much to their dismay that Michael's subjects had mean RTs which were significantly shorter than those of Karen's subjects. In an effort to explain this discrepancy, they looked at the correlation between reaction time and the number of errors for each subject. Table 16.2 presents the correlation coefficients from each experiment.

TABLE 16.2

Pearson Product Moment Correlation Coefficients between RT and Errors for Two Experimenters

Karen's Data	Michael's Data
$r_1 = -0.12$	$r_2 = -0.38$
$N_1 = 20$	$N_2 = 20$
$Z_1 = $ _____	$Z_2 = $ _____

(a) Is there a significant correlation between speed (RT) and accuracy (errors) in Karen's experiment?

_____

(b) Is there a significant correlation between speed and accuracy in Michael's experiment?

_____

(c) Are these two speed-accuracy correlations significantly different from each other?

_____

_____

_____

(d) Using the available information, give a plausible explanation for the original discrepancy between Michael's data and Karen's data. Which section of the experiment should be redone?

_____

_____

_____

_____

3. Dr. Bernice Stanley wished to test the reliability and validity of her new technique designed to measure sentence comprehension. To test its reliability, she administered two forms of this test to a group of college sophomores (Group 1) and then calculated the Pearson product moment correlation coefficient between forms A and B. As an added check she tested these two forms on an additional group of subjects (Group 2). To test the validity of this technique, she administered her test to a group of college sophomores and then administered an older, previously validated test of sentence comprehension to the same group of subjects (Group 3). The correlation coefficients used to test reliability and validity are reported in Table 16.3.

TABLE 16.3

Correlation Coefficients to Test the Reliability and Validity of Dr. Bernice Stanley's New Technique

Test-Retest Reliability		Content Validity
Group 1	Group 2	Group 3
$r_1 = 0.83$	$r_2 = 0.91$	$r_3 = 0.48$
$N_1 = 15$	$N_2 = 18$	$N_3 = 22$
$Z = $ _____	$Z = $ _____	$Z = $ _____

(a) Is there a significant correlation between the two forms of Dr. Bernice Stanley's technique for Group 1?

_____

(b) Is there a significant positive correlation between the two test forms for Group 2?

_____

(c) Is there a significant difference between the correlation coefficients of Groups 1 and 2?

_____

_____

_____

(d) Evaluate the correlation between this new technique and the older, previously validated method.

_____

(e) Dr. Bernice Stanley was a bit disturbed about the low and only marginally significant correlation between her technique and this older technique. She discovered that this older technique was considered valid when its correlation coefficient was equal to 0.38 and $N = 35$. Are these two correlation coefficients (0.48 and 0.38) significantly different?

_____

_____

_____

4. Dr. Paul Levy hypothesized that musical aptitude is positively correlated with the ability to learn foreign languages. Using a variety of tests, he ranked 15 children and 12 adults on their aptitudes in both music and foreign languages. Using these data he calculated a Spearman rho of 0.83 for the children and 0.35 for the adults.

(a) Is Dr. Levy's hypothesis substantiated with his adult subjects?

_____

(b) Do children show a significant correlation between musical ability and the ability to learn foreign languages?

_____

Formulas

Arc sine transform

$$\emptyset = 2 \text{ arc sine } \sqrt{P}$$

Testing whether Pearson r is significantly different from zero

$$df = N - 2$$

Testing whether two Pearson r's are significantly different from each other

Fisher $Z = 1/2 \log_e \left[\dfrac{1 + r}{1 - r} \right]$

$$z = \frac{Z_1 - Z_2}{\sigma_{z_1 - z_2}}$$

$$\sigma_{z_1 - z_2} = \sqrt{\frac{1}{N_1 - 3} + \frac{1}{N_2 - 3}}$$

Testing whether Spearman rho is significantly different from zero

$$N = \text{The number of pairs}$$

Relationships among distributions

—Normal and chi-square distributions

$$\chi^2(n) = \sum^n z^2$$

$$\chi^2(1) = z^2$$

—F and chi-square distributions

$$F(n_1, n_2) = \frac{\chi^2(n_1)/n_1}{\chi^2(n_2)/n_2}$$

—F and t distributions

$$F(1, n) = t^2(n)$$

—t and chi-square distributions

$$t^2(n) = \frac{\chi^2(1)/1}{\chi^2(n)/n}$$

$$t^2(n) = \frac{z^2}{\chi^2(n)/n}$$

$$t(n) = \frac{z}{\sqrt{\chi^2(n)/n}}$$

Rules of Summation

NOTATION

We let the symbols X and Y stand for various values of a variable, and the symbols a, b, and c stand for values of a constant. X and Y will normally be values of some attributes of an individual, so that we could speak of the value of the attribute we are calling X for the ith individual in a sample as X_i. The summation sign, Σ (capital Greek sigma), is used to denote the operation of summation. For example, the instruction to sum all the values of the variable X from the 1st in the sample to the Nth in the sample may be written:

$$\sum_{i=1}^{N} X_i$$

Since N is used to stand for the total number of values in a sample, this instructs us to obtain the sum of the entire set of values in the sample. If we were interested in the sum of only the first five values in the sample, we could write

$$\sum_{i=1}^{5} X_i$$

Normally we are interested in the sum of all the values in the sample; in such a case, we often drop the subscripts and superscripts on the summation sign and on X and write simply

$$\Sigma X$$

An understanding of the rules of summation is necessary to follow many of the procedures outlined in this book. These rules are listed below.

(1) THE SUM OF A CONSTANT

The sum of a constant, a, added to itself N times, is simply the constant a multipled by N, or

$$\sum_{i=1}^{N} a = Na$$

For example, if $a = 2$ and $N = 20$

$$\sum_{i=1}^{20} a = Na = 20 \times 2 = 40$$

This reflects the simple fact that multiplication is a shortcut to adding the same thing to itself N times.

(2) THE SUM OF A CONSTANT TIMES A VARIABLE

The sum of a constant times a variable is equal to the constant times the sum of the variable, or

$$\sum_{i=1}^{3} aX_i = a \sum_{i=1}^{3} X_i$$

For example, if $X_1 = 10$, $X_2 = 20$, $X_3 = 30$, and $a = \frac{1}{2}$, then we compute this either as

$$\sum_{i=1}^{3} aX_i = (\frac{1}{2})(10) + (\frac{1}{2})(20) + (\frac{1}{2})(30) = 5 + 10 + 15 = 30$$

or by

$$a \sum_{i=1}^{3} X_i = (\frac{1}{2})(10 + 20 + 30) = (\frac{1}{2})(60) = 30$$

(3) ORDER OF OPERATIONS IN A SUM

Any operation on the term being summed is done prior to the summation. For example

$$\sum_{i=1}^{3} X_i^2 = X_1^2 + X_2^2 + X_3^2$$

whereas

$$\left(\sum_{i=1}^{3} X_i \right)^2 = (X_1 + X_2 + X_3)^2$$

Thus

$$\Sigma X^2 \neq (\Sigma X)^2$$

Similarly

$$\sum_{i=1}^{3} X_i Y_i = X_1 Y_1 + X_2 Y_2 + X_3 Y_3$$

whereas

$$\left(\sum_{i=1}^{3} X_i\right)\left(\sum_{i=1}^{3} Y_i\right) = (X_1 + X_2 + X_3)(Y_1 + Y_2 + Y_3)$$

Thus

$$\Sigma XY \neq (\Sigma X)(\Sigma Y)$$

A more complicated example is shown below:

$$\Sigma(X - a)^2 = \Sigma(X^2 - 2aX + a^2)$$

The expression in parentheses is squared before the summation is performed.

(4) DISTRIBUTING THE SUMMATION SIGN

If the terms to be summed are themselves a sum or difference, as in the last example of the previous rule, it is then possible to distribute (i.e., apply) the summation sign to each term, as follows:

$$\Sigma(X - a)^2 = \Sigma(X^2 - 2aX + a^2) = \Sigma X^2 - \Sigma 2aX + \Sigma a^2$$

Applying Rule (1) to the third term and Rule (2) to the second term results in

$$\Sigma X^2 - 2a \Sigma X + Na^2$$

A particularly important application of this rule occurs when the constant a is the mean of the sample, $\bar{X}$. Then

$$\Sigma(X - \bar{X})^2 = \Sigma(X^2 - 2\bar{X}X + \bar{X}^2) = \Sigma X^2 - \Sigma 2\bar{X}X + \Sigma \bar{X}^2$$

Applying Rules (1) and (2) results in

$$\Sigma X^2 - 2\bar{X}\Sigma X + N\bar{X}^2$$

Since $\Sigma X = N\bar{X}$, this can be further simplified by

$$\Sigma X^2 - 2N\bar{X}^2 + N\bar{X}^2 = \Sigma X^2 - N\bar{X}^2$$

The preceding application of summation rules is important in deriving the raw score formula for the standard deviation (see Chapter 3).

SUMMATION OF DOUBLY CLASSIFIED VARIABLES

It is often convenient to use double subscripts on a variable which can be classified along each of two dimensions. If each of five subjects participated in each of three conditions of an experiment, a particular test score from that experiment must be classified according to which subject it belongs to and

TABLE A.1

Scores for Five Subjects under Three Conditions of an Experiment, Illustrating Double Classification Notation

Subject (i)	Condition (j) 1	2	3	Row Sums
1	$X_{11} = 10$	$X_{12} = 15$	$X_{13} = 20$	$\sum_{j=1}^{3} X_{1j} = 45$
2	$X_{21} = 12$	$X_{22} = 17$	$X_{23} = 22$	$\sum_{j=1}^{3} X_{2j} = 51$
3	$X_{31} = 14$	$X_{32} = 19$	$X_{33} = 24$	$\sum_{j=1}^{3} X_{3j} = 57$
4	$X_{41} = 16$	$X_{42} = 21$	$X_{43} = 26$	$\sum_{j=1}^{3} X_{4j} = 63$
5	$X_{51} = 18$	$X_{52} = 23$	$X_{53} = 28$	$\sum_{j=1}^{3} X_{5j} = 69$
Column Sums	$\sum_{i=1}^{5} X_{i1} = 70$	$\sum_{i=1}^{5} X_{i2} = 95$	$\sum_{i=1}^{5} X_{i3} = 120$	Total Sum $\sum_{i=1}^{5}\sum_{j=1}^{3} X_{ij} = 285$

which condition of the experiment it came from. We denote this double-subscripted variable as X_{ij}, where i is the subject number and j is the condition number.

Table A.1 shows a set of hypothetical scores for five subjects under three conditions of an experiment. Each score has been labeled with its appropriate subscripts. Note that the first subscript refers to subject number and the second subscript to condition number. The notation and values for each column and row sum are also shown in the table.

It is convenient, particularly for the analysis of variance, to use subscript notation to denote summation of scores in a particular column, in a particular row, or across the entire table. Summation of all the scores in the table is written

$$\sum_{i=1}^{5}\sum_{j=1}^{3} X_{ij} = X_{11} + X_{12} + \cdots + X_{53}$$

where the dots indicate omitted scores that should be obvious from the context. The total number of scores to be summed is given by the *product* of the two indexes, i and j, or $5 \times 3 = 15$. The expression above instructs us to sum all 15 scores in the table together. It is also written more simply as $\Sigma\Sigma X$.

To indicate the summation of a particular column, we write

$$\sum_{i=1}^{5} X_{i1} = X_{11} + X_{21} + X_{31} + X_{41} + X_{51}$$

This instructs us to sum the scores in the first column (i.e., for $j = 1$).

To indicate summation of a particular row, we write

$$\sum_{j=1}^{3} X_{4j} = X_{41} + X_{42} + X_{43}$$

This instructs us to sum the scores in the fourth row, or the scores for the fourth subject.

The following expression instructs us to sum the scores in each column, square those sums, and then sum the squared sums:

$$\sum_{i=1}^{5} \left(\sum_{j=1}^{3} X_{ij} \right)^2 = \left(\sum_{j=1}^{3} X_{1j} \right)^2 + \left(\sum_{j=1}^{3} X_{2j} \right)^2 + \cdots + \left(\sum_{j=1}^{3} X_{5j} \right)^2$$

Finally, the following expression instructs us to square each score and sum the squared scores for all 15 values in the table:

$$\sum_{i=1}^{5} \sum_{j=1}^{3} X_{ij}^2 = X_{11}^2 + X_{12}^2 + \cdots + X_{53}^2$$

The numerical values for the following expressions are based on the scores in Table A.1. The student should also compute these values to test his or her understanding of how the double classification notation scheme works.

Numerical Examples

$$\sum_{i=1}^{4} X_{i2} = 72$$

$$\sum_{j=1}^{2} X_{3j} = 33$$

$$\sum_{j=1}^{2} \sum_{i=1}^{5} X_{ij} = 165$$

$$\sum_{j=1}^{3} \left(\sum_{i=1}^{5} X_{ij} \right)^2 = 28{,}325$$

$$\sum_{i=1}^{5} \left(\sum_{j=1}^{3} X_{ij} \right)^2 = 16{,}605$$

$$\sum_{j=1}^{3} X_{2j}^2 = 917$$

$$\sum_{i=1}^{5} X_{i3}^2 = 2{,}920$$

Computational Methods for Pocket Calculators

Because of the proliferation of pocket electronic calculators in recent years, it seems likely that most students enrolled in a statistics course will either own an electronic calculator or have access to one. This section is included to help you make the maximum use of the calculator at hand or to help you select a calculator that will be of most use in solving statistical problems.

Calculators will include some or all of the following functions. We list them in their order of importance in solving statistics problems. Functions at the beginning of the list will be found in virtually all calculators, whereas those at the end will be found in only some.

(1) Floating decimal point.

(2) The arithmetic functions [+], [−], [×], and [÷].

(3) A square root function, [√]. Some calculators replace the contents of memory with the results of $\sqrt{X}$; for these, it is important to carry out chains of computations in such an order that $\sqrt{X}$ need not be performed while something else is being stored in the memory (see the calculation of Pearson r for an example).

(4) A reciprocal function, [1/X]. This function may be somewhat awkwardly replaced by putting X in memory, entering a 1 into the display, then dividing 1 by the contents of memory. This is usually a rather unsatisfactory alternative because we often use the reciprocal function to divide the contents of memory by a number in the display by multiplying the memory by $1/X$.

(5) A direct square function, [X^2]. This function is very simply replaced by

213

a series of the following two operations: some number X [×] [=]; the result is X^2.

(6) A single memory, [M]. Calculators vary the most in the way memory is addressed. If only a single memory function exists, [M], then pressing [M] will automatically recall the contents of memory and place them in the register *or* will replace the contents of memory with whatever number is in the register if [M] is pressed after an explicit equals operation, [=], or an implicit equals operation, [X^2], [$\sqrt{X}$], or [$1/X$].

A more elaborate calculator might have four memory functions: [CM], [RM], [M+], and [M−]. [CM] clears memory of its contents, [RM] recalls what is stored in the memory and places it in the display without destroying the contents of memory, [M+] adds the contents in the display to memory, and [M−] subtracts the contents in the display from memory.

To simplify notation of the computational steps, we will use the more elaborate four memory functions listed above. The equivalent series of operations when only a single [M] function exists are shown below.

[CM] → 0 [=] [M] (this replaces the contents of memory with 0).

[RM] → [M] (but do not press [M] after an explicit or implicit equals operation; use clear [C] or clear entry [CE] to avoid replacing memory contents with contents of register).

[M+] → some number X[+] [M] [=] [M].

[M−] → some number X[CHG SIGN] [+] [M] [=] [M].

(7) An operation to change the sign of the number in the register, making it negative if it is a positive number and positive if it is a negative number, [CHG SIGN] or [+/−]. The change sign function can be replaced by multiplying by −1: some number X [×] [−] 1 [=].

In the following section, we first present some general rules for calculations, and then present specific applications to statistics problems. To simplify notation, we use a written number or symbol without brackets to indicate which number should be entered into the keyboard, and an operation in square brackets to indicate which operation button should be pressed. If your calculator does not have the operation listed, refer back to the beginning of this section for the equivalent series of substitute operations.

GENERAL RULES

Order of Operations

Most calculators embody a "natural" order of operations, in that the order in which arithmetic operations are written is identical to the order in which they are entered in the calculator. Each of the numbers will appear as it is entered in the display; the final answer is given by the last entry in each line, and will appear in the display after the preceding operation button is pressed. Numbers in ordinary type (5, 16, etc.) are entered by the user; numbers in *italics* (*21, 116*, etc.) appear in the display as the result of an operation. Since calculators differ in the number of decimal places available, intermediate and final results will be given to only four or five places.

Addition: 5 [+] 16 [=] *21*
Subtraction: 272 [−] 156 [=] *116*
Multiplication: 2.5 [×] 92 [=] *230*
Division: 98 [÷] 5 [=] *19.6*

Division When the Divisor is Already in the Display

For example, 100 ÷ 3.4321 when 3.4321, the divisor, has been obtained after a series of calculations and still appears in the display.

3.4321 [1/X] *0.29136* ⋯ [×] 100 [=] *29.13668* ⋯

Rounding

For calculations with electronic calculators all intermediate calculations should be retained with the fullest degree of accuracy the device is capable of. That is, no intermediate calculations should be rounded. This will automatically be true when the entire series of calculations is done within the calculator, so that no intermediate answers need be recorded on paper. When intermediate answers need to be recorded, record them to the number of decimals given by the device (usually 10 to 12 digits).

The only rounding that will be done is in reporting the results. Generally speaking, statistics are reported to two or three decimal places beyond the number in the original data. Thus, when the original data are reported as whole numbers, the statistics calculated from them are reported to two or three decimal places. Means, medians, and variances are often reported to two decimal places, whereas standard deviations are often reported to three. Statistics that are bounded by 0 and 1.0, such as correlation coefficients, regression coefficients, and proportion or probability, are usually reported to three decimal places.

Rule for Rounding. When rounding to the nth decimal place, round up if the number in the $n + 1$st position is greater than 5, and drop the remainder if the number is less than 5. To round the following to two decimal places:

$$50.178 = 50.18$$
$$11.222 = 11.22$$

When the $n + 1$st position is *exactly* 5, neither rule applies. We need a convention that will round up about half the time and drop the remainder the other half. One convention is to drop the $n + 1$st digit when the nth digit is *even* and to round up when the nth digit is *odd*. For example:

$$55.550 = 55.6$$
$$55.450 = 55.4$$

APPLICATIONS TO STATISTICS PROBLEMS

The following are some practical applications to computing statistics.

1. Percentile Ranks and Percentiles

Computing percentile ranks and computing percentiles are examples of chains of computation in which it is important to perform the operations in the correct sequence.

Percentile ranks.

$$PR(X) = \frac{cf_u + \left(\dfrac{X - X_u}{i}\right)f_i}{N} \times 100$$

We compute $PR(X)$ for the following data; $cf_u = 84$, $X = 72$, $X_u = 69.5$, $i = 5, f_i = 20$, and $N = 176$. The order of operations is

$$X \; [-] \; X_u \; [\div] \; i \; [\times] \; f_i \; [+] \; cf_u \; [\div] \; N \; [\times] \; 100 \; [=] \; PR$$
$$72 \; [-] \; 69.5 \; [\div] \; 5 \; [\times] \; 20 \; [+] \; 84 \; [\div] \; 176 \; [\times] \; 100 \; [=] \; 53.40909$$

Percentiles.

$$X = X_u + \frac{i\left(\dfrac{PR \times N}{100} - cf_u\right)}{f_i}$$

The order of operations is:

$$PR \; [\times] \; N \; [\div] \; 100 \; [-] \; cf_u \; [\times] \; i \; [\div] \; f_i \; [+] \; X_u \; [=] \; X$$

For the same data as above, but when X is the unknown and $PR(X) = 53.41$:

$$53.41 \; [\times] \; 176 \; [\div] \; 100 \; [-] \; 84 \; [\times] \; 5 \; [\div] \; 20 \; [+] \; 69.5 \; [=] \; 72.0004$$

2. Mean

To compute the mean of $(4, 20, 6, 8, 19)$, find $\bar{X} = \Sigma X/N$:

$$4 \; [+] \; 20 \; [+] \; 6 \; [+] \; 8 \; [+] \; 19 \; [\div] \; 5 \; [=] \; 11.4$$

To compute the mean of the following ungrouped frequency distribution:

X	f
1	10
2	16
3	20
4	11
5	5

$$\bar{X} = \Sigma fX/N$$

For ΣfX: [CM]

$\quad\quad\quad\quad\quad\quad\quad\quad$ 1 [×] 10 [=] *10* [M+]
$\quad\quad\quad\quad\quad\quad\quad\quad$ 2 [×] 16 [=] *32* [M+]
$\quad\quad\quad\quad\quad\quad\quad\quad$ 3 [×] 20 [=] *60* [M+]
$\quad\quad\quad\quad\quad\quad\quad\quad$ 4 [×] 11 [=] *44* [M+]
$\quad\quad\quad\quad\quad\quad\quad\quad$ 5 [×] 5 [=] *25* [M+]

(Now memory contains 171, or ΣfX.)

Find N

$\quad\quad\quad\quad$ 10 [+] 16 [+] 20 [+] 11 [+] 5 [=] *62*

Find $\bar{X}$

$\quad\quad\quad\quad$ [1/X] *0.01612* $\cdots$ [×] [RM] [=] *2.75806* $\cdots$

Answer: $\bar{X} = 2.76$

To compute the mean for a grouped frequency distribution follow the previous operations, substituting the interval midpoint, X', for X.

3. Variance and Standard Deviation

To compute s^2 and s of (4, 20, 6, 8, 19):

$$s^2 = \Sigma X^2/N - \bar{X}^2$$

Find ΣX^2:   [CM]

$\quad\quad\quad\quad\quad\quad\quad\quad$ 4 [X^2] *16* [M+]
$\quad\quad\quad\quad\quad\quad\quad\quad$ 20 [X^2] *400* [M+]
$\quad\quad\quad\quad\quad\quad\quad\quad$ 6 [X^2] *36* [M+]
$\quad\quad\quad\quad\quad\quad\quad\quad$ 8 [X^2] *64* [M+]
$\quad\quad\quad\quad\quad\quad\quad\quad$ 19 [X^2] *361* [M+]

(Now memory contains 877, or ΣX^2.)

Find $\Sigma X^2/N$

$\quad\quad\quad\quad$ [RM] [÷] 5 [=] *175.4* [CM] [M+]

Find $\bar{X}^2$ and then s^2 and s (note, $\bar{X} = 11.4$)

$\quad\quad\quad\quad$ 11.4 [X^2] *129.96* [M−] [RM] *45.44* [$\sqrt{X}$] *6.7409* $\cdots$

Answer: $s^2 = 45.44$; $s = 6.741$.

To compute s^2 and s of the following ungrouped frequency distribution:

X	f
1	10
2	16
3	20
4	11
5	5

$$s^2 = \Sigma fX^2/N - \bar{X}^2; \quad \bar{X} = 2.75806$$

Find ΣfX^2 [CM]

                1 [X^2] *1* [$\times$] 10 [=] *10* [M+]

                2 [X^2] *4* [$\times$] 16 [=] *64* [M+]

                3 [X^2] *9* [$\times$] 20 [=] *180* [M+]

                4 [X^2] *16* [$\times$] 11 [=] *176* [M+]

                5 [X^2] *25* [$\times$] 5 [=] *125* [M+]

(Now memory contains 555, or ΣfX^2.)
Find $\Sigma fX^2/N$
    First find N

$$10 \, [+] \, 16 \, [+] \, 20 \, [+] \, 11 \, [+] \, 5 \, [=] \, \mathit{62}$$

$$[1/X] \, [\times] \, [RM] \, [=] \, \mathit{8.9516} \cdots [CM] \, [M+]$$

Find $\bar{X}^2$

$$2.75806 \; [X^2] \; \mathit{7.60689} \cdots$$

$$[M-] \; [RM] \; \mathit{1.3447} \cdots [\sqrt{X}] \; \mathit{1.1596} \cdots$$

Answer: $s^2 = \mathit{1.34}$; $s = \mathit{1.160}$

4. Correlation Coefficients (Pearson r) and Regression Coefficients

    To compute r:

$$r = \frac{\Sigma XY - \dfrac{(\Sigma X)(\Sigma Y)}{N}}{\sqrt{\left[\Sigma X^2 - \dfrac{(\Sigma X)^2}{N}\right]\left[\Sigma Y^2 - \dfrac{(\Sigma Y)^2}{N}\right]}}$$

For calculators with only a single memory, the four quantities ΣX, ΣY, ΣX^2, and ΣY^2 must be calculated ahead of time and recorded. We show the steps in the calculations for the following set of paired X, Y scores.

X	Y
10	12
14	15
17	18
20	17
16	20

Compute ΣX, ΣY, ΣX^2, ΣY^2 by the methods described for means and variances: $N = 5$, $\Sigma X = 77$, $\Sigma Y = 82$, $\Sigma X^2 = 1241$, $\Sigma Y^2 = 1382$.
Find $\Sigma X^2 - (\Sigma X)^2/N$:

     77 [X^2] [$\div$] 5 [=] *1185.8* [CHG SIGN] [+] 1241 [=] *55.2*

Find $\Sigma Y^2 - (\Sigma Y)^2/N$:

82 [X²] [÷] 5 [=] *1344.8* [CHG SIGN] [+] 1382 [=] *37.2*

Find ΣXY: [CM]

10 [×] 12 [=] *120* [M+]

14 [×] 15 [=] *210* [M+]

17 [×] 18 [=] *306* [M+]

20 [×] 17 [=] *340* [M+]

16 [×] 20 [=] *320* [M+]

(Now memory contains 1296, or ΣXY.)

Find denominator of r:

55.2 [×] 37.2 [=] *2053.44* [√X̄] *45.3148* ···

[CM] [M+]

Find numerator of r, then r:

77 [×] 82 [÷] 5 [=] *1262.8* [CHG SIGN] [+] 1296 [÷] [RM] [=] *0.73265* ···

Answer: $r = +0.733$

To compute the regression coefficients b_y and a_y (using raw score formulas)

$$b_y = \frac{N\Sigma XY - (\Sigma X)(\Sigma Y)}{N\Sigma X^2 - (\Sigma X)^2}$$

$$a_y = \frac{(\Sigma X^2)(\Sigma Y) - (\Sigma XY)(\Sigma X)}{N \Sigma X^2 - (\Sigma X)^2}$$

We will use data from the calculation of r, so that:

$N = 5$, $\Sigma X = 77$, $\Sigma Y = 82$, $\Sigma X^2 \doteq 1241$, $\Sigma Y^2 = 1382$, $\Sigma XY = 1296$

Find denominator of b_y

5 [×] 1241 [=] *6205* [CM] [M+]

77 [X²] *5929* [M−] [RM] *276*

Find numerator of b_y, then b_y

5 [×] 1296 [=] *6480* [CM] [M+]

77 [×] 82 [=] *6314* [M−] [RM] *166* [÷] 276 [=] *0.601449* ···

Answer: $b_y = +0.601$

Find numerator of a_y, then a_y

1241 [×] 82 [=] *101,762* [CM] [M+] 1296 [×] 77 [=] *99,792*

[M−] [RM] *1970* [÷] 276 [=] *7.1376* ⋯

Answer: $a_y = +7.14$

The regression equation is thus

$$\hat{Y} = b_y X + a_y$$
$$\hat{Y} = 0.601X + 7.14$$

Tables

ACKNOWLEDGMENTS

The author wishes to thank the following authors and publishers for their kind permission to adapt from the following tables:

Table C.1. Table III of A. L. Edwards, *Experimental Design in Psychological Research*, 3rd edition. New York: Holt, Rinehart and Winston, 1968.

Table C.2. Table 12 of E. S. Pearson and H. O. Hartley (Eds.), *Biometrika Tables for Statisticians*, vol. I, 2nd edition. London: Cambridge University Press, 1958.

Table C.3. Table 5 of E. S. Pearson and H. O. Hartley (Eds.), *Biometrika Tables for Statisticians*, vol. II, 3rd edition. London: Cambridge University Press, 1972.

Table C.4. Table 29 of E. S. Pearson and H. O. Hartley (Eds.), *Biometrika Tables for Statisticians*, vol. I, 3rd edition. London: Cambridge University Press, 1966.

Table C.5. Table IV of R. A. Fisher and F. Yates, *Statistical Tables for Biological, Agricultural, and Medical Research*, 6th edition. London: Longman Group, 1974.

Table C.7. Table 11.4 in D. B. Owen, *Handbook of Statistical Tables*. Reading, Mass.: Addison-Wesley, 1962. D. Auble, Extended tables for the Mann-Whitney statistic. *Bulletin of the Institute of Educational Research at Indiana University, 1*, No. 2, 1953.

Table C.8. Table J of R. P. Runyon and A. Haber, *Fundamentals of Behavioral Statistics*. Reading, Mass.: Addison-Wesley, 1968. Based on values in: F. Wilcoxon, S. Katti, and R. A. Wilcox, *Critical values and probability levels for the Wilcoxon rank sum test and the Wilcoxon signed rank test*. New York: American Cyanamid Co., 1963; and F. Wilcoxon and R. A. Wilcox, *Some rapid approximate statistical procedures*. New York: Lederle Laboratories, 1964.

Table C.9. M. Friedman, The use of ranks to avoid the assumption of normality implicit in the analysis of variance. *Journal of the American Statistical Association*, 1937, *32*, 688–689.

Table C.11. Table VII of R. A. Fisher and F. Yates, *Statistical Tables for Biological, Agricultural, and Medical Research*, 6th edition. London: Longman Group, 1974.

Table C.12. Table G of R. P. Runyon and A. Haber, *Fundamentals of Behavioral Statistics*. Reading, Mass.: Addison-Wesley, 1968; based on values from E. G. Olds, The 5 percent significance levels of sums of squares of rank differences and a correction. *Annals of Mathematical Statistics*, 1949, *20*, 117–118, and E. G. Olds, Distribution of the sum of squares of rank differences for small numbers of individuals. *Annals of Mathematical Statistics*, 1938, *9*, 133–148.

Table C.15. Table XXXIII of R. A. Fisher and F. Yates, *Statistical Tables for Biological, Agricultural, and Medical Research*, 6th edition. London: Longman Group, 1974.

Table C.16. Table XXXIII$_1$ and XXXIII$_2$ of R. A. Fisher and F. Yates, *Statistical Tables for Biological, Agricultural, and Medical Research*, 6th edition. London: Longman Group, 1974.

TABLE C.1
Areas and Ordinates of the Normal Distribution

z	(1) $A(0, z)$ or $A(-z, 0)$	(2) $A(-\infty, z)$ or $A(-z, +\infty)$	(3) $A(z, +\infty)$ or $A(-\infty, -z)$	(4) $f(z)$ or $f(-z)$
0.00	0.0000	0.5000	0.5000	0.3989
0.01	0.0040	0.5040	0.4960	0.3989
0.02	0.0080	0.5080	0.4920	0.3989
0.03	0.0120	0.5120	0.4880	0.3988
0.04	0.0160	0.5160	0.4840	0.3986
0.05	0.0199	0.5199	0.4801	0.3984
0.06	0.0239	0.5239	0.4761	0.3982
0.07	0.0279	0.5279	0.4721	0.3980
0.08	0.0319	0.5319	0.4681	0.3977
0.09	0.0359	0.5359	0.4641	0.3973
0.10	0.0398	0.5398	0.4602	0.3970
0.11	0.0438	0.5438	0.4562	0.3965
0.12	0.0478	0.5478	0.4522	0.3961
0.13	0.0517	0.5517	0.4483	0.3956
0.14	0.0557	0.5557	0.4443	0.3951
0.15	0.0596	0.5596	0.4404	0.3945
0.16	0.0636	0.5636	0.4364	0.3939
0.17	0.0675	0.5675	0.4325	0.3932
0.18	0.0714	0.5714	0.4286	0.3925
0.19	0.0753	0.5753	0.4247	0.3918
0.20	0.0793	0.5793	0.4207	0.3910
0.21	0.0832	0.5832	0.4168	0.3902
0.22	0.0871	0.5871	0.4129	0.3894
0.23	0.0910	0.5910	0.4090	0.3885
0.24	0.0948	0.5948	0.4052	0.3876
0.25	0.0987	0.5987	0.4013	0.3867
0.26	0.1026	0.6026	0.3974	0.3857
0.27	0.1064	0.6064	0.3936	0.3847
0.28	0.1103	0.6103	0.3897	0.3836
0.29	0.1141	0.6141	0.3859	0.3825
0.30	0.1179	0.6179	0.3821	0.3814
0.31	0.1217	0.6217	0.3783	0.3802
0.32	0.1255	0.6255	0.3745	0.3790
0.33	0.1293	0.6293	0.3707	0.3778
0.34	0.1331	0.6331	0.3669	0.3765
0.35	0.1368	0.6368	0.3632	0.3752
0.36	0.1406	0.6406	0.3594	0.3739
0.37	0.1443	0.6443	0.3557	0.3725
0.38	0.1480	0.6480	0.3520	0.3712
0.39	0.1517	0.6517	0.3483	0.3697

TABLE C.1, Continued

z	(1) A(0, z) or A(−z, 0),	(2) A(−∞, z) or A(−z, +∞)	(3) A(z, +∞) or A(−∞, −z)	(4) f(z) or f(−z)
0.40	0.1554	0.6554	0.3446	0.3683
0.41	0.1591	0.6591	0.3409	0.3668
0.42	0.1628	0.6628	0.3372	0.3653
0.43	0.1664	0.6664	0.3336	0.3637
0.44	0.1700	0.6700	0.3300	0.3621
0.45	0.1736	0.6736	0.3264	0.3605
0.46	0.1772	0.6772	0.3228	0.3589
0.47	0.1808	0.6808	0.3192	0.3572
0.48	0.1844	0.6844	0.3156	0.3555
0.49	0.1879	0.6879	0.3121	0.3538
0.50	0.1915	0.6915	0.3085	0.3521
0.51	0.1950	0.6950	0.3050	0.3503
0.52	0.1985	0.6985	0.3015	0.3485
0.53	0.2019	0.7019	0.2981	0.3467
0.54	0.2054	0.7054	0.2946	0.3448
0.55	0.2088	0.7088	0.2912	0.3429
0.56	0.2123	0.7123	0.2877	0.3410
0.57	0.2157	0.7157	0.2843	0.3391
0.58	0.2190	0.7190	0.2810	0.3372
0.59	0.2224	0.7224	0.2776	0.3352
0.60	0.2257	0.7257	0.2743	0.3332
0.61	0.2291	0.7291	0.2709	0.3312
0.62	0.2324	0.7324	0.2676	0.3292
0.63	0.2357	0.7357	0.2643	0.3271
0.64	0.2389	0.7389	0.2611	0.3251
0.65	0.2422	0.7422	0.2578	0.3230
0.66	0.2454	0.7454	0.2546	0.3209
0.67	0.2486	0.7486	0.2514	0.3187
0.68	0.2517	0.7517	0.2483	0.3166
0.69	0.2549	0.7549	0.2451	0.3144
0.70	0.2580	0.7580	0.2420	0.3123
0.71	0.2611	0.7611	0.2389	0.3101
0.72	0.2642	0.7642	0.2358	0.3079
0.73	0.2673	0.7673	0.2327	0.3056
0.74	0.2704	0.7704	0.2296	0.3034
0.75	0.2734	0.7734	0.2266	0.3011
0.76	0.2764	0.7764	0.2236	0.2989
0.77	0.2794	0.7794	0.2206	0.2966
0.78	0.2823	0.7823	0.2177	0.2943
0.79	0.2852	0.7852	0.2148	0.2920

z	(1) $A(0, z)$ or $A(-z, 0)$	(2) $A(-\infty, z)$ or $A(-z, +\infty)$	(3) $A(z, +\infty)$ or $A(-\infty, -z)$	(4) $f(z)$ or $f(-z)$
0.80	0.2881	0.7881	0.2119	0.2897
0.81	0.2910	0.7910	0.2090	0.2874
0.82	0.2939	0.7939	0.2061	0.2850
0.83	0.2967	0.7967	0.2033	0.2827
0.84	0.2995	0.7995	0.2005	0.2803
0.85	0.3023	0.8023	0.1977	0.2780
0.86	0.3051	0.8051	0.1949	0.2756
0.87	0.3078	0.8078	0.1922	0.2732
0.88	0.3106	0.8106	0.1894	0.2709
0.89	0.3133	0.8133	0.1867	0.2685
0.90	0.3159	0.8159	0.1841	0.2661
0.91	0.3186	0.8186	0.1814	0.2637
0.92	0.3212	0.8212	0.1788	0.2613
0.93	0.3238	0.8238	0.1762	0.2589
0.94	0.3264	0.8264	0.1736	0.2565
0.95	0.3289	0.8289	0.1711	0.2541
0.96	0.3315	0.8315	0.1685	0.2516
0.97	0.3340	0.8340	0.1660	0.2492
0.98	0.3365	0.8365	0.1635	0.2468
0.99	0.3389	0.8389	0.1611	0.2444
1.00	0.3413	0.8413	0.1587	0.2420
1.01	0.3438	0.8438	0.1562	0.2396
1.02	0.3461	0.8461	0.1539	0.2371
1.03	0.3485	0.8485	0.1515	0.2347
1.04	0.3508	0.8508	0.1492	0.2323
1.05	0.3531	0.8531	0.1469	0.2299
1.06	0.3554	0.8554	0.1446	0.2275
1.07	0.3577	0.8577	0.1423	0.2251
1.08	0.3599	0.8599	0.1401	0.2227
1.09	0.3621	0.8621	0.1379	0.2203
1.10	0.3643	0.8643	0.1357	0.2179
1.11	0.3665	0.8665	0.1335	0.2155
1.12	0.3686	0.8686	0.1314	0.2131
1.13	0.3708	0.8708	0.1292	0.2107
1.14	0.3729	0.8729	0.1271	0.2083
1.15	0.3749	0.8749	0.1251	0.2059
1.16	0.3770	0.8770	0.1230	0.2036
1.17	0.3790	0.8790	0.1210	0.2012
1.18	0.3810	0.8810	0.1190	0.1989
1.19	0.3830	0.8830	0.1170	0.1965

TABLE C.1, *Continued*

z	(1) $A(0, z)$ or $A(-z, 0)$	(2) $A(-z \, \infty,)$ or $A(-z, +\infty)$	(3) $A(z, +\infty)$ or $A(-\infty, -z)$	(4) $f(z)$ or $f(-z)$
1.20	0.3849	0.8849	0.1151	0.1942
1.21	0.3869	0.8869	0.1131	0.1919
1.22	0.3888	0.8888	0.1112	0.1895
1.23	0.3907	0.8907	0.1093	0.1872
1.24	0.3925	0.8925	0.1075	0.1849
1.25	0.3944	0.8944	0.1056	0.1826
1.26	0.3962	0.8962	0.1038	0.1804
1.27	0.3980	0.8980	0.1020	0.1781
1.28	0.3997	0.8997	0.1003	0.1758
1.29	0.4015	0.9015	0.0985	0.1736
1.30	0.4032	0.9032	0.0968	0.1714
1.31	0.4049	0.9049	0.0951	0.1691
1.32	0.4066	0.9066	0.0934	0.1669
1.33	0.4082	0.9082	0.0918	0.1647
1.34	0.4099	0.9099	0.0901	0.1626
1.35	0.4115	0.9115	0.0885	0.1604
1.36	0.4131	0.9131	0.0869	0.1582
1.37	0.4147	0.9147	0.0853	0.1561
1.38	0.4162	0.9162	0.0838	0.1539
1.39	0.4177	0.9177	0.0823	0.1518
1.40	0.4192	0.9192	0.0808	0.1497
1.41	0.4207	0.9207	0.0793	0.1476
1.42	0.4222	0.9222	0.0778	0.1456
1.43	0.4236	0.9236	0.0764	0.1435
1.44	0.4251	0.9251	0.0749	0.1415
1.45	0.4265	0.9265	0.0735	0.1394
1.46	0.4279	0.9279	0.0721	0.1374
1.47	0.4292	0.9292	0.0708	0.1354
1.48	0.4306	0.9306	0.0694	0.1334
1.49	0.4319	0.9319	0.0681	0.1315
1.50	0.4332	0.9332	0.0668	0.1295
1.51	0.4345	0.9345	0.0655	0.1276
1.52	0.4357	0.9357	0.0643	0.1257
1.53	0.4370	0.9370	0.0630	0.1238
1.54	0.4382	0.9382	0.0618	0.1219
1.55	0.4394	0.9394	0.0606	0.1200
1.56	0.4406	0.9406	0.0594	0.1182
1.57	0.4418	0.9418	0.0582	0.1163
1.58	0.4429	0.9429	0.0571	0.1145
1.59	0.4441	0.9441	0.0559	0.1127

TABLE C.1, *Continued*

z	(1) $A(0, z)$ or $A(-z, 0)$	(2) $A(-\infty, z)$ or $A(-z, +\infty)$	(3) $A(z, +\infty)$ or $A(-\infty, -z)$	(4) $f(z)$ or $f(-z)$
1.60	0.4452	0.9452	0.0548	0.1109
1.61	0.4463	0.9463	0.0537	0.1092
1.62	0.4474	0.9474	0.0526	0.1074
1.63	0.4484	0.9484	0.0516	0.1057
1.64	0.4495	0.9495	0.0505	0.1040
1.65	0.4505	0.9505	0.0495	0.1023
1.66	0.4515	0.9515	0.0485	0.1006
1.67	0.4525	0.9525	0.0475	0.0989
1.68	0.4535	0.9535	0.0465	0.0973
1.69	0.4545	0.9545	0.0455	0.0957
1.70	0.4554	0.9554	0.0446	0.0940
1.71	0.4564	0.9564	0.0436	0.0925
1.72	0.4573	0.9573	0.0427	0.0909
1.73	0.4582	0.9582	0.0418	0.0893
1.74	0.4591	0.9591	0.0409	0.0878
1.75	0.4599	0.9599	0.0401	0.0863
1.76	0.4608	0.9608	0.0392	0.0848
1.77	0.4616	0.9616	0.0384	0.0833
1.78	0.4625	0.9625	0.0375	0.0818
1.79	0.4633	0.9633	0.0367	0.0804
1.80	0.4641	0.9641	0.0359	0.0790
1.81	0.4649	0.9649	0.0351	0.0775
1.82	0.4656	0.9656	0.0344	0.0761
1.83	0.4664	0.9664	0.0336	0.0748
1.84	0.4671	0.9671	0.0329	0.0734
1.85	0.4678	0.9678	0.0322	0.0721
1.86	0.4686	0.9686	0.0314	0.0707
1.87	0.4693	0.9693	0.0307	0.0694
1.88	0.4699	0.9699	0.0301	0.0681
1.89	0.4706	0.9706	0.0294	0.0669
1.90	0.4713	0.9713	0.0287	0.0656
1.91	0.4719	0.9719	0.0281	0.0644
1.92	0.4726	0.9726	0.0274	0.0632
1.93	0.4732	0.9732	0.0268	0.0620
1.94	0.4738	0.9738	0.0262	0.0608
1.95	0.4744	0.9744	0.0256	0.0596
1.96	0.4750	0.9750	0.0250	0.0584
1.97	0.4756	0.9756	0.0244	0.0573
1.98	0.4761	0.9761	0.0239	0.0562
1.99	0.4767	0.9767	0.0233	0.0551

TABLE C.1, *Continued*

z	(1) $A(0, z)$ or $A(-z, 0)$	(2) $A(-\infty, z)$ or $A(-z, +\infty)$	(3) $A(z, +\infty)$ or $A(-\infty, -z)$	(4) $f(z)$ or $f(-z)$
2.00	0.4772	0.9772	0.0228	0.0540
2.01	0.4778	0.9778	0.0222	0.0529
2.02	0.4783	0.9783	0.0217	0.0519
2.03	0.4788	0.9788	0.0212	0.0508
2.04	0.4793	0.9793	0.0207	0.0498
2.05	0.4798	0.9798	0.0202	0.0488
2.06	0.4803	0.9803	0.0197	0.0478
2.07	0.4808	0.9808	0.0192	0.0468
2.08	0.4812	0.9812	0.0188	0.0459
2.09	0.4817	0.9817	0.0183	0.0449
2.10	0.4821	0.9821	0.0179	0.0440
2.11	0.4826	0.9826	0.0174	0.0431
2.12	0.4830	0.9830	0.0170	0.0422
2.13	0.4834	0.9834	0.0166	0.0413
2.14	0.4838	0.9838	0.0162	0.0404
2.15	0.4842	0.9842	0.0158	0.0396
2.16	0.4846	0.9846	0.0154	0.0387
2.17	0.4850	0.9850	0.0150	0.0379
2.18	0.4854	0.9854	0.0146	0.0371
2.19	0.4857	0.9857	0.0143	0.0363
2.20	0.4861	0.9861	0.0139	0.0355
2.21	0.4864	0.9864	0.0136	0.0347
2.22	0.4868	0.9868	0.0132	0.0339
2.23	0.4871	0.9871	0.0129	0.0332
2.24	0.4875	0.9875	0.0125	0.0325
2.25	0.4878	0.9878	0.0122	0.0317
2.26	0.4881	0.9881	0.0119	0.0310
2.27	0.4884	0.9884	0.0116	0.0303
2.28	0.4887	0.9887	0.0113	0.0297
2.29	0.4890	0.9890	0.0110	0.0290
2.30	0.4893	0.9893	0.0107	0.0283
2.31	0.4896	0.9896	0.0104	0.0277
2.32	0.4898	0.9898	0.0102	0.0270
2.33	0.4901	0.9901	0.0099	0.0264
2.34	0.4904	0.9904	0.0096	0.0258
2.35	0.4906	0.9906	0.0094	0.0252
2.36	0.4909	0.9909	0.0091	0.0246
2.37	0.4911	0.9911	0.0089	0.0241
2.38	0.4913	0.9913	0.0087	0.0235
2.39	0.4916	0.9916	0.0084	0.0229

TABLE C.1, *Continued*

z	(1) $A(0, z)$ or $A(-z, 0)$	(2) $A(-\infty, z)$ or $A(-z, +\infty)$	(3) $A(z, +\infty)$ or $A(-\infty, -z)$	(4) $f(z)$ or $f(-z)$
2.40	0.4918	0.9918	0.0082	0.0224
2.41	0.4920	0.9920	0.0080	0.0219
2.42	0.4922	0.9922	0.0078	0.0213
2.43	0.4925	0.9925	0.0075	0.0208
2.44	0.4927	0.9927	0.0073	0.0203
2.45	0.4929	0.9929	0.0071	0.0198
2.46	0.4931	0.9931	0.0069	0.0194
2.47	0.4932	0.9932	0.0068	0.0189
2.48	0.4934	0.9934	0.0066	0.0184
2.49	0.4936	0.9936	0.0064	0.0180
2.50	0.4938	0.9938	0.0062	0.0175
2.51	0.4940	0.9940	0.0060	0.0171
2.52	0.4941	0.9941	0.0059	0.0167
2.53	0.4943	0.9943	0.0057	0.0163
2.54	0.4945	0.9945	0.0055	0.0158
2.55	0.4946	0.9946	0.0054	0.0154
2.56	0.4948	0.9948	0.0052	0.0151
2.57	0.4949	0.9949	0.0051	0.0147
2.58	0.4951	0.9951	0.0049	0.0143
2.59	0.4952	0.9952	0.0048	0.0139
2.60	0.4953	0.9953	0.0047	0.0136
2.61	0.4955	0.9955	0.0045	0.0132
2.62	0.4956	0.9956	0.0044	0.0129
2.63	0.4957	0.9957	0.0043	0.0126
2.64	0.4959	0.9959	0.0041	0.0122
2.65	0.4960	0.9960	0.0040	0.0119
2.66	0.4961	0.9961	0.0039	0.0116
2.67	0.4962	0.9962	0.0038	0.0113
2.68	0.4963	0.9963	0.0037	0.0110
2.69	0.4964	0.9964	0.0036	0.0107
2.70	0.4965	0.9965	0.0035	0.0104
2.71	0.4966	0.9966	0.0034	0.0101
2.72	0.4967	0.9967	0.0033	0.0099
2.73	0.4968	0.9968	0.0032	0.0096
2.74	0.4969	0.9969	0.0031	0.0093
2.75	0.4970	0.9970	0.0030	0.0091
2.76	0.4971	0.9971	0.0029	0.0088
2.77	0.4972	0.9972	0.0028	0.0086
2.78	0.4973	0.9973	0.0027	0.0084
2.79	0.4974	0.9974	0.0026	0.0081

TABLE C.1, *Continued*

z	(1) $A(0, z)$ or $A(-z, 0)$	(2) $A(-\infty, z)$ or $A(-z, +\infty)$	(3) $A(z, +\infty)$ or $A(-\infty, -z)$	(4) $f(z)$ or $f(-z)$
2.80	0.4974	0.9974	0.0026	0.0079
2.81	0.4975	0.9975	0.0025	0.0077
2.82	0.4976	0.9976	0.0024	0.0075
2.83	0.4977	0.9977	0.0023	0.0073
2.84	0.4977	0.9977	0.0023	0.0071
2.85	0.4978	0.9978	0.0022	0.0069
2.86	0.4979	0.9979	0.0021	0.0067
2.87	0.4979	0.9979	0.0021	0.0065
2.88	0.4980	0.9980	0.0020	0.0063
2.89	0.4981	0.9981	0.0019	0.0061
2.90	0.4981	0.9981	0.0019	0.0060
2.91	0.4982	0.9982	0.0018	0.0058
2.92	0.4982	0.9982	0.0018	0.0056
2.93	0.4983	0.9983	0.0017	0.0055
2.94	0.4984	0.9984	0.0016	0.0053
2.95	0.4984	0.9984	0.0016	0.0051
2.96	0.4985	0.9985	0.0015	0.0050
2.97	0.4985	0.9985	0.0015	0.0048
2.98	0.4986	0.9986	0.0014	0.0047
2.99	0.4986	0.9986	0.0014	0.0046
3.00	0.4987	0.9987	0.0013	0.0044
3.01	0.4987	0.9987	0.0013	0.0043
3.02	0.4987	0.9987	0.0013	0.0042
3.03	0.4988	0.9988	0.0012	0.0040
3.04	0.4988	0.9988	0.0012	0.0039
3.05	0.4989	0.9989	0.0011	0.0038
3.06	0.4989	0.9989	0.0011	0.0037
3.07	0.4989	0.9989	0.0011	0.0036
3.08	0.4990	0.9990	0.0010	0.0035
3.09	0.4990	0.9990	0.0010	0.0034
3.10	0.4990	0.9990	0.0010	0.0033
3.11	0.4991	0.9991	0.0009	0.0032
3.12	0.4991	0.9991	0.0009	0.0031
3.13	0.4991	0.9991	0.0009	0.0030
3.14	0.4992	0.9992	0.0008	0.0029

TABLE C.2

Critical Values of t

	Level of Significance for One-Tailed Test						
	0.10	0.05	0.025	0.01	0.005	0.001	0.0005
	Level of Significance for Two-Tailed Test						
df	0.20	0.10	0.05	0.02	0.01	0.002	0.001
1	3.078	6.314	12.706	31.821	63.657	318.31	636.62
2	1.886	2.920	4.303	6.965	9.925	22.326	31.598
3	1.638	2.353	3.182	4.541	5.841	10.213	12.924
4	1.533	2.132	2.776	3.747	4.604	7.173	8.610
5	1.476	2.015	2.571	3.365	4.032	5.893	6.869
6	1.440	1.943	2.447	3.143	3.707	5.208	5.959
7	1.415	1.895	2.365	2.998	3.499	4.785	5.408
8	1.397	1.860	2.306	2.896	3.355	4.501	5.041
9	1.383	1.833	2.262	2.821	3.250	4.297	4.781
10	1.372	1.812	2.228	2.764	3.169	4.144	4.587
11	1.363	1.796	2.201	2.718	3.106	4.025	4.437
12	1.356	1.782	2.179	2.681	3.055	3.930	4.318
13	1.350	1.771	2.160	2.650	3.012	3.852	4.221
14	1.345	1.761	2.145	2.624	2.977	3.787	4.140
15	1.341	1.753	2.131	2.602	2.947	3.733	4.073
16	1.337	1.746	2.120	2.583	2.921	3.686	4.015
17	1.333	1.740	2.110	2.567	2.898	3.646	3.965
18	1.330	1.734	2.101	2.552	2.878	3.610	3.922
19	1.328	1.729	2.093	2.539	2.861	3.579	3.883
20	1.325	1.725	2.086	2.528	2.845	3.552	3.850
21	1.323	1.721	2.080	2.518	2.831	3.527	3.819
22	1.321	1.717	2.074	2.508	2.819	3.505	3.792
23	1.319	1.714	2.069	2.500	2.807	3.485	3.767
24	1.318	1.711	2.064	2.492	2.797	3.467	3.745
25	1.316	1.708	2.060	2.485	2.787	3.450	3.725
26	1.315	1.706	2.056	2.479	2.779	3.435	3.707
27	1.314	1.703	2.052	2.473	2.771	3.421	3.690
28	1.313	1.701	2.048	2.467	2.763	3.408	3.674
29	1.311	1.699	2.045	2.462	2.756	3.396	3.659
30	1.310	1.697	2.042	2.457	2.750	3.385	3.646
40	1.303	1.684	2.021	2.423	2.704	3.307	3.551
60	1.296	1.671	2.000	2.390	2.660	3.232	3.460
120	1.289	1.658	1.980	2.358	2.617	3.160	3.373
∞	1.282	1.645	1.960	2.326	2.576	3.090	3.291

TABLE C.3
Critical Values of F

The first F ratio is the critical value for α = .05, the second for α = .01, and the third for α = .001.

df for denominator	α	df for numerator 1	2	3	4	5	6	7	8	9	10	12	15	20	24	30	40	60	∞
3	.05	10.1	9.55	9.28	9.12	9.01	8.94	8.89	8.85	8.81	8.79	8.74	8.70	8.66	8.64	8.62	8.59	8.57	8.53
	.01	34.1	30.8	29.5	28.7	28.2	27.9	27.7	27.5	27.3	27.2	27.1	26.9	26.7	26.6	26.5	26.4	26.3	26.1
	.001	167	148	141	137	135	133	132	131	130	129	128	127	126	126	125	125	124	123
4	.05	7.71	6.94	6.59	6.39	6.26	6.16	6.09	6.04	6.00	5.96	5.91	5.86	5.80	5.77	5.75	5.72	5.69	5.63
	.01	21.2	18.0	16.7	16.0	15.5	15.2	15.0	14.8	14.7	14.5	14.4	14.2	14.0	13.9	13.8	13.7	13.7	13.5
	.001	74.1	61.2	56.2	53.4	51.7	50.5	49.7	49.0	48.5	48.1	47.4	46.8	46.1	45.8	45.4	45.1	44.7	44.1
5	.05	6.61	5.79	5.41	5.19	5.05	4.95	4.88	4.82	4.77	4.74	4.68	4.62	4.56	4.53	4.50	4.46	4.43	4.36
	.01	16.3	13.3	12.1	11.4	11.0	10.7	10.5	10.3	10.2	10.1	9.89	9.72	9.55	9.47	9.38	9.29	9.20	9.02
	.001	47.2	37.1	33.2	31.1	29.8	28.8	28.2	27.6	27.2	26.9	26.4	25.9	25.4	25.1	24.9	24.6	24.3	23.8
6	.05	5.99	5.14	4.76	4.53	4.39	4.28	4.21	4.15	4.10	4.06	4.00	3.94	3.87	3.84	3.81	3.77	3.74	3.67
	.01	13.7	10.9	9.78	9.15	8.75	8.47	8.26	8.10	7.98	7.87	7.72	7.56	7.40	7.31	7.23	7.14	7.06	6.88
	.001	35.5	27.0	23.7	21.9	20.8	20.0	19.5	19.0	18.7	18.4	18.0	17.6	17.1	16.9	16.7	16.4	16.2	15.7
7	.05	5.59	4.74	4.35	4.12	3.97	3.87	3.79	3.73	3.68	3.64	3.57	3.51	3.44	3.41	3.38	3.34	3.30	3.23
	.01	12.2	9.55	8.45	7.85	7.46	7.19	6.99	6.84	6.72	6.62	6.47	6.31	6.16	6.07	5.99	5.91	5.82	5.65
	.001	29.2	21.7	18.8	17.2	16.2	15.5	15.0	14.6	14.3	14.1	13.7	13.3	12.9	12.7	12.5	12.3	12.1	11.7
8	.05	5.32	4.46	4.07	3.84	3.69	3.58	3.50	3.44	3.39	3.35	3.28	3.22	3.15	3.12	3.08	3.04	3.01	2.93
	.01	11.3	8.65	7.59	7.01	6.63	6.37	6.18	6.03	5.91	5.81	5.67	5.52	5.36	5.28	5.20	5.12	5.03	4.86
	.001	25.4	18.5	15.8	14.4	13.5	12.9	12.4	12.0	11.8	11.5	11.2	10.8	10.5	10.3	10.1	9.92	9.73	9.33
9	.05	5.12	4.26	3.86	3.63	3.48	3.37	3.29	3.23	3.18	3.14	3.07	3.01	2.94	2.90	2.86	2.83	2.79	2.71
	.01	10.6	8.02	6.99	6.42	6.06	5.80	5.61	5.47	5.35	5.26	5.11	4.96	4.81	4.73	4.65	4.57	4.48	4.31
	.001	22.9	16.4	13.9	12.6	11.7	11.1	10.7	10.4	10.1	9.89	9.57	9.24	8.90	8.72	8.55	8.37	8.19	7.81

	10	11	12	13	14	15	16	17	18									
10 .05	2.54	2.62	2.66	2.70	2.74	2.77	2.85	2.91	2.98	3.02	3.07	3.14	3.22	3.33	3.48	3.71	4.10	4.96
.01	3.91	4.08	4.17	4.25	4.33	4.41	4.56	4.71	4.85	4.94	5.06	5.20	5.39	5.64	5.99	6.55	7.56	10.0
.001	6.76	7.12	7.30	7.47	7.64	7.80	8.13	8.45	8.75	8.96	9.20	9.52	9.93	10.5	11.3	12.6	14.9	21.0
11 .05	2.40	2.49	2.53	2.57	2.61	2.65	2.72	2.79	2.85	2.90	2.95	3.01	3.09	3.20	3.36	3.59	3.98	4.84
.01	3.60	3.78	3.86	3.94	4.02	4.10	4.25	4.40	4.54	4.63	4.74	4.89	5.07	5.32	5.67	6.22	7.21	9.65
.001	6.00	6.35	6.52	6.68	6.85	7.01	7.32	7.63	7.92	8.12	8.35	8.66	9.05	9.58	10.3	11.6	13.8	19.7
12 .05	2.30	2.38	2.43	2.47	2.51	2.54	2.62	2.69	2.75	2.80	2.85	2.91	3.00	3.11	3.26	3.49	3.89	4.75
.01	3.36	3.54	3.62	3.70	3.78	3.86	4.01	4.16	4.30	4.39	4.50	4.64	4.82	5.06	5.41	5.95	6.93	9.33
.001	5.42	5.76	5.93	6.09	6.25	6.40	6.71	7.00	7.29	7.48	7.71	8.00	8.38	8.89	9.63	10.8	13.0	18.6
13 .05	2.21	2.30	2.34	2.38	2.42	2.46	2.53	2.60	2.67	2.71	2.77	2.83	2.92	3.03	3.18	3.41	3.81	4.67
.01	3.17	3.34	3.43	3.51	3.59	3.66	3.82	3.96	4.10	4.19	4.30	4.44	4.62	4.86	5.21	5.74	6.70	9.07
.001	4.97	5.30	5.47	5.63	5.78	5.93	6.23	6.52	6.80	6.98	7.21	7.49	7.86	8.35	9.07	10.2	12.3	17.8
14 .05	2.13	2.22	2.27	2.31	2.35	2.39	2.46	2.53	2.60	2.65	2.70	2.76	2.85	2.96	3.11	3.34	3.74	4.60
.01	3.00	3.18	3.27	3.35	3.43	3.51	3.66	3.80	3.94	4.03	4.14	4.28	4.46	4.70	5.04	5.56	6.51	8.86
.001	4.60	4.94	5.10	5.25	5.41	5.56	5.85	6.13	6.40	6.58	6.80	7.08	7.44	7.92	8.62	9.73	11.8	17.1
15 .05	2.07	2.16	2.20	2.25	2.29	2.33	2.40	2.48	2.54	2.59	2.64	2.71	2.79	2.90	3.06	3.29	3.68	4.54
.01	2.87	3.05	3.13	3.21	3.29	3.37	3.52	3.67	3.80	3.89	4.00	4.14	4.32	4.56	4.89	5.42	6.36	8.68
.001	4.31	4.64	4.80	4.95	5.10	5.25	5.54	5.81	6.08	6.26	6.47	6.74	7.09	7.57	8.25	9.34	11.3	16.6
16 .05	2.01	2.11	2.15	2.19	2.24	2.28	2.35	2.42	2.49	2.54	2.59	2.66	2.74	2.85	3.01	3.24	3.63	4.49
.01	2.75	2.93	3.02	3.10	3.18	3.26	3.41	3.55	3.69	3.78	3.89	4.03	4.20	4.44	4.77	5.29	6.23	8.53
.001	4.06	4.39	4.54	4.70	4.85	4.99	5.27	5.55	5.81	5.98	62.0	6.46	6.80	7.27	7.94	9.01	11.0	16.1
17 .05	1.96	2.06	2.10	2.15	2.19	2.23	2.31	2.38	2.45	2.49	2.55	2.61	2.70	2.81	2.96	3.20	3.59	4.45
.01	2.65	2.83	2.92	3.00	3.08	3.16	3.31	3.46	3.59	3.68	3.79	3.93	4.10	4.34	4.67	5.18	6.11	8.40
.001	3.85	4.18	4.33	4.48	4.63	4.78	5.05	5.32	5.58	5.75	5.96	6.22	6.56	7.02	7.68	8.73	10.7	15.7
18 .05	1.92	2.02	2.06	2.11	2.15	2.19	2.27	2.34	2.41	2.46	2.51	2.58	2.66	2.77	2.93	3.16	3.55	4.41
.01	2.57	2.75	2.84	2.92	3.00	3.08	3.23	3.37	3.51	3.60	3.71	3.84	4.01	4.25	4.58	5.09	6.01	8.29
.001	3.67	4.00	4.15	4.30	4.45	4.59	4.87	5.13	5.39	5.56	5.76	6.02	6.35	6.81	7.46	8.49	10.4	15.4

TABLE C.3, Continued

df for denominator	α	1	2	3	4	5	6	7	8	9	10	12	15	20	24	30	40	60	∞
19	.05	4.38	3.52	3.13	2.90	2.74	2.63	2.54	2.48	2.42	2.38	2.31	2.23	2.16	2.11	2.07	2.03	1.98	1.88
	.01	8.18	5.93	5.01	4.50	4.17	3.94	3.77	3.63	3.52	3.43	3.30	3.15	3.00	2.92	2.84	2.76	2.67	2.49
	.001	15.1	10.2	8.28	7.27	6.62	6.18	5.85	5.59	5.39	5.22	4.97	4.70	4.43	4.29	4.14	3.99	3.84	3.51
20	.05	4.35	3.49	3.10	2.87	2.71	2.60	2.51	2.45	2.39	2.35	2.28	2.20	2.12	2.08	2.04	1.99	1.95	1.84
	.01	8.10	5.85	4.94	4.43	4.10	3.87	3.70	3.56	3.46	3.37	3.23	3.09	2.94	2.86	2.78	2.69	2.61	2.42
	.001	14.8	9.95	8.10	7.10	6.46	6.02	5.69	5.44	5.24	5.08	4.82	4.56	4.29	4.15	4.00	3.86	3.70	3.38
21	.05	4.32	3.47	3.07	2.84	2.68	2.57	2.49	2.42	2.37	2.32	2.25	2.18	2.10	2.05	2.01	1.96	1.92	1.81
	.01	8.02	5.78	4.87	4.37	4.04	3.81	3.64	3.51	3.40	3.31	3.17	3.03	2.88	2.80	2.72	2.64	2.55	2.36
	.001	14.6	9.77	7.94	6.95	6.32	5.88	5.56	5.31	5.11	4.95	4.70	4.44	4.17	4.03	3.88	3.74	3.58	3.26
22	.05	4.30	3.44	3.05	2.82	2.66	2.55	2.46	2.40	2.34	2.30	2.23	2.15	2.07	2.03	1.98	1.94	1.89	1.78
	.01	7.95	5.72	4.82	4.31	3.99	3.76	3.59	3.45	3.35	3.26	3.12	2.98	2.83	2.75	2.67	2.58	2.50	2.31
	.001	14.4	9.61	7.80	6.81	6.19	5.76	5.44	5.19	4.99	4.83	4.58	4.33	4.06	3.92	3.78	3.63	3.48	3.15
23	.05	4.28	3.42	3.03	2.80	2.64	2.53	2.44	2.37	2.32	2.27	2.20	2.13	2.05	2.01	1.96	1.91	1.86	1.76
	.01	7.88	5.66	4.76	4.26	3.94	3.71	3.54	3.41	3.30	3.21	3.07	2.93	2.78	2.70	2.62	2.54	2.45	2.26
	.001	14.2	9.47	7.67	6.70	6.08	5.65	5.33	5.09	4.89	4.73	4.48	4.23	3.96	3.82	3.68	3.53	3.38	3.05
24	.05	4.26	3.40	3.01	2.78	2.62	2.51	2.42	2.36	2.30	2.25	2.18	2.11	2.03	1.98	1.94	1.89	1.84	1.73
	.01	7.82	5.61	4.72	4.22	3.90	3.67	3.50	3.36	3.26	3.17	3.03	2.89	2.74	2.66	2.58	2.49	2.40	2.21
	.001	14.0	9.34	7.55	6.59	5.98	5.55	5.23	4.99	4.80	4.64	4.39	4.14	3.87	3.74	3.59	3.45	3.29	2.97
25	.05	4.24	3.39	2.99	2.76	2.60	2.49	2.40	2.34	2.28	2.24	2.16	2.09	2.01	1.96	1.92	1.87	1.82	1.71
	.01	7.77	5.57	4.68	4.18	3.86	3.63	3.46	3.32	3.22	3.13	2.99	2.85	2.70	2.62	2.54	2.45	2.36	2.17
	.001	13.9	9.22	7.45	6.49	5.89	5.46	5.15	4.91	4.71	4.56	4.31	4.06	3.79	3.66	3.52	3.37	3.22	2.89
26	.05	4.23	3.37	2.98	2.74	2.59	2.47	2.39	2.32	2.27	2.22	2.15	2.07	1.99	1.95	1.90	1.85	1.80	1.69
	.01	7.72	5.53	4.64	4.14	3.82	3.59	3.42	3.29	3.18	3.09	2.96	2.82	2.66	2.58	2.50	2.42	2.33	2.13
	.001	13.7	9.12	7.36	6.41	5.80	5.38	5.07	4.83	4.64	4.48	4.24	3.99	3.72	3.59	3.44	3.30	3.15	2.82

(df for numerator)

ν₂	p																			
27	.05	1.67	1.79	1.84	1.88	1.93	1.97	2.06	2.13	2.20	2.25	2.31	2.37	2.46	2.57	2.73	2.96	3.35	4.21
	.01	2.10	2.29	2.38	2.47	2.55	2.63	2.78	2.93	3.06	3.15	3.26	3.39	3.56	3.78	4.11	4.60	5.49	7.68
	.001	2.75	3.08	3.23	3.38	3.52	3.66	3.92	4.17	4.41	4.57	4.76	5.00	5.31	5.73	6.33	7.27	9.02	13.6
28	.05	1.65	1.77	1.82	1.87	1.91	1.96	2.04	2.12	2.19	2.24	2.29	2.36	2.45	2.56	2.71	2.95	3.34	4.20
	.01	2.06	2.26	2.35	2.44	2.52	2.60	2.75	2.90	3.03	3.12	3.23	3.36	3.53	3.75	4.07	4.57	5.45	7.64
	.001	2.69	3.02	3.18	3.32	3.46	3.60	3.86	4.11	4.35	4.50	4.69	4.93	5.24	5.66	6.25	7.19	8.93	13.5
29	.05	1.64	1.75	1.81	1.85	1.90	1.94	2.03	2.10	2.18	2.22	2.28	2.35	2.43	2.55	2.70	2.93	3.33	4.18
	.01	2.03	2.23	2.33	2.41	2.49	2.57	2.73	2.87	3.00	3.09	3.20	3.33	3.50	3.73	4.04	4.54	5.42	7.60
	.001	2.64	2.97	3.12	3.27	3.41	3.54	3.80	4.05	4.29	4.45	4.64	4.87	5.18	5.59	6.19	7.12	8.85	13.4
30	.05	1.62	1.74	1.79	1.84	1.89	1.93	2.01	2.09	2.16	2.21	2.27	2.33	2.42	2.53	2.69	2.92	3.32	4.17
	.01	2.01	2.21	2.30	2.39	2.47	2.55	2.70	2.84	2.98	3.07	3.17	3.30	3.47	3.70	4.02	4.51	5.39	7.56
	.001	2.59	2.92	3.07	3.22	3.36	3.49	3.75	4.00	4.24	4.39	4.58	4.82	5.12	5.53	6.12	7.05	8.77	13.3
40	.05	1.51	1.64	1.69	1.74	1.79	1.84	1.92	2.00	2.08	2.12	2.18	2.25	2.34	2.45	2.61	2.84	3.23	4.08
	.01	1.80	2.02	2.11	2.20	2.29	2.37	2.52	2.66	2.80	2.89	2.99	3.12	3.29	3.51	3.83	4.31	5.18	7.31
	.001	2.23	2.57	2.73	2.87	3.01	3.15	3.40	3.64	3.87	4.02	4.21	4.44	4.74	5.13	5.70	6.59	8.25	12.6
60	.05	1.39	1.53	1.59	1.65	1.70	1.75	1.84	1.92	1.99	2.04	2.10	2.18	2.25	2.37	2.53	2.76	3.15	4.00
	.01	1.60	1.84	1.94	2.03	2.12	2.20	2.35	2.50	2.63	2.72	2.82	2.95	3.12	3.34	3.65	4.13	4.98	7.08
	.001	1.89	2.25	2.41	2.55	2.69	2.83	3.08	3.32	3.54	3.69	3.86	4.09	4.37	4.76	5.31	6.17	7.76	12.0
120	.05	1.25	1.43	1.50	1.55	1.61	1.66	1.75	1.83	1.91	1.96	2.02	2.09	2.18	2.29	2.45	2.68	3.07	3.92
	.01	1.38	1.66	1.76	1.86	1.95	2.03	2.19	2.34	2.47	2.56	2.66	2.79	2.96	3.17	3.48	3.95	4.79	6.85
	.001	1.54	1.95	2.11	2.26	2.40	2.53	2.78	3.02	3.24	3.38	3.55	3.77	4.04	4.42	4.95	5.78	7.32	11.4
∞	.05	1.00	1.32	1.39	1.46	1.52	1.57	1.67	1.75	1.83	1.88	1.94	2.01	2.10	2.21	2.37	2.60	3.00	3.84
	.01	1.00	1.47	1.59	1.70	1.79	1.88	2.04	2.18	2.32	2.41	2.51	2.64	2.80	3.02	3.32	3.78	4.61	6.63
	.001	1.00	1.66	1.84	1.99	2.13	2.27	2.51	2.74	2.96	3.10	3.27	3.47	3.74	4.10	4.62	5.42	6.91	10.8

TABLE C.4
Critical Values of the Studentized Range Statistic, q_r

df_{err}	α	r = Number of Steps between Ordered Means								
		2	3	4	5	6	7	8	9	10
5	0.05	3.64	4.60	5.22	5.67	6.03	6.33	6.58	6.80	6.99
	0.01	5.70	6.98	7.80	8.42	8.91	9.32	9.67	9.97	10.24
6	0.05	3.46	4.34	4.90	5.30	5.63	5.90	6.12	6.32	6.49
	0.01	5.24	6.33	7.03	7.56	7.97	8.32	8.61	8.87	9.10
7	0.05	3.34	4.16	4.68	5.06	5.36	5.61	5.82	6.00	6.16
	0.01	4.95	5.92	6.54	7.01	7.37	7.68	7.94	8.17	8.37
8	0.05	3.26	4.04	4.53	4.89	5.17	5.40	5.60	5.77	5.92
	0.01	4.75	5.64	6.20	6.62	6.96	7.24	7.47	7.68	7.86
9	0.05	3.20	3.95	4.41	4.76	5.02	5.24	5.43	5.59	5.74
	0.01	4.60	5.43	5.96	6.35	6.66	6.91	7.13	7.33	7.49
10	0.05	3.15	3.88	4.33	4.65	4.91	5.12	5.30	5.46	5.60
	0.01	4.48	5.27	5.77	6.14	6.43	6.67	6.87	7.05	7.21
11	0.05	3.11	3.82	4.26	4.57	4.82	5.03	5.20	5.35	5.49
	0.01	4.39	5.15	5.62	5.97	6.25	6.48	6.67	6.84	6.99
12	0.05	3.08	3.77	4.20	4.51	4.75	4.95	5.12	5.27	5.39
	0.01	4.32	5.05	5.50	5.84	6.10	6.32	6.51	6.67	6.81
13	0.05	3.06	3.73	4.15	4.45	4.69	4.88	5.05	5.19	5.32
	0.01	4.26	4.96	5.40	5.73	5.98	6.19	6.37	6.53	6.67
14	0.05	3.03	3.70	4.11	4.41	4.64	4.83	4.99	5.13	5.25
	0.01	4.21	4.89	5.32	5.63	5.88	6.08	6.26	6.41	6.54
15	0.05	3.01	3.67	4.08	4.37	4.59	4.78	4.94	5.08	5.20
	0.01	4.17	4.84	5.25	5.56	5.80	5.99	6.16	6.31	6.44
16	0.05	3.00	3.65	4.05	4.33	4.56	4.74	4.90	5.03	5.15
	0.01	4.13	4.79	5.19	5.49	5.72	5.92	6.08	6.22	6.35
17	0.05	2.98	3.63	4.02	4.30	4.52	4.70	4.86	4.99	5.11
	0.01	4.10	4.74	5.14	5.43	5.66	5.85	6.01	6.15	6.27
18	0.05	2.97	3.61	4.00	4.28	4.49	4.67	4.82	4.96	5.07
	0.01	4.07	4.70	5.09	5.38	5.60	5.79	5.94	6.08	6.20
19	0.05	2.96	3.59	3.98	4.25	4.47	4.65	4.79	4.92	5.04
	0.01	4.05	4.67	5.05	5.33	5.55	5.73	5.89	6.02	6.14
20	0.05	2.95	3.58	3.96	4.23	4.45	4.62	4.77	4.90	5.01
	0.01	4.02	4.64	5.02	5.29	5.51	5.69	5.84	5.97	6.09
24	0.05	2.92	3.53	3.90	4.17	4.37	4.54	4.68	4.81	4.92
	0.01	3.96	4.55	4.91	5.17	5.37	5.54	5.69	5.81	5.92
30	0.05	2.89	3.49	3.85	4.10	4.30	4.46	4.60	4.72	4.82
	0.01	3.89	4.45	4.80	5.05	5.24	5.40	5.54	5.65	5.76
40	0.05	2.86	3.44	3.79	4.04	4.23	4.39	4.52	4.63	4.73
	0.01	3.82	4.37	4.70	4.93	5.11	5.26	5.39	5.50	5.60
60	0.05	2.83	3.40	3.74	3.98	4.16	4.31	4.44	4.55	4.65
	0.01	3.76	4.28	4.59	4.82	4.99	5.13	5.25	5.36	5.45
120	0.05	2.80	3.36	3.68	3.92	4.10	4.24	4.36	4.47	4.56
	0.01	3.70	4.20	4.50	4.71	4.87	5.01	5.12	5.21	5.30
∞	0.05	2.77	3.31	3.63	3.86	4.03	4.17	4.29	4.39	4.47
	0.01	3.64	4.12	4.40	4.60	4.76	4.88	4.99	5.08	5.16

TABLE C.5
Critical Values of χ^2

	Level of Significance for One-Tailed Test					
	0.10	0.05	0.025	0.01	0.005	0.0005
	Level of Significance for Two-Tailed Test					
df	0.20	0.10	0.05	0.02	0.01	0.001
1	1.64	2.71	3.84	5.41	6.64	10.83
2	3.22	4.60	5.99	7.82	9.21	13.82
3	4.64	6.25	7.82	9.84	11.34	16.27
4	5.99	7.78	9.49	11.67	13.28	18.47
5	7.29	9.24	11.07	13.39	15.09	20.52
6	8.56	10.64	12.59	15.03	16.81	22.46
7	9.80	12.02	14.07	16.62	18.48	24.32
8	11.03	13.36	15.51	18.17	20.09	26.12
9	12.24	14.68	16.92	19.68	21.67	27.88
10	13.44	15.99	18.31	21.16	23.21	29.59
11	14.63	17.28	19.68	22.62	24.72	31.26
12	15.81	18.55	21.03	24.05	26.22	32.91
13	16.98	19.81	22.36	25.47	27.69	34.53
14	18.15	21.06	23.68	26.87	29.14	36.12
15	19.31	22.31	25.00	28.26	30.58	37.70
16	20.46	23.54	26.30	29.63	32.00	39.25
17	21.62	24.77	27.59	31.00	33.41	40.79
18	22.76	25.99	28.87	32.35	34.80	42.31
19	23.90	27.20	30.14	33.69	36.19	43.82
20	25.04	28.41	31.41	35.02	37.57	45.32
21	26.17	29.62	32.67	36.34	38.93	46.80
22	27.30	30.81	33.92	37.66	40.29	48.27
23	28.43	32.01	35.17	38.97	41.64	49.73
24	29.55	33.20	36.42	40.27	42.98	51.18
25	30.68	34.38	37.65	41.57	44.31	52.62
26	31.80	35.56	38.88	42.86	45.64	54.05
27	32.91	36.74	40.11	44.14	46.96	55.48
28	34.03	37.92	41.34	45.42	48.28	56.89
29	35.14	39.09	42.56	46.69	49.59	58.30
30	36.25	40.26	43.77	47.96	50.89	59.70
40	47.27	51.80	55.76	60.44	63.69	73.40
50	58.16	63.17	67.50	72.61	76.15	86.66
60	68.97	74.40	79.08	84.58	88.38	99.61
70	79.72	85.53	90.53	96.39	100.42	112.32

TABLE C.6

Critical Values of r for the Sign Test

Dashes indicate there is no value of *r* small enough for significance.

	Level of Significance for One-Tailed Test						
	0.10	0.05	0.025	0.01	0.005	0.001	0.0005
	Level of Significance for Two-Tailed Test						
N	0.20	0.10	0.05	0.02	0.01	0.002	0.001
5	0	0	—	—	—	—	—
6	0	0	0	—	—	—	—
7	1	0	0	0	—	—	—
8	1	1	0	0	0	—	—
9	2	1	1	0	0	—	—
10	2	1	1	0	0	0	—
11	2	2	1	1	0	0	0
12	3	2	2	1	1	0	0
13	3	3	2	1	1	0	0
14	4	3	2	2	1	1	0
15	4	3	3	2	2	1	1
16	4	4	3	2	2	1	1
17	5	4	4	3	2	1	1
18	5	5	4	3	3	2	1
19	6	5	4	4	3	2	2
20	6	5	5	4	3	2	2
21	7	6	5	4	4	3	2
22	7	6	5	5	4	3	3
23	7	7	6	5	4	3	3
24	8	7	6	5	5	4	3
25	8	7	7	6	5	4	4
26	9	8	7	6	6	4	4
27	9	8	7	7	6	5	4
28	10	9	8	7	6	5	5
29	10	9	8	7	7	5	5
30	10	10	9	8	7	6	5
31	11	10	9	8	7	6	6
32	11	10	9	8	8	6	6
33	12	11	10	9	8	7	6
34	12	11	10	9	9	7	7
35	13	12	11	10	9	8	7

TABLE C.7

Critical Values of U for the Mann-Whitney Test for 0.05 (First Value) and 0.01 (Second Value) Significance Levels for Two-Tailed Test and for 0.025 and 0.005 Levels for One-Tailed Test[a]

N_1 / N_2	1	2	3	4	5	6	7	8	9	10	11	12	13	14	15	16	17	18	19	20
1	—	—	—	—	—	—	—	—	—	—	—	—	—	—	—	—	—	—	—	—
	—	—	—	—	—	—	—	—	—	—	—	—	—	—	—	—	—	—	—	—
2	—	—	—	—	—	—	—	0	0	0	0	1	1	1	1	1	2	2	2	2
	—	—	—	—	—	—	—	—	—	—	—	—	—	—	—	—	—	—	0	0
3	—	—	—	—	0	1	1	2	2	3	3	4	4	5	5	6	6	7	7	8
	—	—	—	—	—	—	—	—	0	0	0	1	1	1	2	2	2	2	3	3
4	—	—	—	0	1	2	3	4	4	5	6	7	8	9	10	11	11	12	13	14
	—	—	—	—	0	0	1	1	2	2	3	3	4	5	5	6	6	7	7	8
5	—	—	0	1	2	3	5	6	7	8	9	11	12	13	14	15	17	18	19	20
	—	—	—	0	1	1	2	3	4	5	6	7	7	8	9	10	11	12	13
6	—	—	1	2	3	5	6	8	10	11	13	14	16	17	19	21	22	24	25	27
	—	—	0	1	2	3	4	5	6	7	9	10	11	12	13	15	16	17	18
7	—	—	1	3	5	6	8	10	12	14	16	18	20	22	24	26	28	30	32	34
	—	—	0	1	3	4	6	7	9	10	12	13	15	16	18	19	21	22	24
8	—	0	2	4	6	8	10	13	15	17	19	22	24	26	29	31	34	36	38	41
	—	—	1	2	4	6	7	9	11	13	15	17	18	20	22	24	26	28	30
9	—	0	2	4	7	10	12	15	17	20	23	26	28	31	34	37	39	42	45	48
	—	0	1	3	5	7	9	11	13	16	18	20	22	24	27	29	31	33	36
10	—	0	3	5	8	11	14	17	20	23	26	29	33	36	39	42	45	48	52	55
	—	—	0	2	4	6	9	11	13	16	18	21	24	26	29	31	34	37	39	42
11	—	0	3	6	9	13	16	19	23	26	30	33	37	40	44	47	51	55	58	62
	—	—	0	2	5	7	10	13	16	18	21	24	27	30	33	36	39	42	45	48
12	—	1	4	7	11	14	18	22	26	29	33	37	41	45	49	53	57	61	65	69
	—	—	1	3	6	9	12	15	18	21	24	27	31	34	37	41	44	47	51	54
13	—	1	4	8	12	16	20	24	28	33	37	41	45	50	54	59	63	67	72	76
	—	—	1	3	7	10	13	17	20	24	27	31	34	38	42	45	49	53	57	60
14	—	1	5	9	13	17	22	26	31	36	40	45	50	55	59	64	69	74	78	83
	—	—	1	4	7	11	15	18	22	26	30	34	38	42	46	50	54	58	63	67
15	—	1	5	10	14	19	24	29	34	39	44	49	54	59	64	70	75	80	85	90
	—	—	2	5	8	12	16	20	24	29	33	37	42	46	51	55	60	64	69	73
16	—	1	6	11	15	21	26	31	37	42	47	53	59	64	70	75	81	86	92	98
	—	—	2	5	9	13	18	22	27	31	36	41	45	50	55	60	65	70	74	79

TABLE C.7, *Continued*

N_1 / N_2	1	2	3	4	5	6	7	8	9	10	11	12	13	14	15	16	17	18	19	20
17	—	2	6	11	17	22	28	34	39	45	51	57	63	69	75	81	87	93	99	105
	—	—	2	6	10	15	19	24	29	34	39	44	49	54	60	65	70	75	81	86
18	—	2	7	12	18	24	30	36	42	48	55	61	67	74	80	86	93	99	106	112
	—	—	2	6	11	16	21	26	31	37	42	47	53	58	64	70	75	81	87	92
19	—	2	7	13	19	25	32	38	45	52	58	65	72	78	85	92	99	106	113	119
	—	0	3	7	12	17	22	28	33	39	45	51	57	63	69	74	81	87	93	99
20	—	2	8	14	20	27	34	41	48	55	62	69	76	83	90	98	105	112	119	127
	—	0	3	8	13	18	24	30	36	42	48	54	60	67	73	79	86	92	99	105

[a] U must be equal to or *less than* the stated value. Dashes indicate there is no value of U small enough for significance.

TABLE C.8

Critical Values of T for the Wilcoxon Signed-Ranks Test

	Level of Significance for One-Tailed Test					Level of Significance for One-Tailed Test			
	0.05	0.025	0.01	0.005		0.05	0.025	0.01	0.005
	Level of Significance for Two-Tailed Test					Level of Significance for Two-Tailed Test			
N	0.10	0.05	0.02	0.01	N	0.10	0.05	0.02	0.01
5	0	—	—	—	28	130	116	101	91
6	2	0	—	—	29	140	126	110	100
7	3	2	0	—	30	151	137	120	109
8	5	3	1	0	31	163	147	130	118
9	8	5	3	1	32	175	159	140	128
10	10	8	5	3	33	187	170	151	138
11	13	10	7	5	34	200	182	162	148
12	17	13	9	7	35	213	195	173	159
13	21	17	12	9	36	227	208	185	171
14	25	21	15	12	37	241	221	198	182
15	30	25	19	15	38	256	235	211	194
16	35	29	23	19	39	271	249	224	207
17	41	34	27	23	40	286	264	238	220
18	47	40	32	27	41	302	279	252	233
19	53	46	37	32	42	319	294	266	247
20	60	52	43	37	43	336	310	281	261
21	67	58	49	42	44	353	327	296	276
22	75	65	55	48	45	371	343	312	291
23	83	73	62	54	46	389	361	328	307
24	91	81	69	61	47	407	378	345	322
25	100	89	76	68	48	426	396	362	339
26	110	98	84	75	49	446	415	379	355
27	119	107	92	83	50	466	434	397	373

TABLE C.9

Critical Values of χ_r^2 for the Friedman Test

N	k = 3		k = 4	
	$\alpha = 0.05$	$\alpha = 0.01$	$\alpha = 0.05$	$\alpha = 0.01$
2	—	—	6.000	—
3	6.000	—	7.400	9.000
4	6.500	8.000	7.800	9.600
5	6.400	8.400		
6	7.000	9.000		
7	7.143	8.857		
8	6.250	9.000		
9	6.222	8.667		

TABLE C.10

Arc Sine Transforms of Proportions, P, Where $\Phi = 2\ Arc\ Sine\sqrt{P}$

P	φ	P	φ	P	φ	P	φ	P	φ
0.001	0.0633	0.041	0.4078	0.36	1.2870	0.76	2.1176	0.971	2.7993
0.002	0.0895	0.042	0.4128	0.37	1.3078	0.77	2.1412	0.972	2.8053
0.003	0.1096	0.043	0.4178	0.38	1.3284	0.78	2.1652	0.973	2.8115
0.004	0.1266	0.044	0.4227	0.39	1.3490	0.79	2.1895	0.974	2.8177
0.005	0.1415	0.045	0.4275	0.40	1.3694	0.80	2.2143	0.975	2.8240
0.006	0.1551	0.046	0.4323	0.41	1.3898	0.81	2.2395	0.976	2.8305
0.007	0.1675	0.047	0.4371	0.42	1.4101	0.82	2.2653	0.977	2.8371
0.008	0.1791	0.048	0.4418	0.43	1.4303	0.83	2.2916	0.978	2.8438
0.009	0.1900	0.049	0.4464	0.44	1.4505	0.84	2.3186	0.979	2.8507
0.010	0.2003	0.050	0.4510	0.45	1.4706	0.85	2.3462	0.980	2.8578
0.011	0.2101	0.06	0.4949	0.46	1.4907	0.86	2.3746	0.981	2.8650
0.012	0.2195	0.07	0.5355	0.47	1.5108	0.87	2.4039	0.982	2.8725
0.013	0.2285	0.08	0.5735	0.48	1.5308	0.88	2.4341	0.983	2.8801
0.014	0.2372	0.09	0.6094	0.49	1.5508	0.89	2.4655	0.984	2.8879
0.015	0.2456	0.10	0.6435	0.50	1.5708	0.90	2.4981	0.985	2.8960
0.016	0.2537	0.11	0.6761	0.51	1.5908	0.91	2.5322	0.986	2.9044
0.017	0.2615	0.12	0.7075	0.52	1.6108	0.92	2.5681	0.987	2.9131
0.018	0.2691	0.13	0.7377	0.53	1.6308	0.93	2.6061	0.988	2.9221
0.019	0.2766	0.14	0.7670	0.54	1.6509	0.94	2.6467	0.989	2.9314
0.020	0.2838	0.15	0.7954	0.55	1.6710	0.95	2.6906	0.990	2.9413
0.021	0.2909	0.16	0.8230	0.56	1.6911	0.951	2.6952	0.991	2.9516
0.022	0.2977	0.17	0.8500	0.57	1.7113	0.952	2.6998	0.992	2.9625
0.023	0.3045	0.18	0.8763	0.58	1.7315	0.953	2.7045	0.993	2.9741
0.024	0.3111	0.19	0.9021	0.59	1.7518	0.954	2.7093	0.994	2.9865
0.025	0.3176	0.20	0.9273	0.60	1.7722	0.955	2.7141	0.995	3.0001
0.026	0.3239	0.21	0.9521	0.61	1.7926	0.956	2.7189	0.996	3.0150
0.027	0.3301	0.22	0.9764	0.62	1.8132	0.957	2.7238	0.997	3.0320
0.028	0.3362	0.23	1.0004	0.63	1.8338	0.958	2.7288	0.998	3.0521
0.029	0.3423	0.24	1.0239	0.64	1.8546	0.959	2.7338	0.999	3.0783
0.030	0.3482	0.25	1.0472	0.65	1.8755	0.960	2.7389	1.000	3.1416
0.031	0.3540	0.26	1.0701	0.66	1.8965	0.961	2.7440		
0.032	0.3597	0.27	1.0928	0.67	1.9177	0.962	2.7492		
0.033	0.3653	0.28	1.1152	0.68	1.9391	0.963	2.7545		
0.034	0.3709	0.29	1.1374	0.69	1.9606	0.964	2.7598		
0.035	0.3764	0.30	1.1593	0.70	1.9823	0.965	2.7652		
0.036	0.3818	0.31	1.1810	0.71	2.0042	0.966	2.7707		
0.037	0.3871	0.32	1.2025	0.72	2.0264	0.967	2.7762		
0.038	0.3924	0.33	1.2239	0.73	2.0488	0.968	2.7819		
0.039	0.3976	0.34	1.2451	0.74	2.0715	0.969	2.7876		
0.040	0.4027	0.35	1.2661	0.75	2.0944	0.970	2.7934		

TABLE C.11

Critical Values of Pearson r

df[a]	Level of Significance for One-Tailed Test				
	0.05	0.025	0.01	0.005	0.0005
	Level of Significance for Two-Tailed Test				
	0.10	0.05	0.02	0.01	0.001
2	0.9000	0.9500	0.9800	0.9900	0.9990
3	0.8054	0.8783	0.9343	0.9587	0.9912
4	0.7293	0.8114	0.8822	0.9172	0.9741
5	0.6694	0.7545	0.8329	0.8745	0.9507
6	0.6215	0.7067	0.7887	0.8343	0.9249
7	0.5822	0.6664	0.7498	0.7977	0.8982
8	0.5494	0.6319	0.7155	0.7646	0.8721
9	0.5214	0.6021	0.6851	0.7348	0.8471
10	0.4973	0.5760	0.6581	0.7079	0.8233
11	0.4762	0.5529	0.6339	0.6835	0.8010
12	0.4575	0.5324	0.6120	0.6614	0.7800
13	0.4409	0.5139	0.5923	0.6411	0.7603
14	0.4259	0.4973	0.5742	0.6226	0.7420
15	0.4124	0.4821	0.5577	0.6055	0.7246
16	0.4000	0.4683	0.5425	0.5897	0.7084
17	0.3887	0.4555	0.5285	0.5751	0.6932
18	0.3783	0.4438	0.5155	0.5614	0.6787
19	0.3687	0.4329	0.5034	0.5487	0.6652
20	0.3598	0.4227	0.4921	0.5368	0.6524
25	0.3233	0.3809	0.4451	0.4869	0.5974
30	0.2960	0.3494	0.4093	0.4487	0.5541
35	0.2746	0.3246	0.3810	0.4182	0.5189
40	0.2573	0.3044	0.3578	0.3932	0.4896
45	0.2428	0.2875	0.3384	0.3721	0.4648
50	0.2306	0.2732	0.3218	0.3541	0.4433
60	0.2108	0.2500	0.2948	0.3248	0.4078
70	0.1954	0.2319	0.2737	0.3017	0.3799
80	0.1829	0.2172	0.2565	0.2830	0.3568
90	0.1726	0.2050	0.2422	0.2673	0.3375
100	0.1638	0.1946	0.2301	0.2540	0.3211

[a] df $= N - 2$; $N =$ number of pairs.

TABLE C.12

Critical Values of Spearman rho

	Level of Significance for One-Tailed Test			
	0.05	0.025	0.01	0.005
	Level of Significance for Two-Tailed Test			
N^a	0.1	0.05	0.02	0.01
5	0.900	1.000	1.000	—
6	0.829	0.886	0.943	1.000
7	0.714	0.786	0.893	0.929
8	0.643	0.738	0.833	0.881
9	0.600	0.683	0.783	0.833
10	0.564	0.648	0.746	0.794
12	0.506	0.591	0.712	0.777
14	0.456	0.544	0.645	0.715
16	0.425	0.506	0.601	0.665
18	0.399	0.475	0.564	0.625
20	0.377	0.450	0.534	0.591
22	0.359	0.428	0.508	0.562
24	0.343	0.409	0.485	0.537
26	0.329	0.392	0.465	0.515
28	0.317	0.377	0.448	0.496
30	0.306	0.364	0.432	0.478

[a] N is the number of pairs.

TABLE C.13

Values of Z_r for r from 0.00 to 0.99 in 0.01 increments, and from 0.950 to 0.999 in 0.001 increments, where $Z_r = \frac{1}{2}ln\left[(1 + r)/(1 - r)\right]$

r	Z_r	r	Z_r	r	Z_r	r	Z_r	r	Z_r
0.00	0.0000	0.30	0.3095	0.60	0.6931	0.90	1.4722	0.970	2.0923
0.01	0.0100	0.31	0.3205	0.61	0.7089	0.91	1.5275	0.971	2.1095
0.02	0.0200	0.32	0.3316	0.62	0.7250	0.92	1.5890	0.972	2.1273
0.03	0.0300	0.33	0.3428	0.63	0.7414	0.93	1.6584	0.973	2.1457
0.04	0.0400	0.34	0.3541	0.64	0.7582	0.94	1.7380	0.974	2.1649
0.05	0.0500	0.35	0.3654	0.65	0.7753	0.95	1.8318	0.975	2.1847
0.06	0.0601	0.36	0.3769	0.66	0.7928	0.96	1.9459	0.976	2.2054
0.07	0.0701	0.37	0.3884	0.67	0.8107	0.97	2.0923	0.977	2.2269
0.08	0.0802	0.38	0.4001	0.68	0.8291	0.98	2.2976	0.978	2.2494
0.09	0.0902	0.39	0.4118	0.69	0.8480	0.99	2.6467	0.979	2.2729
0.10	0.1003	0.40	0.4236	0.70	0.8673	0.950	1.8318	0.980	2.2976
0.11	0.1104	0.41	0.4356	0.71	0.8872	0.951	1.8421	0.981	2.3235
0.12	0.1206	0.42	0.4477	0.72	0.9076	0.952	1.8527	0.982	2.3507
0.13	0.1307	0.43	0.4599	0.73	0.9287	0.953	1.8635	0.983	2.3796
0.14	0.1409	0.44	0.4722	0.74	0.9505	0.954	1.8745	0.984	2.4101
0.15	0.1511	0.45	0.4847	0.75	0.9730	0.955	1.8857	0.985	2.4427
0.16	0.1614	0.46	0.4973	0.76	0.9962	0.956	1.8972	0.986	2.4774
0.17	0.1717	0.47	0.5101	0.77	1.0203	0.957	1.9090	0.987	2.5147
0.18	0.1820	0.48	0.5230	0.78	1.0454	0.958	1.9210	0.988	2.5550
0.19	0.1923	0.49	0.5361	0.79	1.0714	0.959	1.9333	0.989	2.5987
0.20	0.2027	0.50	0.5493	0.80	1.0986	0.960	1.9459	0.990	2.6467
0.21	0.2132	0.51	0.5627	0.81	1.1270	0.961	1.9588	0.991	2.6996
0.22	0.2237	0.52	0.5763	0.82	1.1568	0.962	1.9721	0.992	2.7587
0.23	0.2342	0.53	0.5901	0.83	1.1881	0.963	1.9857	0.993	2.8257
0.24	0.2448	0.54	0.6042	0.84	1.2212	0.964	1.9996	0.994	2.9031
0.25	0.2554	0.55	0.6184	0.85	1.2562	0.965	2.0139	0.995	2.9945
0.26	0.2661	0.56	0.6328	0.86	1.2933	0.966	2.0287	0.996	3.1063
0.27	0.2769	0.57	0.6475	0.87	1.3331	0.967	2.0439	0.997	3.2504
0.28	0.2877	0.58	0.6625	0.88	1.3758	0.968	2.0595	0.998	3.4534
0.29	0.2986	0.59	0.6777	0.89	1.4219	0.969	2.0756	0.999	3.8002

TABLE C.14

Binomial Coefficients

For $N > 10$, the remaining coefficients may be found by the identity: $\binom{N}{r} = \binom{N}{N-r}$.

For example, $\binom{15}{12} = \binom{15}{15-12} = \binom{15}{3} = 455$.

N	$\binom{N}{0}$	$\binom{N}{1}$	$\binom{N}{2}$	$\binom{N}{3}$	$\binom{N}{4}$	$\binom{N}{5}$	$\binom{N}{6}$	$\binom{N}{7}$	$\binom{N}{8}$	$\binom{N}{9}$	$\binom{N}{10}$
0	1										
1	1	1									
2	1	2	1								
3	1	3	3	1							
4	1	4	6	4	1						
5	1	5	10	10	5	1					
6	1	6	15	20	15	6	1				
7	1	7	21	35	35	21	7	1			
8	1	8	28	56	70	56	28	8	1		
9	1	9	36	84	126	126	84	36	9	1	
10	1	10	45	120	210	252	210	120	45	10	1
11	1	11	55	165	330	462	462	330	165	55	11
12	1	12	66	220	495	792	924	792	495	220	66
13	1	13	78	286	715	1,287	1,716	1,716	1,287	715	286
14	1	14	91	364	1,001	2,002	3,003	3,432	3,003	2,002	1,001
15	1	15	105	455	1,365	3,003	5,005	6,435	6,435	5,005	3,003
16	1	16	120	560	1,820	4,368	8,008	11,440	12,870	11,440	8,008
17	1	17	136	680	2,380	6,188	12,376	19,448	24,310	24,310	19,448
18	1	18	153	816	3,060	8,568	18,564	31,824	43,758	48,620	43,758
19	1	19	171	969	3,876	11,628	27,132	50,388	75,582	92,378	92,378
20	1	20	190	1,140	4,845	15,504	38,760	77,520	125,970	167,960	184,756

TABLE C.15

Random Digits

03 47 43 73 86	36 96 47 36 61	46 98 63 71 62	33 26 16 80 45	60 11 14 10 95
97 74 24 67 62	42 81 14 57 20	42 53 32 37 32	27 07 36 07 51	24 51 79 89 73
16 76 62 27 66	56 50 26 71 07	32 90 79 78 53	13 55 38 58 59	88 97 54 14 10
12 56 85 99 26	96 96 68 27 31	05 03 72 93 15	57 12 10 14 21	88 26 49 81 76
55 59 56 35 64	38 54 82 46 22	31 62 43 09 90	06 18 44 32 53	23 83 01 30 30
16 22 77 94 39	49 54 43 54 82	17 37 93 23 78	87 35 20 96 43	84 26 34 91 64
84 42 17 53 31	57 24 55 06 88	77 04 74 47 67	21 76 33 50 25	83 92 12 06 76
63 01 63 78 59	16 95 55 67 19	98 10 50 71 75	12 86 73 58 07	44 39 52 38 79
33 21 12 34 29	78 64 56 07 82	52 42 07 44 38	15 51 00 13 42	99 66 02 79 54
57 60 86 32 44	09 47 27 96 54	49 17 46 09 62	90 52 84 77 27	08 02 73 43 28
18 18 07 92 46	44 17 16 58 09	79 83 86 19 62	06 76 50 03 10	55 23 64 05 05
26 62 38 97 75	84 16 07 44 99	83 11 46 32 24	20 14 85 88 45	10 93 72 88 71
23 42 40 64 74	82 97 77 77 81	07 45 32 14 08	32 98 94 07 72	93 85 79 10 75
12 36 28 19 95	50 92 26 11 97	00 56 76 31 38	80 22 02 53 53	86 60 42 04 53
37 85 94 35 12	83 39 50 08 30	42 34 07 96 88	54 42 06 87 98	35 85 29 48 39
70 29 17 12 13	40 33 20 38 26	13 89 51 03 74	17 76 37 13 04	07 74 21 19 30
56 62 18 37 35	96 83 50 87 75	97 12 25 93 47	70 33 24 03 54	97 77 46 44 80
99 49 57 22 77	88 42 95 45 72	16 64 36 16 00	04 43 18 66 79	94 77 24 21 90
16 08 15 04 72	33 27 14 34 09	45 59 34 68 49	12 72 07 34 45	99 27 72 95 14
31 16 93 32 43	50 27 89 87 19	20 15 37 00 49	52 85 66 60 44	38 68 88 11 80
68 34 30 13 70	55 74 30 77 40	44 22 78 84 26	04 33 46 09 52	68 07 97 06 57
74 57 25 65 76	59 29 97 68 60	71 91 38 67 54	13 58 18 24 76	15 54 55 95 52
27 42 37 86 53	48 55 90 65 72	96 57 69 36 10	96 46 92 42 45	97 60 49 04 91
00 39 68 29 61	66 37 32 20 30	77 84 57 03 29	10 45 65 04 26	11 04 06 67 24
29 94 98 94 24	68 49 69 10 82	53 75 91 93 30	34 25 20 57 27	40 48 73 51 92
16 90 82 66 59	83 62 64 11 12	67 19 00 71 74	60 47 21 29 68	02 02 37 03 31
11 27 94 75 06	06 09 19 74 66	02 94 37 34 02	76 70 90 30 86	38 45 94 30 38
35 24 10 16 20	33 32 51 26 38	79 78 45 04 91	16 92 53 56 16	02 75 50 95 98
38 23 16 86 38	42 38 97 01 50	87 75 66 81 41	40 01 74 91 62	48 51 84 08 32
31 96 25 91 47	96 44 33 49 13	34 86 82 53 91	00 52 43 48 85	27 55 26 89 62
66 67 40 67 14	64 05 71 95 86	11 05 65 09 68	76 83 20 37 90	57 16 00 11 66
14 90 84 45 11	75 73 88 05 90	52 27 41 14 86	22 98 12 22 08	07 52 74 95 80
68 05 51 18 00	33 96 02 75 19	07 60 62 93 55	59 33 82 43 90	49 37 38 44 59
20 46 78 73 90	97 51 40 14 02	04 02 33 31 08	39 54 16 49 36	47 95 93 13 30
64 19 58 97 79	15 06 15 93 20	01 90 10 75 06	40 78 78 89 62	02 67 74 17 33
05 26 93 70 60	22 35 85 15 13	92 03 51 59 77	59 56 78 06 83	52 91 05 70 74
07 97 10 88 23	09 98 42 99 64	61 71 62 99 15	06 51 29 16 93	58 05 77 09 51
68 71 86 85 85	54 87 66 47 54	73 32 08 11 12	44 95 92 63 16	29 56 24 29 48
26 99 61 65 53	58 37 78 80 70	42 10 50 67 42	32 17 55 85 74	94 44 67 16 94
14 65 52 68 75	87 59 36 22 41	26 78 63 06 55	13 08 27 01 50	15 29 39 39 43
17 53 77 58 71	71 41 61 50 72	12 41 94 96 26	44 95 27 36 99	02 96 74 30 83
90 26 59 21 19	23 52 23 33 12	96 93 02 18 39	07 02 18 36 07	25 99 32 70 23
41 23 52 55 99	31 04 49 69 96	10 47 48 45 88	13 41 43 89 20	97 17 14 49 17
60 20 50 81 69	31 99 73 68 68	35 81 33 03 76	24 30 12 48 60	18 99 10 72 34
91 25 38 05 90	94 58 28 41 36	45 37 59 03 09	90 35 57 29 12	82 62 54 65 60

TABLE C.15, *Continued*

34 50 57 74 37	98 80 33 00 91	09 77 93 19 82	74 94 80 04 04	45 07 31 66 49
85 22 04 39 43	73 81 53 94 79	33 62 46 86 28	08 31 54 46 31	53 94 13 38 47
09 79 13 77 48	73 82 97 22 21	05 03 27 24 83	72 89 44 05 60	35 80 39 94 88
88 75 80 18 14	22 95 75 42 49	39 32 82 22 49	02 48 07 70 37	16 04 61 67 87
90 96 23 70 00	39 00 03 06 90	55 85 78 38 36	94 37 30 69 32	90 89 00 76 33
53 74 23 99 67	61 32 28 69 84	94 62 67 86 24	98 33 41 19 95	47 53 53 38 09
63 38 06 86 54	99 00 65 26 94	02 82 90 23 07	79 62 67 80 60	75 91 12 81 19
35 30 58 21 46	06 72 17 10 94	25 21 31 75 96	49 28 24 00 49	55 65 79 78 07
63 43 36 82 69	65 51 18 37 88	61 38 44 12 45	32 92 85 88 65	54 34 81 85 35
98 25 37 55 26	01 91 82 81 46	74 71 12 94 97	24 02 71 37 07	03 92 18 66 75
02 63 21 17 69	71 50 80 89 56	38 15 70 11 48	43 40 45 86 98	00 83 26 91 03
64 55 22 21 82	48 22 28 06 00	61 54 13 43 91	82 78 12 23 29	06 66 24 12 27
85 07 26 13 89	01 10 07 82 04	59 63 69 36 03	69 11 15 83 80	13 29 54 19 28
58 54 16 24 15	51 54 44 82 00	62 61 65 04 69	38 18 65 18 97	85 72 13 49 21
34 85 27 84 87	61 48 64 56 26	90 18 48 13 26	37 70 15 42 57	65 65 80 39 07
03 92 18 27 46	57 99 16 96 56	30 33 72 85 22	84 64 38 56 98	99 01 30 98 64
62 95 30 27 59	37 75 41 66 48	86 97 80 61 45	23 53 04 01 63	45 76 08 64 27
08 45 93 15 22	60 21 75 46 91	98 77 27 85 42	28 88 61 08 84	69 62 03 42 73
07 08 55 18 40	45 44 75 13 90	24 94 96 61 02	57 55 66 83 15	73 42 37 11 61
01 85 89 95 66	51 10 19 34 88	15 84 97 19 75	12 76 39 43 78	64 63 91 08 25
72 84 71 14 35	19 11 58 49 26	50 11 17 17 76	86 31 57 20 18	95 60 78 46 75
88 78 28 16 84	13 52 53 94 53	75 45 69 30 96	73 89 65 70 31	99 17 43 48 76
45 17 75 65 57	28 40 19 72 12	25 12 74 75 67	60 40 60 81 19	24 62 01 61 16
96 76 28 12 54	22 01 11 94 25	71 96 16 16 88	68 64 36 74 45	19 59 50 88 92
43 31 67 72 30	24 02 94 08 63	38 32 36 66 02	69 36 38 25 39	48 03 45 15 22
50 44 66 44 21	66 06 58 05 62	68 15 54 35 02	42 35 48 96 32	14 52 41 52 48
22 66 22 15 86	26 63 75 41 99	58 42 36 72 24	58 37 52 18 51	03 37 18 39 11
96 24 40 14 51	23 22 30 88 57	95 67 47 29 83	94 69 40 06 07	18 16 36 78 86
31 73 91 61 19	60 20 72 93 48	98 57 07 23 69	65 95 39 69 58	56 80 30 19 44
78 60 73 99 84	43 89 94 36 45	56 69 47 07 41	90 22 91 07 12	78 35 34 08 72
84 37 90 61 56	70 10 23 98 05	85 11 34 76 60	76 48 45 34 60	01 64 18 39 96
36 67 10 08 23	98 93 35 08 86	99 29 76 29 81	33 34 91 58 93	63 14 52 32 52
07 28 59 07 48	89 64 58 89 75	83 85 62 27 89	30 14 78 56 27	86 63 59 80 02
10 15 83 87 60	79 24 31 66 56	21 48 24 06 93	91 98 94 05 49	01 47 59 38 00
55 19 68 97 65	03 73 52 16 56	00 53 55 90 27	33 42 29 38 87	22 13 88 83 34
53 81 29 13 39	35 01 20 71 34	62 33 74 82 14	53 73 19 09 03	56 54 29 56 93
51 86 32 68 92	33 98 74 66 99	40 14 71 94 58	45 94 19 38 81	14 44 99 81 07
35 91 70 29 13	80 03 54 07 27	96 94 78 32 66	50 95 52 74 33	13 80 55 62 54
37 71 67 95 13	20 02 44 95 94	64 85 04 05 72	01 32 90 76 14	53 89 74 60 41
93 66 13 83 27	92 79 64 64 72	28 54 96 53 84	48 14 52 98 94	56 07 93 89 30
02 96 08 45 65	13 05 00 41 84	93 07 54 72 59	21 45 57 09 77	19 48 56 27 44
49 83 43 48 35	82 88 33 69 96	72 36 04 19 76	47 45 15 18 60	82 11 08 95 97
84 60 71 62 46	40 80 81 30 37	34 39 23 05 38	25 15 35 71 30	88 12 57 21 77
18 17 30 88 71	44 91 14 88 47	89 23 30 63 15	56 34 20 47 89	99 82 93 24 98
79 69 10 61 78	71 32 76 95 62	87 00 22 58 40	92 54 01 75 25	43 11 71 99 31

TABLE C.16A
Permutations for N = 10

03528 49761	28071 39465	97041 52683	45167 82093	35421 09867	71345 06982	47286 10359	83567 49102	94170 65328	46789 02531	56471 93208	65132 74809	18294 50376	73618 04952	89714 02365
80219 43657	29485 70361	85093 24176	45687 30129	32579 48016	52867 03194	70851 29463	03621 94587	51490 32768	53180 76924	76283 90451	90287 56314	34605 12879	67295 10834	82906 45137
36524 97801	07561 98234	67820 13459	20739 58146	68045 13782	54978 36102	90317 48562	64529 78301	57319 64802	74861 39502	94816 05723	10798 32546	06431 29857	53984 16072	07196 32584
56913 84027	06289 51734	64527 80193	30265 49718	43209 81675	84152 69307	69183 47250	01278 39546	41973 25068	03471 56829	85014 27639	01628 73954	42016 58379	90164 53827	90418 73625
70523 68194	83297 60541	81239 06745	05913 68742	75206 38491	18350 67924	81623 07549	59327 64081	08317 56492	39581 60247	45736 19802	12987 54360	40568 23917	20915 48367	40819 32367
59208 13674	56078 31492	74268 09351	54981 27630	12573 68490	51246 38097	43985 27160	04628 97531	54670 32918	93108 67542	86341 95207	10678 42593	70468 51239	53920 74618	91478 32650
40329 71568	15237 98604	65897 13402	18693 20547	43709 58612	10783 95426	41237 89605	72168 35904	87194 23506	80472 69351	38125 46970	23945 10687	73981 06254	31749 26580	52831 49760
78136 09452	62531 84097	92143 05876	28935 46107	98410 75236	78059 61432	76901 35482	24618 57093	85102 93647	30642 15987	10378 24956	61739 08245	41980 25763	59761 42803	65943 80172
58236 10974	29871 64350	53107 89264	50762 41839	47103 69852	81973 65042	35716 42089	83924 67501	21593 40678	98432 57601	95260 84371	83496 17250	27810 95634	82193 67450	24851 90367

35710	34620	58037	13450	13064	36809	41059	24538	49168	79431
98624	87915	92164	97286	58927	14275	62738	60917	53270	05628
72850	82439	96408	27386	39274	10578	18594	13864	92810	76915
94316	16075	57123	90514	86105	34269	07236	07529	34576	84023
02698	80129	94786	57493	84961	53076	89631	23695	50628	64192
43517	65374	02315	20681	75203	92184	07524	04817	39417	85307
73294	23057	67983	97813	47605	89710	76523	79358	28940	48307
86015	94168	02514	04625	81239	54236	91408	42061	65317	15269
76581	06417	37198	60125	26039	69210	58302	32781	74269	71893
24309	58329	65240	84937	78145	37485	41679	50469	03851	02546
68102	71306	20935	15230	93802	28947	27149	31970	84715	07423
53794	94258	78641	84679	47651	16053	30586	28564	23069	89165
16248	24150	15894	02538	93028	57408	06384	56192	12674	16732
97305	63987	06723	67419	54176	63219	95721	73048	03895	84590
57346	25301	23461	95342	43960	29064	40519	50139	28730	16720
82019	78649	80957	01786	78521	87513	28736	74286	51946	45983
74312	52839	57819	82401	31748	90758	60274	17096	54867	14379
85960	70614	04623	93756	96250	34621	18359	34258	30912	56802
72896	01325	32516	92017	48721	74590	43895	17620	93618	90132
43105	74896	07498	64538	63905	31286	20167	98543	25470	68547
78542	82167	84067	27845	28754	21875	93605	15237	67984	39425
13069	49053	51923	16093	61039	69403	72148	86094	01325	86107
71358	36489	64530	32647	32940	27615	47395	61348	32891	25684
90246	17502	81972	85091	68751	40839	01628	72509	64057	17309
19562	52193	21035	02391	31250	60895	94652	87162	71896	71692
38704	04687	64789	68574	47896	23714	18073	45930	20453	84305
26179	25789	45961	69345	13897	87529	15203	32816	45982	59762
45038	31460	80723	17820	45260	61403	47689	50749	70316	81340
83417	48210	67439	25481	59816	03957	69012	57693	69407	20531
29065	79365	10285	70963	47023	84612	74385	48012	52138	98746

TABLE C.16B

Permutations for N = 20

TABLE C.17
Squares, Square Roots, and Reciprocals of Numbers from 1 to 1000

N	N^2	$\sqrt{N}$	$1/N$	N	N^2	$\sqrt{N}$	$1/N$
0	0	.0000	∞	50	2500	7.0711	.020000
1	1	1.0000	1.000000	51	2601	7.1414	.019608
2	4	1.4142	.500000	52	2704	7.2111	.019231
3	9	1.7321	.333333	53	2809	7.2801	.018868
4	16	2.0000	.250000	54	2916	7.3485	.018519
5	25	2.2361	.200000	55	3025	7.4162	.018182
6	36	2.4495	.166667	56	3136	7.4833	.017857
7	49	2.6458	.142857	57	3249	7.5498	.017544
8	64	2.8284	.125000	58	3364	7.6158	.017241
9	81	3.0000	.111111	59	3481	7.6811	.016949
10	100	3.1623	.100000	60	3600	7.7460	.016667
11	121	3.3166	.090909	61	3721	7.8102	.016393
12	144	3.4641	.083333	62	3844	7.8740	.016129
13	169	3.6056	.076923	63	3969	7.9373	.015873
14	196	3.7417	.071429	64	4096	8.0000	.015625
15	225	3.8730	.066667	65	4225	8.0623	.015385
16	256	4.0000	.062500	66	4356	8.1240	.015152
17	289	4.1231	.058824	67	4489	8.1854	.014925
18	324	4.2426	.055556	68	4624	8.2462	.014706
19	361	4.3589	.052632	69	4761	8.3066	.014493
20	400	4.4721	.050000	70	4900	8.3666	.014286
21	441	4.5826	.047619	71	5041	8.4261	.014085
22	484	4.6904	.045455	72	5184	8.4853	.013889
23	529	4.7958	.043478	73	5329	8.5440	.013699
24	576	4.8990	.041667	74	5476	8.6023	.013514
25	625	5.0000	.040000	75	5625	8.6603	.013333
26	676	5.0990	.038462	76	5776	8.7178	.013158
27	729	5.1962	.037037	77	5929	8.7750	.012987
28	784	5.2915	.035714	78	6084	8.8318	.012821
29	841	5.3852	.034483	79	6241	8.8882	.012658
30	900	5.4772	.033333	80	6400	8.9443	.012500
31	961	5.5678	.032258	81	6561	9.0000	.012346
32	1024	5.6569	.031250	82	6724	9.0554	.012195
33	1089	5.7446	.030303	83	6889	9.1104	.012048
34	1156	5.8310	.029412	84	7056	9.1652	.011905
35	1225	5.9161	.028571	85	7225	9.2195	.011765
36	1296	6.0000	.027778	86	7396	9.2736	.011628
37	1369	6.0828	.027027	87	7569	9.3274	.011494
38	1444	6.1644	.026316	88	7744	9.3808	.011364
39	1521	6.2450	.025641	89	7921	9.4340	.011236
40	1600	6.3246	.025000	90	8100	9.4868	.011111
41	1681	6.4031	.024390	91	8281	9.5394	.010989
42	1764	6.4807	.023810	92	8464	9.5917	.010870
43	1849	6.5574	.023256	93	8649	9.6437	.010753
44	1936	6.6332	.022727	94	8836	9.6954	.010638
45	2025	6.7082	.022222	95	9025	9.7468	.010526
46	2116	6.7823	.021739	96	9216	9.7980	.010417
47	2209	6.8557	.021277	97	9409	9.8489	.010309
48	2304	6.9282	.020833	98	9604	9.8995	.010204
49	2401	7.0000	.020408	99	9801	9.9499	.010101

N	N^2	$\sqrt{N}$	$1/N$	N	N^2	$\sqrt{N}$	$1/N$
100	10000	10.0000	.01000000	150	22500	12.2474	.00666667
101	10201	10.0499	.00990099	151	22801	12.2882	.00662252
102	10404	10.0995	.00980392	152	23104	12.3288	.00657895
103	10609	10.1489	.00970874	153	23409	12.3693	.00653595
104	10816	10.1980	.00961538	154	23716	12.4097	.00649351
105	11025	10.2470	.00952381	155	24025	12.4499	.00645161
106	11236	10.2956	.00943396	156	24336	12.4900	.00641026
107	11449	10.3441	.00934579	157	24649	12.5300	.00636943
108	11664	10.3923	.00925926	158	24964	12.5698	.00632911
109	11881	10.4403	.00917431	159	25281	12.6095	.00628931
110	12100	10.4881	.00909091	160	25600	12.6491	.00625000
111	12321	10.5357	.00900901	161	25921	12.6886	.00621118
112	12544	10.5830	.00892857	162	26244	12.7279	.00617284
113	12769	10.6301	.00884956	163	26569	12.7671	.00613497
114	12996	10.6771	.00877193	164	26896	12.8062	.00609756
115	13225	10.7238	.00869565	165	27225	12.8452	.00606061
116	13456	10.7703	.00862069	166	37556	12.8841	.00602410
117	13689	10.8167	.00854701	167	27889	12.9228	.00598802
118	13924	10.8628	.00847458	168	28224	12.9615	.00595238
119	14161	10.9087	.00840336	169	28561	13.0000	.00591716
120	14400	10.9545	.00833333	170	28900	13.0384	.00588235
121	14641	11.0000	.00826446	171	29241	13.0767	.00584795
122	14884	11.0454	.00819672	172	29584	13.1149	.00581395
123	15129	11.0905	.00813008	173	29929	13.1529	.00578035
124	15376	11.1355	.00806452	174	30276	13.1909	.00574713
125	15625	11.1803	.00800000	175	30625	13.2288	.00571429
126	15876	11.2250	.00793651	176	30976	13.2665	.00568182
127	16129	11.2694	.00787402	177	31329	13.3041	.00564972
128	16384	11.3137	.00781250	178	31684	13.3417	.00561798
129	16641	11.3578	.00775194	179	32041	13.3791	.00558659
130	16900	11.4018	.00769231	180	32400	13.4164	.00555556
131	17161	11.4455	.00763359	181	32761	13.4536	.00552486
132	17424	11.4891	.00757576	182	33124	13.4907	.00549451
133	17689	11.5326	.00751880	183	33489	13.5277	.00546448
134	17956	11.5758	.00746269	184	33856	13.5647	.00543478
135	18225	11.6190	.00740741	185	34225	13.6015	.00540541
136	18496	11.6619	.00735294	186	34596	13.6382	.00537634
137	18769	11.7047	.00729927	187	34969	13.6748	.00534759
138	19044	11.7473	.00724638	188	35344	13.7113	.00531915
139	19321	11.7898	.00719424	189	35721	13.7477	.00529101
140	19600	11.8322	.00714286	190	36100	13.7840	.00526316
141	19881	11.8743	.00709220	191	36481	13.8203	.00523560
142	20164	11.9164	.00704225	192	36864	13.8564	.00520833
143	20449	11.9583	.00699301	193	37249	13.8924	.00518135
144	20736	12.0000	.00694444	194	37636	13.9284	.00515464
145	21025	12.0416	.00689655	195	38025	13.9642	.00512821
146	21316	12.0830	.00684932	196	38416	14.0000	.00510204
147	21609	12.1244	.00680272	197	38809	14.0357	.00507614
148	21904	12.1655	.00675676	198	39204	14.0712	.00505051
149	22201	12.2066	.00671141	199	39601	14.1067	.00502513

N	N^2	$\sqrt{N}$	$1/N$	N	N^2	$\sqrt{N}$	$1/N$
200	40000	14.1421	.00500000	250	62500	15.8114	.00400000
201	40401	14.1774	.00497512	251	63001	15.8430	.00398406
202	40804	14.2127	.00495050	252	63504	15.8745	.00396825
203	41209	14.2478	.00492611	253	64009	15.9060	.00395257
204	41616	14.2829	.00490196	254	64516	15.9374	.00393701
205	42025	14.3178	.00487805	255	65025	15.9687	.00392157
206	42436	14.3527	.00485437	256	65536	16.0000	.00390625
207	42849	14.3875	.00483092	257	66049	16.0312	.00389105
208	43264	14.4222	.00480769	258	66564	16.0624	.00387597
209	43681	14.4568	.00478469	259	67081	16.0935	.00386100
210	44100	14.4914	.00476190	260	67600	16.1245	.00384615
211	44521	14.5258	.00473934	261	68121	16.1555	.00383142
212	44944	14.5602	.00471698	262	68644	16.1864	.00381679
213	45369	14.5945	.00469484	263	69169	16.2173	.00380228
214	45796	14.6287	.00467290	264	69696	16.2481	.00378788
215	46225	14.6629	.00465116	265	70225	16.2788	.00377358
216	46656	14.6969	.00462963	266	70756	16.3095	.00375940
217	47089	14.7309	.00460829	267	71289	16.3401	.00374532
218	47524	14.7648	.00458716	268	71824	16.3707	.00373134
219	47961	14.7986	.00456621	269	72361	16.4012	.00371747
220	48400	14.8324	.00454545	270	72900	16.4317	.00370370
221	48841	14.8661	.00452489	271	73441	16.4621	.00369004
222	49284	14.8997	.00450450	272	73984	16.4924	.00367647
223	49729	14.9332	.00448430	273	74529	16.5227	.00366300
224	50176	14.9666	.00446429	274	75076	16.5529	.00364964
225	50625	15.0000	.00444444	275	75625	16.5831	.00363636
226	51076	15.0333	.00442478	276	76176	16.6132	.00362319
227	51529	15.0665	.00440529	277	76729	16.6433	.00361011
228	51984	15.0997	.00438596	278	77284	16.6733	.00359712
229	52441	15.1327	.00436681	279	77841	16.7033	.00358423
230	52900	15.1658	.00434783	280	78400	16.7332	.00357143
231	53361	15.1987	.00432900	281	78961	16.7631	.00355872
232	53824	15.2315	.00431034	282	79524	16.7929	.00354610
233	54289	15.2643	.00429185	283	80089	16.8226	.00353357
234	54756	15.2971	.00427350	284	80656	16.8523	.00352113
235	55225	15.3297	.00425532	285	81225	16.8819	.00350877
236	55696	15.3623	.00423729	286	81796	16.9115	.00349650
237	56169	15.3948	.00421941	287	82369	16.9411	.00348432
238	56644	15.4272	.00420168	288	82944	16.9706	.00347222
239	57121	15.4596	.00418410	289	83521	17.0000	.00346021
240	57600	15.4919	.00416667	290	84100	17.0294	.00344828
241	58081	15.5242	.00414938	291	84681	17.0587	.00343643
242	58564	15.5563	.00413223	292	85264	17.0880	.00342466
243	59049	15.5885	.00411523	293	85849	17.1172	.00341297
244	59536	15.6205	.00409836	294	86436	17.1464	.00340136
245	60025	15.6525	.00408163	295	87025	17.1756	.00338983
246	60516	15.6844	.00406504	296	87616	17.2047	.00337838
247	61009	15.7162	.00404858	297	88209	17.2337	.00336700
248	61504	15.7480	.00403226	298	88804	17.2627	.00335570
249	62001	15.7797	.00401606	299	89401	17.2916	.00334448

N	N^2	$\sqrt{N}$	$1/N$	N	N^2	$\sqrt{N}$	$1/N$
300	90000	17.3205	.00333333	350	122500	18.7083	.00285714
301	90601	17.3494	.00332226	351	123201	18.7350	.00284900
302	91204	17.3781	.00331126	352	123904	18.7617	.00284091
303	91809	17.4069	.00330033	353	124609	18.7883	.00283286
304	92416	17.4356	.00328947	354	125316	18.8149	.00282486
305	93025	17.4642	.00327869	355	126025	18.8414	.00281690
306	93636	17.4929	.00326797	356	126736	18.8680	.00280899
307	94249	17.5214	.00325733	357	127449	18.8944	.00280112
308	94864	17.5499	.00324674	358	128164	18.9209	.00279330
309	95481	17.5784	.00323625	359	128881	18.9473	.00278552
310	96100	17.6068	.00322581	360	129000	18.9737	.00277778
311	96721	17.6352	.00321543	361	130321	19.0000	.00277008
312	97344	17.6635	.00320513	362	131044	19.0263	.00276243
313	97969	17.6918	.00319489	363	131769	19.0526	.00275482
314	98596	17.7200	.00318471	364	132496	19.0788	.00274725
315	99225	17.7482	.00317460	365	133225	19.1050	.00273973
316	99856	17.7764	.00316456	366	133956	19.1311	.00273224
317	100489	17.8045	.00315457	367	134689	19.1572	.00272480
318	101124	17.8326	.00314465	368	135424	19.1833	.00271739
319	101761	17.8606	.00313480	369	136161	19.2094	.00271003
320	102400	17.8885	.00312500	370	136900	19.2354	.00270270
321	103041	17.9165	.00311526	371	137641	19.2614	.00269542
322	103684	17.9444	.00310559	372	138384	19.2873	.00268817
323	104329	17.9722	.00309598	373	139129	19.3132	.00268097
324	104976	18.0000	.00308642	374	139876	19.3391	.00267380
325	105625	18.0278	.00307692	375	140625	19.3649	.00266667
326	106276	18.0555	.00306748	376	141376	19.3907	.00265957
327	106929	18.0831	.00305810	377	142129	19.4165	.00265252
328	107584	18.1108	.00304878	378	142884	19.4422	.00264550
329	108241	18.1384	.00303951	379	143641	19.4679	.00263852
330	108900	18.1659	.00303030	380	144400	19.4936	.00263158
331	109561	18.1934	.00302115	381	145161	19.5192	.00262467
332	110224	18.2209	.00301205	382	145924	19.5448	.00261780
333	110889	18.2483	.00300300	383	146689	19.5704	.00261097
334	111556	18.2757	.00299401	384	147456	19.5959	.00260417
335	112225	18.3030	.00298507	385	148225	19.6214	.00259740
336	112896	18.3303	.00297619	386	148996	19.6469	.00259067
337	113569	18.3576	.00296736	387	149769	19.6723	.00258398
338	114244	18.3848	.00295858	388	150544	19.6977	.00257732
339	114921	18.4120	.00294985	389	151321	19.7231	.00257069
340	115600	18.4391	.00294118	390	152100	19.7484	.00256410
341	116281	18.4662	.00293255	391	152881	19.7737	.00255754
342	116964	18.4932	.00292398	392	153664	19.7990	.00255102
343	117649	18.5203	.00291545	393	154449	19.8242	.00254453
344	118336	18.5472	.00290698	394	155236	19.8494	.00253807
345	119025	18.5742	.00289855	395	156025	19.8746	.00253165
346	119716	18.6011	.00289017	396	156816	19.8997	.00252525
347	120409	18.6279	.00288184	397	157609	19.9249	.00251889
348	121104	18.6548	.00287356	398	158404	19.9499	.00251256
349	121801	18.6815	.00286533	399	159201	19.9750	.00250627

N	N^2	$\sqrt{N}$	$1/N$	N	N^2	$\sqrt{N}$	$1/N$
400	160000	20.0000	.00250000	450	202500	21.2132	.00222222
401	160801	20.0250	.00249377	451	203401	21.2368	.00221729
402	161604	20.0499	.00248756	452	204304	21.2603	.00221239
403	162409	20.0749	.00248139	453	205209	21.2838	.00220751
404	163216	20.0998	.00247525	454	206116	21.3073	.00220264
405	164025	20.1246	.00246914	455	207025	21.3307	.00219780
406	164836	20.1494	.00246305	456	207936	21.3542	.00219298
407	165649	20.1742	.00245700	457	208849	21.3776	.00218818
408	166464	20.1990	.00245098	458	209764	21.4009	.00218341
409	167281	20.2237	.00244499	459	210681	21.4243	.00217865
410	168100	20.2485	.00243902	460	211600	21.4476	.00217391
411	168921	20.2731	.00243309	461	212521	21.4709	.00216920
412	169744	20.2978	.00242718	462	213444	21.4942	.00216450
413	170569	20.3224	.00242131	463	214369	21.5174	.00215983
414	171396	20.3470	.00241546	464	215296	21.5407	.00215517
415	172225	20.3715	.00240964	465	216225	21.5639	.00215054
416	173056	20.3961	.00240385	466	217156	21.5870	.00214592
417	173889	20.4206	.00239808	467	218089	21.6102	.00214133
418	174724	20.4450	.00239234	468	219024	21.6333	.00213675
419	175561	20.4695	.00238663	469	219961	21.6564	.00213220
420	176400	20.4939	.00238095	470	220900	21.6795	.00212766
421	177241	20.5183	.00237530	471	221841	21.7025	.00212314
422	178084	20.5426	.00236967	472	222784	21.7256	.00211864
423	178929	20.5670	.00236407	473	223729	21.7486	.00211416
424	179776	20.5913	.00235849	474	224676	21.7715	.00210970
425	180625	20.6155	.00235294	475	225625	21.7945	.00210526
426	181476	20.6398	.00234742	476	226576	21.8174	.00210084
427	182329	20.6640	.00234192	477	227529	21.8403	.00209644
428	183184	20.6882	.00233645	478	228484	21.8632	.00209205
429	184041	20.7123	.00233100	479	229441	21.8861	.00208768
430	184900	20.7364	.00232558	480	230400	21.9089	.00208333
431	185761	20.7605	.00232019	481	231361	21.9317	.00207900
432	186624	20.7846	.00231481	482	232324	21.9545	.00207469
433	187489	20.8087	.00230947	483	233289	21.9773	.00207039
434	188356	20.8327	.00230415	484	234256	22.0000	.00206612
435	189225	20.8567	.00229885	485	235225	22.0227	.00206186
436	190096	20.8806	.00229358	486	236196	22.0454	.00205761
437	190969	20.9045	.00228833	487	237169	22.0681	.00205339
438	191844	20.9284	.00228311	488	238144	22.0907	.00204918
439	192721	20.9523	.00227790	489	239121	22.1133	.00204499
440	193600	20.9762	.00227273	490	240100	22.1359	.00204082
441	194481	21.0000	.00226757	491	241081	22.1585	.00203666
442	195364	21.0238	.00226244	492	242064	22.1811	.00203252
443	196249	21.0476	.00225734	493	243049	22.2036	.00202840
444	197136	21.0713	.00225225	494	244036	22.2261	.00202429
445	198025	21.0950	.00224719	495	245025	22.2486	.00202020
446	198916	21.1187	.00224215	496	246016	22.2711	.00201613
447	199809	21.1424	.00223714	497	247009	22.2935	.00201207
448	200704	21.1660	.00223214	498	248004	22.3159	.00200803
449	201601	21.1896	.00222717	499	249001	22.3383	.00200401

N	N^2	$\sqrt{N}$	$1/N$	N	N^2	$\sqrt{N}$	$1/N$
500	250000	22.3607	.00200000	550	302500	23.4521	.00181818
501	251001	22.3830	.00199601	551	303601	23.4734	.00181488
502	252004	22.4054	.00199203	552	304704	23.4947	.00181159
503	253009	22.4277	.00198807	553	305809	23.5160	.00180832
504	254016	22.4499	.00198413	554	306916	23.5372	.00180505
505	255025	22.4722	.00198020	555	308025	23.5584	.00180180
506	256036	22.4944	.00197628	556	309136	23.5797	.00179856
507	257049	22.5167	.00197239	557	310249	23.6008	.00179533
508	258064	22.5389	.00196850	558	311364	23.6220	.00179211
509	259081	22.5610	.00196464	559	312481	23.6432	.00178891
510	260100	22.5832	.00196078	560	313600	23.6643	.00178571
511	261121	22.6053	.00195695	561	314721	23.6854	.00178253
512	262144	22.6274	.00195312	562	315844	23.7065	.00177936
513	263169	22.6495	.00194932	563	316969	23.7276	.00177620
514	264196	22.6716	.00194553	564	318096	23.7487	.00177305
515	265225	22.6936	.00194175	565	319225	23.7697	.00176991
516	266256	22.7156	.00193798	566	320356	23.7908	.00176678
517	267289	22.7376	.00193424	567	321489	23.8118	.00176367
518	268324	22.7596	.00193050	568	322624	23.8328	.00176056
519	269361	22.7816	.00192678	569	323761	23.8537	.00175747
520	270400	22.8035	.00192308	570	324900	23.8747	.00175439
521	271441	22.8254	.00191939	571	326041	23.8956	.00175131
522	272484	22.8473	.00191571	572	327184	23.9165	.00174825
523	273529	22.8692	.00191205	573	328329	23.9374	.00174520
524	274576	22.8910	.00190840	574	329476	23.9583	.00174216
525	275625	22.9129	.00190476	575	330625	23.9792	.00173913
526	276676	22.9347	.00190114	576	331776	24.0000	.00173611
527	277729	22.9565	.00189753	577	332929	24.0208	.00173310
528	278784	22.9783	.00189394	578	334084	24.0416	.00173010
529	279841	23.0000	.00189036	579	335241	24.0624	.00172712
530	280900	23.0217	.00188679	580	336400	24.0832	.00172414
531	281961	23.0434	.00188324	581	337561	24.1039	.00172117
532	283024	23.0651	.00187970	582	338724	24.1247	.00171821
533	284089	23.0868	.00187617	583	339889	24.1454	.00171527
534	285156	23.1084	.00187266	584	341056	24.1661	.00171233
535	286225	23.1301	.00186916	585	342225	24.1868	.00170940
536	287296	23.1517	.00186567	586	343396	24.2074	.00170648
537	288369	23.1733	.00186220	587	344569	24.2281	.00170358
538	289444	23.1948	.00185874	588	345744	24.2487	.00170068
539	290521	23.2164	.00185529	589	346921	24.2693	.00169779
540	291600	23.2379	.00185185	590	348100	24.2899	.00169492
541	292681	23.2594	.00184843	591	349281	24.3105	.00169205
542	293764	23.2809	.00184502	592	350464	24.3311	.00168919
543	294849	23.3024	.00184162	593	351649	24.3516	.00168634
544	295936	23.3238	.00183824	594	352836	24.3721	.00168350
545	297025	23.3452	.00183486	595	354025	24.3926	.00168067
546	298116	23.3666	.00183150	596	355216	24.4131	.00167785
547	299209	23.3880	.00182815	597	356409	24.4336	.00167504
548	300304	23.4094	.00182482	598	357604	24.4540	.00167224
549	301401	23.4307	.00182149	599	358801	24.4745	.00166945

N	N^2	$\sqrt{N}$	$1/N$	N	N^2	$\sqrt{N}$	$1/N$
600	360000	24.4949	.00166667	650	422500	25.4951	.00153846
601	361201	24.5153	.00166389	651	423801	25.5147	.00153610
602	362404	24.5357	.00166113	652	425104	25.5343	.00153374
603	363609	24.5561	.00165837	653	426409	25.5539	.00153139
604	364816	24.5764	.00165563	654	427716	25.5734	.00152905
605	366025	24.5967	.00165289	655	429025	25.5930	.00152672
606	367236	24.6171	.00165017	656	430336	25.6125	.00152439
607	368449	24.6374	.00164745	657	431649	25.6320	.00152207
608	369664	24.6577	.00164474	658	432964	25.6515	.00151976
609	370881	24.6779	.00164204	659	434281	25.6710	.00151745
610	372100	24.6982	.00163934	660	435600	25.6905	.00151515
611	373321	24.7184	.00163666	661	436921	25.7099	.00151286
612	374544	24.7386	.00163399	662	438244	25.7294	.00151057
613	375769	24.7588	.00163132	663	439569	25.7488	.00150830
614	376996	24.7790	.00162866	664	440896	25.7682	.00150602
615	378225	24.7992	.00162602	665	442225	25.7876	.00150376
616	379456	24.8193	.00162338	666	443556	25.8070	.00150150
617	380689	24.8395	.00162075	667	444889	25.8263	.00149925
618	381924	24.8596	.00161812	668	446224	25.8457	.00149701
619	383161	24.8797	.00161551	669	447561	25.8650	.00149477
620	384400	24.8998	.00161290	670	448900	25.8844	.00149254
621	385641	24.9199	.00161031	671	450241	25.9037	.00149031
622	386884	24.9399	.00160772	672	451584	25.9230	.00148810
623	388129	24.9600	.00160514	673	452929	25.9422	.00148588
624	389376	24.9800	.00160256	674	454276	25.9615	.00148368
625	390625	25.0000	.00160000	675	455625	25.9808	.00148148
626	391876	25.0200	.00159744	676	456976	26.0000	.00147929
627	393129	25.0400	.00159490	677	458329	26.0192	.00147710
628	394384	25.0599	.00159236	678	459684	26.0384	.00147493
629	395641	25.0799	.00158983	679	461041	26.0576	.00147275
630	396900	25.0998	.00158730	680	462400	26.0768	.00147059
631	398161	25.1197	.00158479	681	463761	26.0960	.00146843
632	399424	25.1396	.00158228	682	465124	26.1151	.00146628
633	400689	25.1595	.00157978	683	466489	26.1343	.00146413
634	401956	25.1794	.00157729	684	467856	26.1534	.00146199
635	403225	25.1992	.00157480	685	469225	26.1725	.00145985
636	404496	25.2190	.00157233	686	470596	26.1916	.00145773
637	405769	25.2389	.00156986	687	471969	26.2107	.00145560
638	407044	25.2587	.00156740	688	473344	26.2298	.00145349
639	408321	25.2784	.00156495	689	474721	26.2488	.00145138
640	409600	25.2982	.00156250	690	476100	26.2679	.00144928
641	410881	25.3180	.00156006	691	477481	26.2869	.00144718
642	412164	25.3377	.00155763	692	478864	26.3059	.00144509
643	413449	25.3574	.00155521	693	480249	26.3249	.00144300
644	414736	25.3772	.00155280	694	481636	26.3439	.00144092
645	416025	25.3969	.00155039	695	483025	26.3629	.00143885
646	417316	25.4165	.00154799	696	484416	26.3818	.00143678
647	418609	25.4362	.00154560	697	485809	26.4008	.00143472
648	419904	25.4558	.00154321	698	487204	26.4197	.00143266
649	421201	25.4755	.00154083	699	488601	26.4386	.00143062

N	N^2	$\sqrt{N}$	$1/N$	N	N^2	$\sqrt{N}$	$1/N$
700	490000	26.4575	.00142857	750	562500	27.3861	.00133333
701	491401	26.4764	.00142653	751	564001	27.4044	.00133156
702	492804	26.4953	.00142450	752	565504	27.4226	.00132979
703	494209	26.5141	.00142248	753	567009	27.4408	.00132802
704	495616	26.5330	.00142045	754	568516	27.4591	.00132626
705	497025	26.5518	.00141844	755	570025	27.4773	.00132450
706	498436	26.5707	.00141643	756	571536	27.4955	.00132275
707	499849	26.5895	.00141443	757	573049	27.5136	.00132100
708	501264	26.6083	.00141243	758	574564	27.5318	.00131926
709	502681	26.6271	.00141044	759	576081	27.5500	.00131752
710	504100	26.6458	.00140845	760	577600	27.5681	.00131579
711	505521	26.6646	.00140647	761	579121	27.5862	.00131406
712	506944	26.6833	.00140449	762	580644	27.6043	.00131234
713	508369	26.7021	.00140252	763	582169	27.6225	.00131062
714	509796	26.7208	.00140056	764	583696	27.6405	.00130890
715	511225	26.7395	.00139860	765	585225	27.6586	.00130719
716	512656	26.7582	.00139665	766	586756	27.6767	.00130548
717	514089	26.7769	.00139470	767	588289	27.6948	.00130378
718	515524	26.7955	.00139276	768	589824	27.7128	.00130208
719	516961	26.8142	.00139082	769	591361	27.7308	.00130039
720	518400	26.8328	.00138889	770	592900	27.7489	.00129870
721	519841	26.8514	.00138696	771	594441	27.7669	.00129702
722	521284	26.8701	.00138504	772	595984	27.7849	.00129534
723	522729	26.8887	.00138313	773	597529	27.8029	.00129366
724	524176	26.9072	.00138122	774	599076	27.8209	.00129199
725	525625	26.9258	.00137931	775	600625	27.8388	.00129032
726	527076	26.9444	.00137741	776	602176	27.8568	.00128866
727	528529	26.9629	.00137552	777	603729	27.8747	.00128700
728	529984	26.9815	.00137363	778	605284	27.8927	.00128535
729	531441	27.0000	.00137174	779	606841	27.9106	.00128370
730	532900	27.0185	.00136986	780	608400	27.9285	.00128205
731	534361	27.0370	.00136799	781	609961	27.9464	.00128041
732	535824	27.0555	.00136612	782	611524	27.9643	.00127877
733	537289	27.0740	.00136426	783	613089	27.9821	.00127714
734	538756	27.0924	.00136240	784	614656	28.0000	.00127551
735	540225	27.1109	.00136054	785	616225	28.0179	.00127389
736	541696	27.1293	.00135870	786	617796	28.0357	.00127226
737	543169	27.1477	.00135685	787	619369	28.0535	.00127065
738	544644	27.1662	.00135501	788	620944	28.0713	.00126904
739	546121	27.1846	.00135318	789	622521	28.0891	.00126743
740	547600	27.2029	.00135135	790	624100	28.1069	.00126582
741	549081	27.2213	.00134953	791	625681	28.1247	.00126422
742	550564	27.2397	.00134771	792	627264	28.1425	.00126263
743	552049	27.2580	.00134590	793	628849	28.1603	.00126103
744	553536	27.2764	.00134409	794	630436	28.1780	.00125945
745	555025	27.2947	.00134228	795	632025	28.1957	.00125786
746	556516	27.3130	.00134048	796	633616	28.2135	.00125628
747	558009	27.3313	.00133869	797	635209	28.2312	.00125471
748	559504	27.3496	.00133690	798	636804	28.2489	.00125313
749	561001	27.3679	.00133511	799	638401	28.2666	.00125156

N	N²	√N	1/N	N	N²	√N	1/N
800	640000	28.2843	.00125000	850	722500	29.1548	.00117647
801	641601	28.3019	.00124844	851	724201	29.1719	.00117509
802	643204	28.3196	.00124688	852	725904	29.1890	.00117371
803	644809	28.3373	.00124533	853	727609	29.2062	.00117233
804	646416	28.3549	.00124378	854	729316	29.2233	.00117096
805	648025	28.3725	.00124224	855	731025	29.2404	.00116959
806	649636	28.3901	.00124069	856	732736	29.2575	.00116822
807	651249	28.4077	.00123916	857	734449	29.2746	.00116686
808	652864	28.4253	.00123762	858	736164	29.2916	.00116550
809	654481	28.4429	.00123609	859	737881	29.3087	.00116414
810	656100	28.4605	.00123457	860	739600	29.3258	.00116279
811	657721	28.4781	.00123305	861	741321	29.3428	.00116144
812	659344	28.4956	.00123153	862	743044	29.3598	.00116009
813	660969	28.5132	.00123001	863	744769	29.3769	.00115875
814	662596	28.5307	.00122850	864	746496	29.3939	.00115741
815	664225	28.5482	.00122699	865	748225	29.4109	.00115607
816	665856	28.5657	.00122549	866	749956	29.4279	.00115473
817	667489	28.5832	.00122399	867	751689	29.4449	.00115340
818	669124	28.6007	.00122249	868	753424	29.4618	.00115207
819	670761	28.6182	.00122100	869	755161	29.4788	.00115075
820	672400	28.6356	.00121951	870	756900	29.4958	.00114943
821	674041	28.6531	.00121803	871	758641	29.5127	.00114811
822	675684	28.6705	.00121655	872	760384	29.5296	.00114679
823	677329	28.6880	.00121507	873	762129	29.5466	.00114548
824	678976	28.7054	.00121359	874	763876	29.5635	.00114416
825	680625	28.7228	.00121212	875	765625	29.5804	.00114286
826	682276	28.7402	.00121065	876	767376	29.5973	.00114155
827	683929	28.7576	.00120919	877	769129	29.6142	.00114025
828	685584	28.7750	.00120773	878	770884	29.6311	.00113895
829	687241	28.7924	.00120627	879	772641	29.6479	.00113766
830	688900	28.8097	.00120482	880	774400	29.6648	.00113636
831	690561	28.8271	.00120337	881	776161	29.6816	.00113507
832	692224	28.8444	.00120192	882	777924	29.6985	.00113379
833	693889	28.8617	.00120048	883	779689	29.7153	.00113250
834	695556	28.8791	.00119904	884	781456	29.7321	.00113122
835	697225	28.8964	.00119760	885	783225	29.7489	.00112994
836	698896	28.9137	.00119617	886	784996	29.7658	.00112867
837	700569	28.9310	.00119474	887	786769	29.7825	.00112740
838	702244	28.9482	.00119332	888	788544	29.7993	.00112613
839	703921	28.9655	.00119190	889	790321	29.8161	.00112486
840	705600	28.9828	.00119048	890	792100	29.8329	.00112360
841	707281	29.0000	.00118906	891	793881	29.8496	.00112233
842	708964	29.0172	.00118765	892	795664	29.8664	.00112108
843	710649	29.0345	.00118624	893	797449	29.8831	.00111982
844	712336	29.0517	.00118483	894	799236	29.8998	.00111857
845	714025	29.0689	.00118343	895	801025	29.9166	.00111732
846	715716	29.0861	.00118203	896	802816	29.9333	.00111607
847	717409	29.1033	.00118064	897	804609	29.9500	.00111483
848	719104	29.1204	.00117925	898	806404	29.9666	.00111359
849	720801	29.1376	.00117786	899	808201	29.9833	.00111235

N	N²	√N	1/N	N	N²	√N	1/N
900	810000	30.0000	.00111111	950	902500	30.8221	.00105263
901	811801	30.0167	.00110988	951	904401	30.8383	.00105152
902	813604	30.0333	.00110865	952	906304	30.8545	.00105042
903	815409	30.0500	.00110742	953	908209	30.8707	.00104932
904	817216	30.0666	.00110619	954	910116	30.8869	.00104822
905	819025	30.0832	.00110497	955	912095	30.9031	.00104712
906	820836	30.0998	.00110375	956	913936	30.9192	.00104603
907	822649	30.1164	.00110254	957	915849	30.9354	.00104493
908	824464	30.1330	.00110132	958	917764	30.9516	.00104384
909	826281	30.1496	.00110011	959	919681	30.9677	.00104275
910	828100	30.1662	.00109890	960	921600	30.9839	.00104167
911	829921	30.1828	.00109769	961	923521	31.0000	.00104058
912	831744	30.1993	.00109649	962	925444	31.0161	.00103950
913	833569	30.2159	.00109529	963	927369	31.0322	.00103842
914	835396	30.2324	.00109409	964	929296	31.0483	.00103734
915	837225	30.2490	.00109290	965	931225	31.0644	.00103627
916	839056	30.2655	.00109170	966	933156	31.0805	.00103520
917	840889	30.2820	.00109051	967	935089	31.0966	.00103413
918	842724	30.2985	.00108932	968	937024	31.1127	.00103306
919	844561	30.3150	.00108814	969	938961	31.1288	.00103199
920	846400	30.3315	.00108696	970	940900	31.1448	.00103093
921	848241	30.3480	.00108578	971	942841	31.1609	.00102987
922	850084	30.3645	.00108460	972	944784	31.1769	.00102881
923	851929	30.3809	.00108342	973	946729	31.1929	.00102775
924	853776	30.3974	.00108225	974	948676	31.2090	.00102669
925	855625	30.4138	.00108108	975	950625	31.2250	.00102564
926	857476	30.4302	.00107991	976	952576	31.2410	.00102459
927	859329	30.4467	.00107875	977	954529	31.2570	.00102354
928	861184	30.4631	.00107759	978	956484	31.2730	.00102249
929	863041	30.4795	.00107643	979	958441	31.2890	.00102145
930	864900	30.4959	.00107527	980	960400	31.3050	.00102041
931	866761	30.5123	.00107411	981	962361	31.3209	.00101937
932	868624	30.5287	.00107296	982	964324	31.3369	.00101833
933	870489	30.5450	.00107181	983	966289	31.3528	.00101729
934	872356	30.5614	.00107066	984	968256	31.3688	.00101626
935	874225	30.5778	.00106952	985	970225	31.3847	.00101523
936	876096	30.5941	.00106838	986	972196	31.4006	.00101420
937	877969	30.6105	.00106724	987	974169	31.4166	.00101317
938	879844	30.6268	.00106610	988	976144	31.4325	.00101215
939	881721	30.6431	.00106496	989	978121	31.4484	.00101112
940	883600	30.6594	.00106383	990	980100	31.4643	.00101010
941	885481	30.6757	.00106270	991	982081	31.4802	.00100908
942	887364	30.6920	.00106157	992	984064	31.4960	.00100806
943	889249	30.7083	.00106045	993	986049	31.5119	.00100705
944	891136	30.7246	.00105932	994	988036	31.5278	.00100604
945	893025	30.7409	.00105820	995	990025	31.5436	.00100503
946	894916	30.7571	.00105708	996	992016	31.5595	.00100402
947	896809	30.7734	.00105597	997	994009	31.5753	.00100301
948	898704	30.7896	.00105485	998	996004	31.5911	.00100200
949	900601	30.8058	.00105374	999	998001	31.6070	.00100100
				1000	1000000	31.6228	.00100000

Chapter 1

I.

A. 1. (a) $(12 \div 2) \times (6 - 3) = 18$
    (b) $12 \div (2 \times 6) - 3 = -2$
    (c) $12 \div (2 \times (6 - 3)) = 2$
    (d) $(12 \div 2) \times 6 - 3 = 33$
  2. (a) True
    (b) False
    (c) False
    (d) True
    (e) True
    (f) False

II.

A. 1. (a) False
    (b) True
    (c) True
    (d) True
    (e) False
    (f) True
    (g) True
    (h) True

III.

A. 1. (a) B
    (b) B
    (c) C
    (d) B
    (e) C
    (f) C
    (g) C
    (h) B
    (i) C
    (j) B

IV.

A. 1. (a) 0.80
    (b) 3.50
    (c) 4.375
    (d) 0.75
    (e) 625.0
  2. (a) 3.2%
    (b) 4%
    (c) 0.1%
    (d) 0.46%
    (e) 22%
    (f) 30%

3. (a) 2.30×10^{-4}
   (b) 2.20×10^{1}
   (c) 2.00×10^{-2}
   (d) 1.20×10^{-2}
   (e) 1.60×10^{-1}
   (f) 1.00×10^{-4}

V.

A. 1. (a) (4)
   (b) (1)
   (c) (5)
   (d) (6)
   (e) (2)
   (f) (3)

2.	Row Sums	Column Sums	Total Sums
	61	100	373
	60	96	
	83	121	
	72	56	
	97		

3. (a) 72
   (b) 39
   (c) 53
   (d) 65
   (e) 9
   (f) 22
   (g) 28
   (h) 39
   (i) 44
   (j) 66

Chapter 2

A. 1. (a) Dependent
   (b) Discrete
   (c) Independent
   (d) Dependent
   (e) Continuous
2. (a) Ordinal
   (b) Nominal
   (c) Interval
   (d) Ratio
   (e) Ratio
   (f) Interval
3. (a) Independent: drug versus nothing
       Dependent: temperature, interval scale

(b) Independent: drinking more milk (6 or more glasses) versus less milk (1 or fewer glasses)
    Dependent: height and weight, ratio scale
(c) Independent: number of times GRE exam taken
    Dependent: GRE score, interval scale
(d) Independent: degree of hunger
    Dependent: number of food-related responses, ratio scale
(e) Independent: two systems of betting on horses
    Dependent: amount of money won, ratio scale

B. 1. (a) Nominal
       (b) Ratio
       (c) Interval
       (d) Ordinal
       (e) Nominal
   2. (Table 2.2): (1) 8,   (2) 5,   (3) 6,   (4) 3,   (5) 3
   3. (a) 36%
      (b) 44%
      (c) 20%

   4. TABLE 2.3

Interval	Midpoint	f	Interval	Midpoint	f
145–149	147	1	115–119	117	1
140–144	142	0	110–114	112	4
135–139	137	1	105–109	107	3
130–134	132	2	100–104	102	3
125–129	127	4	95–99	97	3
120–124	122	3			

   5. TABLE 2.4

Class Interval		Midpoint	f	cf	c%
Apparent Limits	Real Limits				
108–110	107.5–110.5	109	1	25	100%
105–107	104.5–107.5	106	1	24	96%
102–104	101.5–104.5	103	4	23	92%
99–101	98.5–101.5	100	4	19	76%
96–98	95.5–98.5	97	5	15	60%
93–95	92.5–95.5	94	3	10	40%
90–92	89.5–92.5	91	2	7	28%
87–89	86.5–89.5	88	4	5	20%
84–86	83.5–86.5	85	1	1	4%

   6. (a) 12th
      (b) 34th
      (c) 89.33th
   7. (a) 91.38 months
      (b) 97.00 months
      (c) 101.31 months

Chapter 3

A. 1. (a) Median
    (b) Mode
    (c) Mean
    (d) Median
    (e) Mode
    (f) Median
    (g) Mean
    (h) Median
    (i) Mean
  2. (a) False
    (b) True
    (c) False
    (d) False
    (e) True
    (f) False
  3. (a) $<$, $<$
    (b) $=$, $=$
    (c) $>$, $>$
    (d) $>$, $>$
    (e) $=$, $=$
    (f) $<$, $<$

B. 1. (a) Mode $= 9$
    (b) Modal interval $= 7$–8, mode $= 7.5$
    (c) Median $= 8$
    (d) Mean $= 7.16$
    (e) 26
    (f) Range $= 10$
    (g) Interquartile range $= 3$; $(9 - 6)$
    (h) $s^2 = 4.694$
    (i) $s = 2.167$
    (j) Mode
  2. (a) TABLE 3.3

Interval		Interval Midpoint (X_m)	f	cf	fX_m	X_m^2	fX_m^2
Apparent Limits	Real Limits						
125–127	124.5–127.5	126	4	50	504	15,876	63,504
122–124	121.5–124.5	123	3	46	369	15,129	45,387
119–121	118.5–121.5	120	4	43	480	14,400	57,600
116–118	115.5–118.5	117	1	39	117	13,689	13,689
113–115	112.5–115.5	114	4	38	456	12,996	51,984
110–112	109.5–112.5	111	5	34	555	12,321	61,605
107–109	106.5–109.5	108	5	29	540	11,664	58,320
104–106	103.5–106.5	105	8	24	840	11,025	88,200
101–103	100.5–103.5	102	6	16	612	10,404	62,424
98–100	97.5–100.5	99	6	10	594	9,801	58,806
95–97	94.5–97.5	96	4	4	384	9,216	36,864

(b) Mode $= 105$
(c) Median $= 107.10$
(d) Mean $= 109.02$
(e) Range $= 33$
(f) Interquartile range $= 115.12 - 101.75 = 13.37$
(g) $s = 9.164$
(h) $s^2 = 82.29$
3. (a) $\bar{X}_{comb} = 12.967$
(b) $s^2_{comb} = 8.256$
(c) $s_{comb} = 2.873$

Chapter 4

A. 1. (a) False
(b) True
(c) True
(d) True
(e) False
(f) False
(g) False
(h) True
(i) False
(j) False
2. (a) (1) Yes, positive
(2) Pearson r
(3) Yes, age causes the ability to learn math to increase.
(b) (1) Yes, negative
(2) Spearman rho
(3) No
(c) (1) Yes, positive
(2) Pearson r
(3) Yes, more studying improves test scores.
(d) (1) Yes, negative
(2) Pearson r
(3) Yes, increased TV watching decreases number of books read.
(e) (1) Yes, positive
(2) Spearman rho
(3) Yes, high temperatures cause more people to go to parks.

B. 1. TABLE 4.1

X	x	z_x	z_x^2
25	2.5	0.304	0.0924
20	-2.5	-0.304	0.0924
29	6.5	0.790	0.6241
32	9.5	1.154	1.3317
11	-11.5	-1.397	1.9516
34	11.5	1.397	1.9516
16	-6.5	-0.790	0.6241
13	-9.5	-1.154	1.3317
$\Sigma X = 180$	$\Sigma x = 0$	$\Sigma z_x = 0$	$\Sigma z_x^2 = 7.9996$

(a) $\bar{z} = \dfrac{\Sigma z}{N} = \dfrac{0}{8} = 0$

(b) $s_z^2 = \dfrac{\Sigma z^2}{N} = \dfrac{7.9996}{8} \simeq 1.0$; $s_z = \sqrt{1.0} = 1.0$

(c) $\Sigma z^2 = 7.996 \simeq N$

2. TABLE 4.3

Day	X	Y	X^2	Y^2	XY
1	90	9	8100	81	810
2	40	7	1600	49	280
3	20	5	400	25	100
4	30	5	900	25	150
5	80	1	6400	1	80
6	60	2	3600	4	120
7	70	8	4900	64	560
8	20	3	400	9	60
9	90	7	8100	49	630
10	10	1	100	1	10
11	40	4	1600	16	160
12	10	2	100	4	20
13	50	3	2500	9	150
14	80	7	6400	49	560
15	40	1	1600	1	40
	$\Sigma X = 730$	$\Sigma Y = 65$	$\Sigma X^2 = 46,700$	$\Sigma Y^2 = 387$	$\Sigma XY = 3730$

(a) $\bar{X} = 48.67$
$\bar{Y} = 4.33$
$s_x^2 = 744.89$
$s_x = 27.293$
$s_y^2 = 7.02$
$s_y = 2.650$
(b) $r = +0.522$

3. TABLE 4.4

Sire/Colt	Sire's Rank (X)	% of Races Won by Colt	Colt's Rank (Y)	$D = X - Y$	D^2
A	2	78%	1	1	1
B	5	42%	4	1	1
C	1	44%	3	−2	4
D	7	30%	7	0	0
E	9	10%	9	0	0
F	3	41%	5	−2	4
G	8	36%	6	2	4
H	6	25%	8	−2	4
I	4	68%	2	2	4
				$\Sigma D = 0$	$\Sigma D^2 = 22$

(a) rho $= +0.817$

Chapter 5

A. 1. (a) Dependent
   (b) r
   (c) $(Y - 2)/4$
   (d) Horizontal
   (e) r^2
   (f) Is not
   (g) 7
   (h) Independent
   (i) Minimize the sum of squared deviations
   (j) r
   (k) $r = 0$
   (l) Vertical
   (m) Standard error of estimate of y ($s_{est\ y}$)
   (n) Lower
   (0) a

  2. (a) Predictor variable: number of letters
   Dependent variable: reading time
   Causal relationship
   (b) Predictor variable: z_y
   Dependent variable: z_x
   Cannot tell
   (c) Predictor variable: personality inventory
   Dependent variable: diagnosis
   Causal relationship
   (d) Predictor variable: aptitude test
   Dependent variable: achievement test
   No causal relationship
   (e) Predictor variable: resume
   Dependent variable: success at a job
   No causal relationship
   (f) Predictor variable: Y
   Dependent variable: X
   Cannot tell
   (g) Predictor variable: distance
   Dependent variable: amount of gas
   Causal relationship
   (h) Predictor variable: high school grades
   Dependent variable: SAT score
   No causal relationship
   (i) Predictor variable: SAT score
   Dependent variable: college grades
   No causal relationship

B. 1. TABLE 5.1

Equation	X	Y	X	Y	X	Y	X	Y	X	Y
(a) $Y = X/10 + 6$	−5	5.50	−1	5.90	−1/2	5.95	0	6.00	3	6.30
(b) $3Y = 2X − 7$	−5	−5.67	−1	−3.00	−1/2	−2.67	0	−2.33	3	−0.33
(c) $4Y = 3X$	−5	−3.75	−1	−0.75	−1/2	−0.38	0	0	3	2.25
(d) $Y = X + 2$	−5	−3.00	−1	1.00	−1/2	1.50	0	2.00	3	5.00
(e) $Y = 0.5X + 1.6$	−5	−0.90	−1	1.10	−1/2	1.35	0	1.60	3	3.10

2. (a) $b_y = 1/10$ $a_y = +6$
   $b_x = 10$ $a_x = -60$
   (b) $b_y = 2/3$ $a_y = -7/3$
   $b_x = 3/2$ $a_x = +3 \, 1/2$
   (c) $b_y = 3/4$ $a_y = 0$
   $b_x = 4/3$ $a_x = 0$
   (d) $b_y = 1$ $a_y = +2$
   $b_x = 1$ $a_x = -2$
   (e) $b_y = 0.5$ $a_y = +1.6$
   $b_x = 2$ $a_x = -3.2$
3. $\hat{z}_y = 0.615$
4. (a) $\hat{X} = 0.32Y + 55.64$
   (b) $\hat{Y} = 2X - 67$
   (c) 113
   (d) 99.80

5. TABLE 5.2

Pair	X	Y	X^2	Y^2	XY	$\hat{X}$	$\hat{Y}$
1	63	59	3969	3481	3717	57.81	64.64
2	72	75	5184	5625	5400	72.11	74.08
3	51	48	2601	2304	2448	47.97	52.07
4	86	88	7396	7744	7568	83.73	88.75
5	28	30	784	900	840	31.88	27.96
6	52	60	2704	3600	3120	58.70	53.12
7	79	88	6241	7744	6952	83.73	81.41
8	63	59	3969	3481	3717	57.81	64.64
9	54	55	2916	3025	2970	54.23	55.21

$\Sigma X = 548$ $\Sigma Y = 562$ $\Sigma X^2 = 35,764$ $\Sigma Y^2 = 37,904$ $\Sigma XY = 36,732$

(a) $\hat{X} = 0.894Y + 5.061$
(b) $\hat{Y} = 1.048X - 1.380$

Chapter 6

A. 1. (a) AND
   (b) $P(A/B)$
   (c) The sample space
   (d) OR
   (e) $P(A)$
   (f) Mutually exclusive
   (g) Equally likely, denumerable
2. (a) 1
   (b) 3
   (c) 4
   (d) 2
   (e) 2
3. (a) Permutations
   (b) Arrangements
   (c) r-tuplets
   (d) Arrangements

    (e) Combinations

    (f) r-tuplets

    (g) Combinations

    (h) Arrangements

B. 1. (a) (1) $(\frac{1}{5})^4$

        (2) $1 - [1 - (\frac{1}{5})^4]^5$

    (b) (1) $(\frac{1}{4})^6$

        (2) $1 - [1 - (\frac{1}{4})^6]^5$

    (c) (1) $(\frac{1}{4})^3$

        (2) $1 - [1 - (\frac{1}{4})^3]^5$

  2. $1 - (11/12)(10/12)$

  3. (a) $(13/52)(12/51)(11/50)$

    (b) $1/13 + 1/52$

    (c) $(1/4)^5$

    (d) $(1/13)(1/51)(1/50)(1/49)$

    (e) $(4/52)(3/52)(2/52)(1/52)$

  4. (a) $\binom{5}{3} \times \binom{10}{2} = 10 \times 45 = 450$

    (b) $\binom{5}{2} \times \binom{10}{3} = 10 \times 120 = 1200$

    (c) $\binom{10}{5} = 252$

  5. (a) $4 \times 2 \times 3 = 24$

    (b) $4 \times 2 \times 4 = 32$

    (c) Number correct − number wrong

    (d) $4 \times 2 \times 3 \times 1 = 24$

    (e) $4 \times 2 \times 4 \times 2 = 64$

  6. (a) $1/36, 35{:}1$

    (b) $1/18, 17{:}1$

    (c) $5/36, 31{:}5$

    (d) $1/6, 5{:}1$

    (e) $1/18, 17{:}1$

  7. (a) $1/7$

    (b) $1/3$

  8. (a) $0.46 + 0.42 - (0.46 \times 0.42) = 0.687$

    (b) $0.53 + 0.48 - (0.53 \times 0.48) = 0.756$

    (c) $0.46 + 0.48 - (0.46 \times 0.48) = 0.719$

Chapter 7

A. 1. (a) Dependent

    (b) Independent

    (c) Statistics

    (d) Dependent

    (e) Five

    (f) One

    (g) Natural

    (h) BAAB

    (i) Frequencies, proportions

    (j) Counterbalanced

    (k) Ordinal

    (l) Random

(m) Stratified
(n) Is not
2. (a) 1
  (b) 4
  (c) 1
  (d) 3
  (e) 4
  (f) 1
3. (a) False
  (b) False
  (c) False
  (d) False
  (e) True
  (f) True
  (g) True
  (h) True
  (i) False
  (j) False
4. (a) 3
  (b) 3
  (c) 1
  (d) 4
  (e) 2
  (f) 2
  (g) 4
  (h) 4
B. 1. (a) An experiment with one independent variable having just two levels.
  (b) Variability among subjects can be subtracted out in a within-subjects design.
  (c) When exposure of subjects to one condition might affect their performance to another condition.
  (d) Because we want to generalize from the sample to a population.
  (e) When the behavior we are studying reflects basic processes common to all humans (or to all animals).
  (f) When one wants to balance practice and/or fatigue effects evenly across conditions and when there is no harm in letting subjects know which condition is next.
  (g) Using a table of random numbers or using a table of permutations and repeating them.
  (h) When it would be confusing to the subject to switch strategies from trial to trial.
2. (a) Matched t test
  (b) Matched t test
  (c) Independent t test
  (d) One-way repeated-measures ANOVA
  (e) One-way randomized ANOVA
  (f) One-way randomized ANOVA
  (g) One-way randomized ANOVA
  (h) Independent t test
  (i) Independent t test
  (j) One-way repeated-measures ANOVA
3. (a) (1) A = level of reading group; B = interest of material
    (2) $A = 3; B = 2$

   (3) A = natural; B = artificial
   (4) A = between; B = within
   (5) Mixed
(b) (1) A = dose prior to training; B = dose prior to test
   (2) A = 2; B = 2
   (3) A = artificial; B = artificial
   (4) A = between; B = between
   (5) Random
(c) (1) A = type of achievement; B = year in school
   (2) A = 2; B = 4
   (3) A = natural; B = natural
   (4) A = within; B = within
   (5) Repeated-measures
(d) (1) A = level of aggressiveness; B = zodiac sign
   (2) A = 2; B = 12
   (3) A = natural; B = natural
   (4) A = between; B = between
   (5) Random
(e) (1) A = incentive level; B = task difficulty
   (2) A = 3; B = 3
   (3) A = artificial; B = artificial
   (4) A = between; B = within
   (5) Mixed
4. (a) (1) Either controlled or method not important
   (2) Controlled
 (b) (1) Random
   (2) Controlled
 (c) (1) Controlled
   (2) Method not important
 (d) (1) Controlled
   (2) Controlled
 (e) (1) Controlled
   (2) Controlled
5.

T	U	V	W	X	Y	Z
U	V	W	X	Y	Z	T
V	W	X	Y	Z	T	U
W	X	Y	Z	T	U	V
X	Y	Z	T	U	V	W
Y	Z	T	U	V	W	X
Z	T	U	V	W	X	Y

 (a) No
 (b) Between-subjects control
 (c) No
 (d) It includes only 7 permutations out of a possible 78 ($= 5040$) permutations.

Chapter 8

A. 1. (a) 3
   (b) 5
   (c) 1
   (d) 4
   (e) 2

2. (a) Bernouilli
   (b) $N + 1$
   (c) Need not
   (d) Must
   (e) p, N
   (f) μ, σ
   (g) Normal, binomial
   (h) 0.50
   (i) Binomial
   (j) Zero
   (k) N, the number of opportunities
   (l) Normal
   (m) More, decreases

B. 1. $(1/6)^5 + 5(1/6)^4(5/6) + 10(1/6)^3(5/6)^2 + 10(1/6)^2(5/6)^3 + 5(1/6)(5/6)^4 + (5/6)^5 =$ $0.00013 + 0.0032 + 0.0322 + 0.1608 + 0.4019 + 0.4019 = 1.000$

2. $(3/5)^4 + 4(3/5)^3(2/5) + 6(3/5)^2(2/5)^2 + 4(3/5)(2/5)^3 + (2/5)^4 = 0.1296 + 0.3456 +$ $0.3456 + 0.1536 + 0.0256 = 1.000$

3. (a) $1/6 + 1/6 = 1/3$
   (b) $10(1/3)^3(2/3)^2 = 0.1646$
   (c) $(2/3)^5 = 0.1317$
   (d) $1 - (2/3)^5 = 0.8683$
   (e) $(1/3)^5 = 0.0041$

4. (a) $(0.25)^6 = 0.00024$
   (b) $15(0.75)^4(0.25)^2 = 0.2966$
   (c) $(0.75)^6 + 6(0.75)^5(0.25) + 15(0.75)^4(0.25)^2 + 20(0.75)^3(0.25)^3 = 0.1780 + 0.3560 +$ $0.2966 + 0.1318 = 0.9624$
   (d) 750
   (e) $\mu_r = 1000 \times 0.75 = 750; \sigma_r = \sqrt{1000 \times 0.75 \times .025} = 13.69$

5. (a) 1.17
   (b) -1.67
   (c) -1.33
   (d) -0.25
   (e) 0.58

6. (a) 81.25
   (b) 71.75
   (c) 76.25
   (d) 79.5
   (e) 68.5

7. (a) 0.2537
   (b) 0.7734
   (c) 0
   (d) 0.7976
   (e) 0.9032

8. (a) 841.40
   (b) 89.2
   (c) 1086.80
   (d) 80.8
   (e) 66.7

Chapter 9

A. 1. (a) Alternative
   (b) Null
   (c) Null

    (d) Null
    (e) Alternative
    (f) Null
    (g) Null
    (h) Alternative
    (i) Alternative
    (j) Alternative
    (k) Null

2. (a) Chance or random sampling
    (b) Null
    (c) Alternative
    (d) Accept
    (e) Reject

3. (a) True
    (b) True
    (c) True
    (d) True
    (e) False
    (f) False
    (g) False
    (h) False
    (i) False

4. (a) Type I
    (b) Type I
    (c) Type II
    (d) Type II
    (e) Type I
    (f) Type I
    (g) Type II
    (h) Type I

5. (a) Interval estimate
    (b) Hypothesis testing
    (c) The independent variable, chance
    (d) Dependent
    (e) One-tailed
    (f) Small
    (g) Increased
    (h) Parameters, statistics
    (i) Decreases
    (j) Standard error
    (k) Null
    (l) Standard error
    (m) Normal
    (n) Increases
    (o) t distribution
    (p) Central limit theorem

6. (a) 4   (h) 2
    (b) 2   (i) 1
    (c) 2   (j) 3
    (d) 1   (k) 2
    (e) 2   (l) 1
    (f) 1   (m) 3
    (g) 4   (n) 4

B. 1. (a) (1) Probability of a one equals 1/6
        (2) Probability of a one does not equal 1/6
        (3) Nondirectional
    (b) (1) Males and females are equal in manual dexterity
        (2) Males and females are not equal in manual dexterity
        (3) Nondirectional
    (c) (1) Cats are equal to or dumber than dogs
        (2) Cats are smarter than dogs
        (3) Directional
    (d) (1) The drug does not reduce or increase anxiety
        (2) The drug decreases anxiety
        (3) Directional
    (e) (1) Children who watch educational TV programs have average or below IQs
        (2) They have above-average IQs
        (3) Directional

2. (a) Because that null hypothesis is diffuse (i.e., can take on a number of different values) and so its sampling distribution is not known exactly
    (b) Our knowledge is not precise enough to postulate "behavioral constants"
    (c) That if one state is true, the other cannot be true and vice versa; and that one of the states must be true
    (d) So if one hypothesis is rejected the other can be accepted, and vice versa
    (e) Because the rejection region is in only one tail of the sampling distribution, a smaller value of the test statistic, and hence a smaller difference in sample means is required for significance
    (f) The probability that if the null hypothesis were true, the experimenter would have observed such extreme differences in his samples
    (g) Because the sampling distribution can only be calculated for specific values of parameter or differences in parameters
    (h) If the alternative hypothesis is true and in the predicted direction, the power of one-tailed test is greater than that of a two-tailed test. Just the opposite holds when a true alternative hypothesis has a value in the opposite direction from that predicted
    (i) In accepting the null hypothesis, the investigator is accepting a specific value or difference in population parameters, one which is very unlikely to be *exactly* true. In failing to reject, the investigator makes no commitment to these exact values.
    (j) To discover characteristics about things we cannot study in their entirety (populations) from characteristics of things we can study in their entirety (samples)
    (k) It is more desirable to compute the theoretical probability because drawing repeated samples would require drawing an infinite number of samples

Chapter 10

A. 1. (a) Population
    (b) Known
    (c) Sampling distribution
    (d) Zero
    (e) Population standard deviations, degree of correlation
    (f) Null
    (g) Degrees of freedom

(h) Homogeneity
(i) Robust
(j) Rejection region

2. (a) Symmetrical
 (b) t
 (c) Within
 (d) t
 (e) Decrease, increase
 (f) Is
 (g) Does
 (h) Does not
 (i) Normal
 (h) t, z
 (k) Increases

3. (a) 1
 (b) 3
 (c) 3
 (d) 1

4. (a) True
 (b) False
 (c) True
 (d) True
 (e) False
 (f) True
 (g) True
 (h) False
 (i) False

B. 1. (a) Yes, $z = 4.67$, $p < 0.001$, two-tailed
 (b) 108.12, 119.88
 (c) 106.26, 121.74
 (d) $t = 1.78$, df $= 24$, n.s. (two-tailed)
 (e) 109.37, 118.63
 (f) $t = 2.52$, df $= 48$, $p < .02$ (two-tailed)
 (g) 110.79, 117.21

2. (a) H_1: unintentional learning has some effect on recognition memory
 H_0: unintentional learning has no effect on recognition memory
 (b) $\Sigma X_1 = 1022$ $\Sigma X_2 = 956$ $\Sigma D = 66$ $\Sigma D^2 = 656$
 $\bar{X}_1 = 85.17$ $\bar{X}_2 = 79.67$ $D = 5.5$
 $s_D^2 = 24.42$
 (c) $t = 3.69$, df $= 11$, $p < 0.01$ (two-tailed)
 (d) H_0: unintentional learning has no or a detrimental effect on recognition memory
 H_1: unintentional learning has a positive effect on recognition memory
 (e) $t = 3.69$, df $= 11$, $p < 0.005$ (one-tailed)
 (f) Unintentional learning improves memory

3. (a) H_1: marijuana affects logical thought processes
 H_0: marijuana does not affect logical thought processes
 (b) $s_{\bar{X}_1 - \bar{X}_2} = 9.885$
 $t = 1.62$
 df $= 49$
 (c) No

    (d) Marijuana has no effect on logical thought processes
4. (a) H_0: order of test has no effect on math scores
       H_1: order of test has some effect
   (b) $s_{\bar{X}_1 - \bar{X}_2} = 3.747$
       $t = 27.22$
       df $= 49$
   (c) Yes, $p < 0.001$ (two-tailed)
   (d) Marijuana has little, if any, effect on math scores, whereas taking the same test again has large effects
5. (a) H_0: children are equally or more lateralized than adults
       H_1: adults are more lateralized than children
   (b) $\Sigma X_1 = 260$ $\Sigma X_1^2 = 5692$ $\Sigma X_2 = 185$ $\Sigma X_2^2 = 2687$
       $\bar{X}_1 = 17.33$ $\bar{X}_2 = 12.33$
       $s_1^2 = 79.022$ $s_2^2 = 27.022$
            $s_{\bar{X}_1 - \bar{X}_2} = 2.752$
            $t = 1.82$, df $= 28$
   (c) Yes, $p < 0.05$ (one-tailed)
   (d) There is some evidence that lateralization develops after puberty.
6. (a) $\Sigma X_1 = 233$ $\Sigma X_1^2 = 5297$ $\Sigma X_2 = 162$ $\Sigma X_2^2 = 2158$
       $\bar{X}_1 = 21.18$ $\bar{X}_2 = 11.57$
       $s_1^2 = 32.953$ $s_2^2 = 20.278$
           $s_{\bar{x}_1 - \bar{x}_2} = 2.136$
           $t = 4.50$, df $= 23$
   (b) Yes, $p < 0.0005$, one-tailed test
   (c) By eliminating left-handed subjects, Ms. Rosafsky has obtained much stronger evidence that lateralization develops after puberty.

Chapter 11

A. 1. (a) Two
   (b) Is not
   (c) Never
   (d) Is
   (e) Accept
   (f) Larger, smaller
   (g) Greater
   (h) Need not
  2. (a) 3
   (b) 1
   (c) 4
   (d) 3
   (e) 2
   (f) 3
B. 1. (a) $df_{68} = 29$; $df_{76} = 24$
   (b) $\hat{s}_{68}^2 = 188.28$; $\hat{s}_{76}^2 = 596.88$
   (c) $F = 3.17$
   (d) $F \geq 2.52$
   (e) 0.025
   (f) Accept their hypothesis by rejecting H_0

2. (a) TABLE 11.2

	1	2	3	4	5
Sums	$\bar{A}_1 = 112.6$ 563	$\bar{A}_2 = 147.2$ 736	$\bar{A}_3 = 104.6$ 523	$\bar{A}_4 = 100.2$ 501	$\bar{A}_5 = 107.2$ 536

$s = 5, a = 5, N = 25$
$T = 2869$
$TS = 341,095$
$C = 326,955.24$
$SS_{tot} = 14,139.76$
$SS_A = 7142.96$
$SS_{err} = 6996.80$

(b) TABLE 11.3

Source of Variance	SS	df	MS	F	p
A (Main Effect)	7,142.96	4	1785.74	5.10	<0.01
Error (Within Groups)	6,996.80	20	349.84		
Total	14,139.76	24			

(c) Yes

(d) 20% A, 80% B because that combination gave the highest yield

3. (a) TABLE 11.4

Sums	116.89	120.33	116.90
	$\bar{A}_1 = 1052$	$\bar{A}_2 = 1444$	$\bar{A}_3 = 1169$
	$s_1 = 9$	$s_2 = 12$	$s_3 = 10; a = 3, N = 31$

$T = 3665$
$TS = 437,439$
$C = 433,297.58$
$SS_{tot} \doteq 4141.42$
$SS_A = 86.96$
$SS_{err} = 4054.46$

(b) TABLE 11.5

Source of Variance	SS	df	MS	F	p
A (main effect)	86.96	2	43.48	<1	n.s.
Error (within groups)	4054.46	28	144.80		
Total	4141.42	30			

(c) No

4. (a) TABLE 11.6

	$\bar{A}_1 = 117.3$	$\bar{A}_2 = 122.5$	$\bar{A}_3 = 116.1$
Sums	1173	1225	1161

S sums: 396, 359, 333, 340, 333, 349, 305, 367, 377, 400
$s = 10, a = 3, N = 21$
$T = 3559$
$TS = 425,599$
$C = 422,216.03$
$SS_{tot} = 3382.97$
$SS_A = 231.47$
$SS_S = 2690.30$
$SS_{A \times S} = 461.20$

4. (b) TABLE 11.7

Source of variance	SS	df	MS	F	p
A (main effect)	231.47	2	115.74	4.52	<0.05
S (subjects)	2690.30	9	298.92		
$A \times S$ (error)	461.20	18	25.62		
Total	3382.97	29			

(c) Yes
(d) Repeated measures designs are more sensitive than randomized designs because they eliminate variance due to individual differences.

Chapter 12

A. 1. (a) 3
  (b) 2
  (c) 1
  (d) 1
  (e) 3
  (f) 4
  (g) 3
2. (a) False
  (b) True
  (c) False
  (d) True
  (e) False
  (f) False
3. (a) F ratio
  (b) Two
  (c) Three
  (d) 2×5
  (e) One, six
  (f) Ten, six
  (g) Cannot
  (h) Can

4. (a) A sig.
   B sig.
   $A \times B$ n.s.
   (b) A n.s.
   B n.s.
   $A \times B$ sig.
   (c) A sig.
   B n.s.
   $A \times B$ sig.
   (d) A n.s.
   B sig.
   $A \times B$ n.s.
   (e) A n.s.
   B sig.
   $A \times B$ sig.
   (f) A n.s.
   B n.s.
   $A \times B$ n.s.
   (g) A sig.
   B n.s.
   $A \times B$ n.s.
   (h) A sig.
   B sig.
   $A \times B$ sig.

B. 1. (a) Mixed
   (b) $\overline{A_1B_1} = 74.00$ $\overline{A_2B_1} = 77.67$
   $\overline{A_1B_2} = 64.00$ $\overline{A_2B_2} = 68.00$
   (d) Drug use decreases depression; females are more depressed than males; there is no interaction between drug condition and sex.

   (e) TABLE 12.2

Drug Condition (Factor B)	Sex	
	Male (a_1)	Female (a_2)
Before Drug (b_1)	72	83
	84	79
	63	80
	75	62
	69	91
	81	71
	$A_1B_1 = 444$	$A_2B_1 = 466$
	$\overline{A_1B_1} = 74.00$	$\overline{A_2B_1} = 77.67$ $B_1 = 910$
With Drug (b_2)	62	71
	73	80
	62	68
	65	54
	50	73
	72	62
	$A_1B_2 = 384$	$A_2B_2 = 408$ $B_2 = 792$
	$\overline{A_1B_2} = 64.00$	$\overline{A_2B_2} = 68.00$
	$A_1 = 828$	$A_2 = 874$ $T = 1{,}702$
		$TS = 122{,}932$

AS matrix

$A_1S_1 = 134$	$A_2S_1 = 154$
$A_1S_2 = 157$	$A_2S_2 = 159$
$A_1S_3 = 125$	$A_2S_3 = 148$
$A_1S_4 = 140$	$A_2S_4 = 116$
$A_1S_5 = 119$	$A_2S_5 = 164$
$A_1S_6 = 153$	$A_2S_6 = 133$

TABLE 12.3

Source of Variance	SS	df	MS	F	p
A (sex)	88.17	1	88.17	0.64	n.s.
S/A	1382.66	10	138.27		
B (drug condition)	580.17	1	580.17	32.11	<0.001
$A \times B$	0.16	1	0.16	0.009	n.s.
$B \times S/A$	180.67	10	18.07		
Total	2231.83	23			

2. (a) completely randomized

  (b) $\overline{A_1B_1} = 82.50$ $\quad \overline{A_2B_1} = 69.25$ $\quad \overline{A_3B_1} = 68.00$
  $\overline{A_1B_2} = 91.25$ $\quad \overline{A_2B_2} = 90.50$ $\quad \overline{A_3B_2} = 90.75$

  (d) Teacher instruction is superior to programmed instruction and programmed instruction of Spanish is superior to that of the other two languages.

  (e) TABLE 12.5

Instruction Condition (Factor B)	Language (Factor A)		
	Spanish (a_1)	French (a_3)	Italian (a_1)
Programmed (b_1)	72	69	63
	83	66	72
	96	78	78
	79	64	59
	$A_1B_1 = 330$	$A_2B_1 = 277$	$A_3B_1 = 272$ $\qquad B_1 = 879$
	$\overline{A_1B_1} = 82.50$	$\overline{A_2B_1} = 69.25$	$\overline{A_3B_1} = 68.00$
Teacher Instructed (b_2)	83	96	89
	95	87	93
	89	93	86
	98	86	95
	$A_1B_2 = 365$	$A_2B_2 = 362$	$A_3B_2 = 363$ $\qquad B_2 = 1090$
	$\overline{A_1B_2} = 91.25$	$\overline{A_2B_2} = 90.50$	$\overline{A_3B_2} = 90.75$
	$A_1 = 695$	$A_2 = 639$	$A_3 = 635$ $\qquad T = 1969$
			$TS = 164,805$

TABLE 12.6

Source of Variance	SS	df	MS	F	p
A (Language)	281.33	2	140.67	5.68	<0.05
B (Instruction)	1855.04	1	1855.04	37.42	<0.001
$A \times B$	236.34	2	118.17	4.77	<0.05
Error	892.25	18	49.57		
Total	3264.96	23			

(f) Teacher instruction is significantly better than programmed instruction ($p < 0.001$); however the instructional technique interacts with language being taught ($p < 0.05$) in that programmed instruction produces better learning for Spanish than either French or Italian.

3. (a) Completely repeated measures

(b) $\overline{A_1B_1} = 68.12$ $\overline{A_2B_1} = 57.50$
    $\overline{A_1B_2} = 86.25$ $\overline{A_2B_2} = 73.12$

(d) Slow presentation of words improves recall of words over fast presentation; high frequency words are recalled better than low frequency words; there is no apparent interaction between presentation rate and frequency.

(e) TABLE 12.8

Frequency (Factor B)	Presentation rate (Factor A)		
	Slow (a_1)	Fast (a_2)	BS matrix
Low (b_1)	75	60	$B_1S_1 = 135$
	70	60	$B_1S_2 = 130$
	75	55	$B_1S_3 = 130$
	60	50	$B_1S_4 = 110$
	60	45	$B_1S_5 = 105$
	60	50	$B_1S_6 = 110$
	70	55	$B_1S_7 = 125$
	75	85	$B_1S_8 = 160$ $B_1 = 1005$
	$A_1B_1 = 545$	$A_2B_1 = 460$	
	$\overline{A_1B_1} = 68.12$	$\overline{A_2B_1} = 57.50$	
High (b_2)	95	80	$B_2S_1 = 175$
	85	70	$B_2S_2 = 155$
	90	80	$B_2S_3 = 170$
	90	75	$B_2S_4 = 165$
	85	70	$B_2S_5 = 155$
	75	65	$B_2S_6 = 140$
	80	65	$B_2S_7 = 145$
	90	80	$B_2S_8 = 170$
	$A_1B_2 = 690$	$A_2B_2 = 585$	$B_2 = 1275$
	$\overline{A_1B_2} = 86.25$	$\overline{A_2B_2} = 73.12$	
	$A_1 = 1235$	$A_2 = 1045$	$T = 2280$
			$TS = 167,850$
		AS matrix	S matrix
	$A_1S_1 = 170$	$A_2S_1 = 140$	$S_1 = 310$
	$A_1S_2 = 155$	$A_2S_2 = 130$	$S_2 = 285$
	$A_1S_3 = 165$	$A_2S_3 = 135$	$S_3 = 300$
	$A_1S_4 = 150$	$A_2S_4 = 125$	$S_4 = 275$
	$A_1S_5 = 145$	$A_2S_5 = 115$	$S_5 = 260$
	$A_1S_6 = 135$	$A_2S_6 = 115$	$S_6 = 250$
	$A_1S_7 = 150$	$A_2S_7 = 120$	$S_7 = 270$
	$A_1S_8 = 165$	$A_2S_8 = 165$	$S_8 = 330$

TABLE 12.9

Source of variance	SS	df	MS	F	p
A (presentation rate)	1128.12	1	1128.12	42.83	<0.001
S	1262.50	7	180.36		
A × S	184.38	7	26.34		
B (frequency)	2278.12	1	2278.12	38.95	<0.001
B × S	409.38	7	58.48		
A × B	12.51	1	12.51	0.70	n.s.
A × B × S	124.99	7	17.86		
Total	5400.00	31			

(f) Both presentation rate and word frequency were highly significant ($p < 0.001$) whereas the interaction between them was not ($F < 1$).

Chapter 13

A. 1. (a) Is not
   (b) Post hoc
   (c) Post hoc
   (d) Three
   (e) Marginal means
   (f) Simple main effects
   (g) Simple main effects
   (h) Post hoc
   (i) Rejecting
   (j) Newman-Keuls
   (k) Cannot
   (l) Tukey
  2. (a) 1
   (b) 3
   (c) 2
   (d) 2
   (e) 4
  3. (a) True
   (b) False
   (c) False
   (d) True
   (e) False
   (f) True
   (g) True
B. 1. (b) 3
   (c) $s = 6, a = 4, N = 24, df_A = 3, df_{err} = 20$
   (d) $SS' = 108.00, F' = 1.15, df = 1, 20$, n.s.
   (e) $SS' = 427.11, F' = 4.55, df = 1, 20, p < 0.05$
   (f) $SS' = 1730.68, F' = 18.44, df = 1, 20, p < 0.001$
   (g) Nonmeaningful and nonpronounceable trigrams have higher thresholds than either meaningful, nonpronounceable or meaningful, pronounceable trigrams.

The latter two do not differ significantly but they have significantly higher higher thresholds than meaningful, pronounceable trigrams.

2. (b) $SS_{A \text{ at } b_1} = 1444.80$, $F_{A \text{ at } b_2} = 5.83$, df = 2, 24, $p < 0.01$

   (c) $SS_A' = 123.27$, $F_A' = 0.99$, df = 1, 24, n.s.

   (d) $SS_A' = 5248.80$, $F_A' = 42.33$, df = 1, 24, $p < 0.001$

   (e) $SS_{A \text{ at } b_2} = 4481.73$, $F_{A \text{ at } b_2} = 18.07$, df = 2, 24, $p < 0.001$

   (f) $SS_B' = 15,686.53$, $F_B' = 126.50$, df = 1, 24, $p < 0.001$

   (g) $SS_{B \text{ at } a_1} = 3,686.40$, $F_{B \text{ at } a_1} = 29.73$, df = 1, 24, $p < 0.001$

   (h) Marginal means comparisons: c, d, f

   Simple main effects comparisons: b, e, g

   (i) Dull rats have longer running times than bright rats; the compatible training condition has a favorable effect on times whereas the incompatible condition has an unfavorable effect compared to a control for both bright and dull rats.

3. (b) $SS_{A \text{ at } b_2} = 0.40$, $F_{A \text{ at } b_2} = 0.04$, df = 1, 8, n.s.

   (c) $SS_{A \text{ at } b_1} = 240.10$, $F_{A \text{ at } b_1} = 24.12$, df = 1, 8, $p < 0.01$

   (d) $SS_{B \text{ at } a_1} = 16.90$, $F_{B \text{ at } a_1} = 38.63$, df = 1, 8, $p < 0.001$

   (e) $SS_{B \text{ at } a_2} = 115.60$, $F_{B \text{ at } a_2} = 264.23$, df = 1, 8, $p < 0.001$

   (f) The old drug slowly decreases hyperactivity as it is taken over time, whereas the new drug initially causes an increase, then a decrease in hyperactivity.

4. (c) $r = 2$; $CD_{0.05} = 12.62$; $CD_{0.01} = 16.87$

   $r = 6$; $CD_{0.05} = 18.68$; $CD_{0.01} = 22.57$

   $r = 4$; $CD_{0.05} = 16.74$; $CD_{0.01} = 20.75$

   (d) $r = 3$; $CD_{0.05} = 19.96$; $CD_{0.01} = 23.80$

   $r = 5$; $CD_{0.05} = 19.96$; $CD_{0.01} = 23.80$

   $r = 8$; $CD_{0.05} = 19.96$; $CD_{0.01} = 23.80$

   (e) TABLE 13.5. (f) only 21 (A_4 versus A_7) is no longer significant.

	A_1	A_2	A_3	A_4	A_5	A_6	A_7	A_8	
				Matrix of Differences					
A_1		12	(36)	(50)	(62)	(69)	(71)	(76)	$r = 8$
A_2			(24)	(38)	(50)	(57)	(59)	(64)	$r = 7$
A_3				14	(26)	(33)	(35)	(40)	$r = 6$
A_4					12	19	(21)	(26)	$r = 5$
A_5						7	9	14	$r = 4$
A_6							2	7	$r = 3$
A_7								6	$r = 2$
A_8									

(g) 12- and 14-year-olds do not differ from one another but are significantly worse than other age groups; 10- and 16-year-olds do not differ from each other, and 16-year-olds don't differ from 20-year-olds, but all are inferior to either 4-, 6-, or 8-year-olds, who in turn do not differ from one another. In summary, the best age to learn languages is between 4 and 8 years of age.

Chapter 14

A. 1. (a) Means

   (b) Frequencies

   (c) Categorical

   (d) Correction for continuity, decrease

   (e) df = 1

    (f) Continuous approximation

    (g) Is not

    (h) Proportions, 1

  2. (a) 1

    (b) 2

    (c) 4

    (d) 2

    (e) 4

  3. (a) True

    (b) False

    (c) False

    (d) True

    (e) False

B. 1. (a) H_0: Females and males are equally afflicted by the disease.

        H_1: Females and males are not equally afflicted by the disease.

    (b) $\chi^2 = 3.025$, df = 1, n.s. (two-tailed test)

    (c) $\chi^2 = 4.50$, df = 1, $p < 0.05$ (two-tailed test)

  2. (b) $\chi^2 = 33.00$, df = 1, $p < 0.001$

    (c) 1100 of 2000 women received degrees in the humanities and 1400 of 3000 men received degrees, so $P_F = 0.55$ and $P_M = 0.467$. $p = 0.500$, $\sigma_{P_1 - P_2} = 0.0144$, $z = 5.745$, $p < 0.001$ (Note that $z^2 = 33.00$, the value obtained for x^2 in b.)

  3. (b) $x^2 = 55.36$, df = 2, $p < 0.001$ (two-tailed tests)

  4. (a) H_0: The new treatment will not affect, or will even increase, the number of cavities.

        H_1: The new treatment will decrease the number of cavities.

    (b) $\chi^2 = 18.28$, df = 2, $p < 0.0005$ (one-tailed test)

    (c) Send your children to Dr. Shechtman.

  5. (b) $\chi^2 = 25.06$, df = 3, $p < 0.0005$ (one-tailed test)

    (c) "You can't tell a book by its cover" is not an appropriate adage in today's world.

Chapter 15

A. 1. (a) Nonparametric

    (b) Normality, homogeneity

    (c) Parametric

    (d) Proportion

    (e) More

    (f) Median

    (g) More

    (h) More

    (i) Correction for continuity

  2. (a) 4

    (b) 1

    (c) 3

    (d) 2

    (e) 1

  3. (a) True

    (b) False

    (c) True

    (d) False

    (e) False

B. 1. (a) Sign test
    (b) No
    (c) Yes, $p < 0.05$ by a one-tailed test
    (d) $z = 2.18$, $p < 0.05$, one-tailed
  2. (a) t test for independent samples
    (b) Median and Mann-Whitney U tests
    (c) $\chi^2 = 1.54$, df $= 1$, n.s.
    (d) T_1 88.5, $T_2 = 211.5$ [Check: $T_1 + T_2 = N(N+1)/2$]
        $U_1 = 106.5$, $U_2 = 33.5$ [Check: $U_1 + U_2 = 140 = N_1N_2$]
        Reject H_0 at $p < 0.05$ since U_2 is smaller than 36.
  3. (a) Friedman test
    (b) $T_1 = 29$, $T_2 = 18$, $T_3 = 19$ [Check: $\Sigma T_1 = 66 = N(k)(k+1)/2$]
        $\chi_r^2 = 6.73$, df $= 2$, $p < 0.025$ (one-tailed test)
    (c) $T_1 = 26$, $T_2 = 15$, $T_3 = 13$ [Check: $\Sigma T_1 = 54 = N(k)(k+1)/2$]
        $\chi_r^2 = 10.89$, $k = 3$, $N = 9$, $p < 0.01$ from Table C.9
  4. (a) Median and Mann-Whitney U tests
    (b) $T_1 = 163.5$, $T_2 = 214.5$ [Check: $T_1 + T_2 = 378 = N(N+1)/2$]
        $U_1 = 109.5$, $U_2 = 72.5$ [Check: $U_1 + U_2 = 182 = N_1N_2$]
        Accept H_0: There is no significant difference in emotional maturity between
          girls and boys.
    (c) $\chi^2 = 0$ since the expected and observed frequencies are equal.
  5. (a) Sign test and Wilcoxon signed-ranks test
    (b) $T_+ = 59.5$, $T_- = 6.5$ [Check: $T_+ + T_- = 66 = N(N+1)/2$]
        $p < 0.01$, one-tailed test
    (c) $r = 2$, $N = 11$, $p < 0.05$, one-tailed test
        It yields the same conclusion, but at a lower level of significance.
  6. (a) Median test and Krusal-Wallis test
    (b) $T_1 = 44$, $T_2 = 43.5$, $T_3 = 63.5$, $T_4 = 80$
        [Check: ΣT: $= 231 = N(N+1)/2$]
        $H = 6.40$, df $= 3$, $p < 0.05$, one-tailed test

Chapter 16

A. 1. (a) More
    (b) Normal
    (c) Decreases
    (d) Maximize
    (e) Minimize
    (f) Fisher Z
  2. (a) False
    (b) True
    (c) False
    (d) True
    (e) False
    (f) False
    (g) True
  3. (a) χ^2
    (b) F
    (c) F
    (d) t
    (e) t

B. 1. (a) Friedman test
   (b) $\bar{X}_1 = 0.138$, $\bar{X}_2 = 0.767$, $\bar{X}_3 = 0.667$
       $\bar{\theta}_1 = 0.6616$, $\bar{\theta}_2 = 2.2189$, $\bar{\theta}_3 = 1.9586$
   (c) One-way analysis of variance
   (d) A parametric test is more powerful
   (e) $\theta(\bar{X}_1) = 0.7611 \neq 0.6616$
       $\theta(\bar{X}_2) = 2.1342 \neq 2.2189$
       $\theta(\bar{X}_3) = 1.9113 \neq 1.9586$
2. (a) No
   (b) Yes, $p < 0.05$ (one-tailed test)
   (c) No, $z = 0.815$, n.s.
   (d) Michael's subjects were sacrificing accuracy for speed and should be run over
       (that is, again).
3. (a) Yes, df $= 13$, $p < 0.0005$ (one-tailed test)
   (b) Yes, df $= 16$, $p < 0.0005$ (one-tailed test)
   (c) No, $z = 0.876$, n.s.
   (d) df $= 20$, $p < 0.025$ (one-tailed test)
       It shows marginally significant validity.
   (e) No, $z = 0.424$
4. (a) No
   (b) Yes, $p < 0.005$ (one-tailed test)